THE HEART OF ISLAM

Also by Seyyed Hossein Nasr

A Young Muslim's Guide to the Modern World
An Introduction to Islamic Cosmological Doctrines
Ideals and Realities of Islam
Islam—Religion, History, and Civilization
Islam and the Plight of Modern Man
Islamic Art and Spirituality
Islamic Life and Thought
Islamic Science—An Illustrated Study
Knowledge and the Sacred
Man and Nature—The Spiritual Crisis of Modern Man
Muhammad—Man of God
Religion and the Order of Nature
Science and Civilization in Islam
Sufi Essays
The Islamic Intellectual Tradition in Persia
The Need for a Sacred Science
Three Muslim Sages
Traditional Islam in the Modern World

THE HEART OF ISLAM

Enduring Values for Humanity

SEYYED HOSSEIN NASR

HarperSanFrancisco
A Division of HarperCollins*Publishers*

All translations of poetry are by S. H. Nasr unless otherwise noted.

HarperCollins books may be purchased for educational, business, or sales promotional use. For information please write: Special Markets Department, HarperCollins Publishers, Inc., 10 East 53rd Street, New York, NY 10022.

HarperCollins Web site: http://www.harpercollins.com
HarperCollins®, ®, and HarperSanFrancisco™ are
trademarks of HarperCollins Publishers, Inc.

FIRST HARPERCOLLINS PAPERBACK EDITION
PUBLISHED IN 2004

Library of Congress Cataloging-in-Publication Data

Nasr, Seyyed Hossein.
Heart of Islam : enduring values for humanity / by Seyyed Hossein Nasr.
p. cm.
Includes bibliographical references and index.
ISBN 0-06-073064-1 (pbk.)
1. Islam—Universality. 2. Islam—Essence, genius, nature. 3. Sufism. I. Title.
BP170.8 .N37 2002
297—dc21

2002068504

07 08 RRD(H) 10 9 8 7

Dedicated to the Sacred and Enduring
Presence of Shaykh Aḥmad ibn Muṣṭafā

al-Shādhilī al-'Alawī

Contents

	Preface	xi
One	One God, Many Prophets *The Unity of Truth and the Multiplicity of Revelations*	1
Two	The Spectrum of Islam *Sunnism, Shī'ism, and Sufism and Traditional, Modernist, and "Fundamentalist" Interpretations of Islam Today*	55
Three	Divine and Human Laws	113
Four	The Vision of Community and Society	157
Five	Compassion and Love, Peace and Beauty	201
Six	Divine and Human Justice *Peace and the Question of War*	237
Seven	Human Responsibilities and Human Rights	273
Epilogue	The Ethical and Spiritual Nature of Human Life, East and West	307
	Notes	317
	Bibliography	319
	Index	325

بسم الله الرحمن الرحيم

In the Name of God, the Infinitely Good, the All-Merciful

Preface

The past few decades have witnessed a growing interest in Islam in the West, increasing with each global event involving the name of Islam: from the Lebanese civil war to the Iranian Revolution of 1979 to the rise of Islamic movements among Palestinians. This rising interest now stands at unprecedented levels since the tragic events of September 11, 2001. The world is thirsty for information about Islam, especially in America, yet this thirst has generally not been quenched with healthy water. In fact, a torrent of "knowledge" has flooded the media from books to journals, radio, and television, much of which is based on ignorance, misinformation, and even disinformation. Not only has this torrent failed the cause of understanding, it has too frequently rendered the greatest disservice to the Western public in order to further particular ideological and political goals.

Of course, distortion of matters Islamic in the West is not new; it has a thousand-year-old history going back to monstrous biographies of the Prophet of Islam written mostly in Latin in France and Germany in the tenth and eleventh centuries. This earlier portrayal of Islam as a Christian heresy, however, still showed an intellectual respect for Islamic civilization and thought. During the Renaissance such figures as Petrarch abandoned even this respect in favor of outright disdain. During the eighteenth and nineteenth centuries, certain figures such as Voltaire tried to use aspects of Islam to attack Christianity, while a number of exceptional figures like Goethe and Emerson held Islamic teachings in great love and esteem. Meanwhile, the new methods of rationalist, historicist, and skeptical scholarship about religion growing out of the so-called Age of Enlightenment (which was in reality an age of the darkening of the soul and eclipse of the intellect) began to apply their methods to the study of Islam in the name of orientalism. Even when they were not serving colonial powers, most of these orientalists studied Islam in the arrogant belief that they possessed a flawless scientific method that applied universally to all religions. The last thing such scholars cared about was what Muslims, or for that matter Hindus or Buddhists, thought about their own religion and how they experienced their own religious universe. Of course, there were exceptions, but these only proved the rule. Orientalist studies of Islam began and ended with the unspoken presumption that Islam was not a revelation, but a phenomenon contrived merely by human agency in a particular historical situation. In this chorus the voices of Louis Massignon, H. A. R. Gibb, and Henry Corbin, followed by a later generation of sympathetic Western scholars such as Annemarie Schimmel, remain truly exceptional.

It was not until the second half of the twentieth century that born Muslims well versed in Western languages and methods of research and expression began to write in-depth works on Islam in European languages to explain the tradition in a serious way to the Western audience. They were joined in this task by a number of Western intellectual and spiritual figures and scholars who had been able to penetrate the Islamic universe of meaning and to speak and write from within the Islamic tradition. As a result of the efforts of these two groups, a number of authentic and profound books on various aspects of Islam appeared in English and other European languages. In contrast to earlier periods, such works were at least available, but their voices continued to be drowned out by the cacophonies of those who rejected Islam from positions of either Christian or Jewish polemicism or secular agnosticism. In fact, there is no religion about which so much has been written in the West by those opposed to it as Islam. No such parallel can be found for Taoism, Confucianism, Hinduism, or Buddhism.

Since the September 11 tragedy, with the rise of interest in Islamic matters, the cacophony has become louder, necessitating an explanation of the authentic teachings of Islam anew in light of the challenges of the present-day situation. This book is a humble effort toward achieving this end. It was commissioned by Harper San Francisco and has been written with the express purpose of explaining certain basic aspects of Islam and widely discussed issues in a manner acceptable to mainstream Islamic thought and comprehensible to the general Western public. It seeks to render a service to all those Westerners genuinely interested in understanding authentic Islam and its relation to the West rather than relying on the distorted images of Islam often presented to them. Needless to say, in a single book of this size it is not possible to deal with all the relevant issues, but I have sought to deal at least with the most significant ones in an effort to open a spiritual and intellectual space for mutual understanding. I also point to principles enabling Muslims and Westerners alike to live in peace and harmony with each other and to join hands against all those from both sides who seek to fan the fire of hatred and to precipitate clashes of civilizations and nations.

I wish to thank Stephen Hanselman of Harper San Francisco for his many suggestions for the book, Katherine O'Brien for helping to prepare the manuscript for publication, and Joseph Lumbard for proofreading the manuscript. May this humble effort serve as a small step toward bringing about better understanding between people of good will in the West and in the Islamic world.

Bethesda, Maryland
March 2002
Dhu'l-ḥijjah A.H. 1423

One

ONE GOD, MANY PROPHETS

The Unity of Truth and the Multiplicity of Revelations

Say: He, God, is One, God the Self-Sufficient Besought of all.
He begetteth not, nor is begotten, and none is like Him.

Quran 112: v.1–4[1]

GOD THE ONE

At the heart of Islam stands the reality of God, the One, the Absolute and the Infinite, the Infinitely Good and All-Merciful, the One Who is at once transcendent and immanent, greater than all we can conceive or imagine, yet, as the Quran, the sacred scripture of Islam, attests, closer to us than our jugular vein. The One God, known by His Arabic Name, Allah, is the central reality of Islam in all of its facets, and attestation to this oneness, which is called *tawḥīd*, is the axis around which all that is Islamic revolves. Allah is beyond all duality and relationality, beyond the differences of gender and of all qualities that distinguish beings from each other in this world. Yet He is the source of all existence and all cosmic and human qualities as well as the End to Whom all things return.

To testify to this oneness lies at the heart of the credo of Islam, and the formula that expresses the truth of this oneness, *Lā ilāha illa'Llāh,* "There is no god but God," is the first of two testifications *(shahādahs)* by which a person bears witness to being a Muslim; the second is *Muḥammadun rasūl Allāh,* "Muḥammad is the messenger of God." The oneness of God is for Muslims not only the heart of their religion, but that of every authentic religion. It is a reassertion of the revelation of God to the Hebrew prophets and to Christ, whom Muslims also consider to be their prophets, the revelation of the truth that "The Lord is one," the reconfirmation of that timeless truth that is also stated in the Catholic creed, *Credo in unum Deum,* "I believe in one God." As the Quran states, "We have never sent a messenger before thee except that We revealed to him, saying, 'There is no god but I, so worship Me'" (21:25). Like countless Muslims, when I read the names of the prophets of old in the Quran or in the traditional prayers, I experience them as living realities in the Islamic universe, while being fully conscious of the fact that they are revered figures in Judaism and Christianity. I also remain fully aware that they are all speaking of the same God Who is One and not of some other deity.

The One God, or Allah, is neither male nor female. However, in the inner teachings of Islam His Essence is often referred to in feminine form and the Divinity is often mentioned as the Beloved, while the Face He has turned to the world as Creator and Sustainer is addressed in the masculine form. Both the male and the female are created by Him and the root of both femininity and masculinity are to be found in the Divine Nature, which transcends the duality between them. Furthermore, the Qualities of God, which are reflected throughout creation, are of a feminine as well as a masculine nature, and the traditional Islamic understanding of the Divinity is not at all confined, as some think, to a purely patriarchal image.

The Quran, which is the verbatim Word of God for Muslims, to be compared to Christ himself in Christianity, reveals not only the Supreme Name of God as Allah, but also mentions other "beautiful Names" of God, considered by traditional sources to be ninety-nine in number, Names revealing different aspects of the Divinity. The Quran states, "To God belong the most beautiful Names *(al-asmā' al-ḥusnā)*. Call on Him thereby" (7:180). These Names are divided into those of Perfection *(Kamāl)*, Majesty *(Jalāl)*, and Beauty *(Jamāl)*, the first relating to the essential oneness of God Himself beyond all polarization and the last two to the masculine and feminine dimensions of reality *in divinis* (in the Divine Order). The Names of Majesty include the Just, the Majestic, the Reckoner, the Giver of Death, the Victorious, and the All-Powerful, and those of Beauty, the All-Merciful, the Forgiver, the Gentle, the Generous, the Beautiful, and Love. For Muslims the whole universe consists of the reflection in various combinations of the Divine Names, and human life is lived amid the polarizations and tensions as well as harmony of the cosmic and human qualities derived from these Names. God at once judges us according to His Justice and forgives us according to His Mercy. He is far beyond our reach, yet resides at the center of the heart of the faithful. He punishes the wicked, but also loves His creatures and forgives them.

The doctrine of God the One, as stated in the Quran, does not only emphasize utter transcendence, although there are powerful expressions of this truth such as *Allāhu akbar*, usually translated as "God is great," but meaning that God is greater than anything we can conceive of Him, which is also attested by the apophatic theology of both the Catholic and Orthodox churches as well as by traditional Judaism. The Quran also accentuates God's nearness to us, stating that He is closer to us than ourselves and that He is present everywhere, as when it states: "Whithersoever ye turn, there is the Face of God" (2:115). The traditional religious life of a Muslim is based on a rhythmic movement between the poles of transcendence and immanence, of rigor and compassion, of justice and forgiveness, of the fear of punishment and hope for mercy based on God's love for us. But the galaxy of Divine Names and the multiplicity of Divine Qualities reflected in the cosmos and within the being of men and women do not distract the Muslim for one moment from the oneness of God, from that Sun before whose light all multiplicity perishes. Striving after the realization of that oneness, or *tawḥīd,* is the heart of Islamic life; and the measure of a successful religious life is the degree to which one is able to realize *tawḥīd,* which means not only oneness, but also the integration of multiplicity into Unity.

Moreover, since there is no official sacerdotal authority in Islam like the magisterium in Roman Catholic Christianity, the authenticity of one's faith in Islam has by and large been determined by the testification of *tawḥīd,* while the degree of inward realization of this truth has remained a matter to be decided by God and not by external authorities. This has been the general norm in Islamic history, but there have also been exceptions, and there are historical instances when a particular group or political authority has taken it upon itself to determine the authenticity or lack thereof of the belief in *tawḥīd* of a particular person or school. But there has never been an Inquisition in Islam, and there has been greater latitude in the acceptance of ideas, especially mystical and esoteric ones, than in most periods of the history of Western Christianity before the penetration of modernism into Christian theology itself.

Now, although Islam is based on the reality of God, the One, in His Absoluteness and Suchness, it also addresses humanity in its essential reality, in its suchness. Man, in the traditional sense of the term corresponding to *insān* in Arabic or *homo* in Greek and not solely the male, is seen in Islam not as a sinful being to whom the message of Heaven is sent to heal the wound of the original sin, but as a being who still carries his primordial nature *(al-fiṭrah)* within himself, although he has forgotten that nature now buried deep under layers of negligence. As the Quran states:

"[God] created man in the best of stature *(aḥsan al-taqwīm)*" (95:4) with an intelligence capable of knowing the One. The message of Islam is addressed to that primordial nature. It is a call for recollection, for the remembrance of a knowledge kneaded into the very substance of our being even before our coming into this world. In a famous verse that defines the relationship between human beings and God, the Quran, in referring to the precosmic existence of man, states, "'Am I not your Lord?' They said: 'Yes, we bear witness'" (7:172). The "they" refers to all the children of Adam, male and female, and the "yes" confirms the affirmation of God's Oneness by us in our pre-eternal ontological reality.

Men and women still bear the echo of this "yes" deep down within their souls, and the call of Islam is precisely to this primordial nature, which uttered the "yes" even before the creation of the heavens and the earth. The call of Islam therefore concerns, above all, the remembrance of a knowledge deeply embedded in our being, the confirmation of a knowledge that saves, hence the soteriological function of knowledge in Islam. Islam addresses the human being not primarily as will, but as intelligence. If the great sin in Christianity is disobedience, which has warped the will, the great sin in Islam is forgetfulness and the resulting inability of the intelligence to function in the way that God created it as the means to know the One. That is why the greatest sin in Islam and the only one God does not forgive is *shirk*, or taking a partner unto God, which means denying the Oneness of God, or *tawḥīd*.

This direct address from God, the One, to each human being in its primordial state requires total surrender to the Majesty of the Absolute, before whom ultimately nothing can in fact exist. In an ordinary sense it means the surrender of ourselves to God, and in the highest sense it means the awareness of our nothingness before Him, for, as the Quran says, "All that dwells in the heavens and the earth perishes, yet there abideth the Face of thy Lord, Majestic, Splendid" (55:26–27). The very name of the religion, Islam, comes from this reality, for the Arabic word *al-islām* means "surrender" as well as the peace that issues from our surrender to God. In fact, Islam is the only major religion, along with Buddhism (if we consider the name of the religion to come from *Budd,* the Divine Intellect, and not the Buddha), whose name is not related to a person or ethnic group, but to the central idea of the religion. Moreover, Islam considers all authentic religions to be based on this surrender, so that *al-islām* means not only the religion revealed through the Quran to the Prophet Muḥammad, but all authentic religions as such. That is why in the Quran the prophet Abraham is also called *muslim,* that is, one who is in the state of *al-islām.*

True surrender is not, however, only concerned with our will. It must involve our whole being. A shallow understanding of surrender can lead to either a passive attitude, in which one does not strive in life as one should according to the promulgations of the religion, or to mistaking one's own imperfect understanding of Islam for the truth and performing acts that are against God's teachings while claiming that one is acting in surrender to God. Islam states that a person must be the perfect servant *('abd)* of God in the sense of following His commands. But since God has given us many faculties, including free will and intelligence, our surrender must be complete and total, not limited to only certain faculties. It must involve the whole of our being. Otherwise, hidden thoughts and emotions as well as false ideas can combine with a fallacious sense of external surrender of one's will to God to produce acts in the name of religion that can have calamitous consequences.

Such acts have appeared from time to time historically and can be seen especially in this day and age, but they are deviations rather than the norm. The norm by which the vast majority of Muslims have lived over the ages has meant surrender to God with one's whole being, following the Divine Law and the ethical teachings of Islam to the extent possible, striving in life according to religious teachings to the extent of one's ability, and then being resigned to consequences that ensue and accepting what destiny has put before us. It is in this sense that the common Arabic saying ***maktūb,*** "It is written," marking the sign of resignation to a particular event or results of one's actions, must be understood. This surrender has certainly not meant either fatalism or an individualistic interpretation of Divine norms in the name of surrender. It has, on the contrary, led to an inward and outward striving combined with serenity that characterizes traditional patterns of Islamic life, in contrast to both modernistic and much of the so-called fundamentalist currents found in the Islamic world today.

CREATION OF THE WORLD AND OF HUMAN BEINGS

Since the One God is Infinite and Absolute as well as the Infinitely Good, He could not but create. His infinitude implies that He contains within Himself all possibilities, including that of negating Himself, and this possibility had to be realized in the form of creation. Moreover, as St. Augustine also stated, it is in the nature of the good to give of itself, and the Infinitely-Good could not but radiate the reality that constitutes the world and, in fact, all the worlds.

But creation or radiation implies separation, and it is this ontological separation from the Source of all goodness that constitutes evil. One might say that evil is nothing but separation from the Good and privation, although it is real on its own level, in a sense as real as our own existential level on which we find it. And yet the good belongs to the pole of being and evil to that of nonbeing.

Throughout the history of Islam there have been numerous profound metaphysical and theological discussions concerning the question of evil, as there have been in other religions, especially Christianity. But in contrast to the modern West, in which many people have turned away from God and religion because they could not understand how a God who is good could create a world in which there is evil, in the Islamic world this question of theodicy has hardly ever bothered the religious conscience of even the most intelligent people or turned them away from God. The emphasis of the Quran upon the reality of evil on the moral plane combined with the sapiential and theological explanations of this question have kept men and women confronted with this problem in the domain of faith. The strong emphasis in Islam on the Will of God has also played a role in resigning Muslims to the presence of evil in the world (which they must nevertheless combat to the extent possible), even when they cannot understand the causes involved.

In any case, God has created the world, in which there is imperfection and evil, but the world itself is considered by the Quran to be good, a view corresponding to that found in the book of Genesis. And creation has a purpose, for, as the Quran says, "O Lord, Thou didst not create this [the world] in vain" (8:190). The deepest purpose of creation is explained by a famous *ḥadīth qudsī* (a sacred saying of the

Prophet not part of the Quran in which God speaks in the first person through the mouth of the Prophet): "I was a hidden treasure. I loved to be known. Therefore, I created the creation so that I would be known." The purpose of creation therefore is God's love for the knowledge of Himself realized through His central agent on earth, humanity. For a human being to know God is to fulfill the purpose of creation. Moreover, God loved to be known. Hence, the love of God and by God permeates the whole universe, and many Islamic mystics of Sufis over the ages have spoken of that love to which Dante refers at the end of the *Divine Comedy* when he speaks of "the love that moves the sun and the stars."

This sacred *ḥadīth (ḥadīth qudsī)* also speaks of God's being "a hidden treasure," which is a symbol of the truth that everything in the universe has its origin in the Divine Reality and is a manifestation of that Reality. Everything in the total cosmos both visible and invisible is a theophany, or manifestation, of the Divine Names and Qualities and is drawn from the "treasury" of God. The Wisdom of God thus permeates the universe, and Muslims in fact see the cosmos as God's primordial revelation. Everything in the universe, in reflecting God's Wisdom, also glorifies Him, for, as the Quran says, "There is nothing but that it hymns His praise" (17:44). In fact, the very existence of beings is nothing but their invocation of God's Names, and the universe itself is nothing but the consequence of the breathing upon the archetypal realities of all beings in the Divine Intellect of the Breath of the Compassionate *(nafas al-Raḥmān)*. It is through His Name *al-Raḥmān,* which means the Infinitely-Good and also Merciful, that the universe has come into being. It is significant to note that much of the Quran is devoted to the cosmos and the world of nature, which play an integral role in the traditional life of Muslims. All Islamic rites are harmonized with natural phenomena, and in general Muslims view the world of creation as God's first revelation, before the Torah, the Gospels, the Quran, and other sacred scriptures were revealed. That is why in Islam, as in medieval Judaism and Christianity, the cosmos is seen as a book in which the "signs of God," the *vestigia Dei* of Christian authors, are to be read.

The Islamic understanding of anthropogenesis, the creation of human beings, resembles those of Judaism and Christianity in many ways, but also differs on certain significant issues. In fact, there are also important differences between Judaism and Christianity when it comes to the question of original sin. As for Adam's original creation, the Quran speaks of God creating Adam from clay and breathing His Spirit into him, "And I breathed into him My Spirit" (15:29). The Quran continues:

> And when thy Lord said unto the angels: "Verily! I am about to place a vicegerent *(khalīfah)* on earth," they said, "Wilt Thou place therein one who will bring corruption therein and will shed blood, while we, we hymn Thy praise and sanctify Thee?" He said: "Surely, I know that which ye know not."
>
> And He taught Adam all the names, then showed them to the angels, saying: "Inform me of the names of these, if ye are truthful."
>
> They said: "Be glorified! We have no knowledge save that which Thou hast taught us." (2:30–32)[2]

The angels were then asked by God to prostrate before Adam, and all did so except Iblīs, that is, the Devil or Satan, who refused because of pride. God placed Adam and his wife in paradise and permitted them to eat of the fruits there, except the fruit of the forbidden tree. But Satan "caused them to deflect therefrom," and the Fall ensued. But a revelation was sent to Adam. He repented and became the first prophet as well as the father of humanity.

The Quranic account contains all the main features of the sacred anthropology of Islam and its view of the nature of men and women. First of all, God chose the human being as His vicegerent *(khalīfah)* on earth, which means that He has given human beings power to dominate the earth, but on the condition that they remain obedient to God, that is, being God's servant, or *'abd Allāh*. There are numerous Quranic references to this truth. The two primary features of being human are servanthood and vicegerency: being passive toward Heaven in submission to God's Will, on the one hand, and being active as God's agent and doing His Will in the world, on the other. Moreover, Adam was taught all the names, which means that God has placed within human nature an intelligence that is central and the means by which he can know all things. It also means that human beings themselves are the theophany, or visible manifestation, of all of God's Names. There is in principle no limit to human intelligence in knowing the nature of things (the question of knowing the Divine Essence is a different matter) unless there is an obstacle that prevents it from functioning correctly. That is why Muslims believe that any normal and wholesome intelligence will be naturally led to the confirmation of Divine Oneness and are at a loss when rationalist skeptics from the West refuse to accept the One (most Muslims are unaware of the obstacles in the soul of such a skeptic that reduce the intelligence to analytical reason and prevent it from functioning in its fullness). Adam, the prototype of humanity, is superior to the angels by virtue of his knowledge of the names of all things as well as by being the reflection of all the Divine Names and Qualities.

As for Iblīs, his rebellion comes from pride in considering his nature, which was made of fire, superior to that of Adam, who was made of clay. He refused to prostrate himself before Adam, because fire is a more noble element than earth or clay. He could not see the effect of the Spirit that God had breathed into Adam. Satan was therefore the first to misuse analogy, to try to replace intelligence with ordinary logical reasoning. His fall was thus also connected to the domain of knowledge. The lack of total knowledge on his part created the sense of pride, which in Islam, as in Christianity, is the source of all other vices.

The Quran mentions Adam's wife, but not her name. *Ḥadīth* sources however confirm that her name was Ḥawwā', or Eve. In fact, the Islamic names for the first parents of humanity, Ādam and Ḥawwā', are the same as in Judaism and Christianity. The Quran, however, does not mention how she was created. Some traditional commentators have repeated the biblical account of her creation from Adam's rib, while other authorities have mentioned that she was created from the same clay from which God created Adam. It is important to note for the Islamic understanding of womanhood and women's roles in both religious and social life that, in contrast to the biblical story, Eve did not tempt Adam to eat the forbidden fruit. Rather, they were tempted together by Iblīs and therefore Eve was not the cause of Adam's expulsion from paradise. He was also responsible; they shared in performing the act that led to their fall, and therefore both men and women are faced equally with its consequences. As far as the forbidden fruit is concerned, again, the Quran does not mention it explicitly, but according to traditional commentaries it was not an apple, as believed by Christians and Jews, but wheat.

The creation of human beings complements the creation of the cosmos and adds to the created order a central being who is God's vicegerent, capable of knowing all things, of dominating the earth, given the power to do good, but also to wreak havoc and, in fact, corrupt the earth. According to a famous *ḥadīth,* "God created man upon His form," although here form does not mean physical image, but rather the reflection of God's Names and Qualities. But human beings are also given the freedom to rebel against God, and Iblīs can exercise power over them. The human being contains, in fact, all possibilities within himself or herself. The soul itself is a vast field in which the signs of God are manifested. As a Quranic verse states, "We shall show them our signs *(āyāt)* upon the horizons and within their souls until it becomes manifest unto them that it is the truth" (41:53). Therefore, in a sense, the human being is itself a revelation like the macrocosm.

It might be said that from the Islamic point of view creation and revelation are inseparable, and that there are in fact three grand revelations: the cosmos, the human state, and religions—all three of which Islam sees as "books." There is, first of all, the cosmic book to be read and deciphered. Then there is the inner book of the soul, which we carry within ourselves. And finally there are sacred scriptures, which have been sent by God through His Mercy to guide humanity throughout the ages and which are the foundations of various religions and keys for reading the other two books, that of the cosmos and that of the soul.

MANY REVELATIONS, MANY PROPHETS

In the Islamic perspective, the oneness of God has as its consequence not the uniqueness of prophecy, but its multiplicity, since God as the Infinite created a world in which there is multiplicity and this includes, of course, the human order. For Islam, revelation and prophecy are both necessary and universal. Humanity, according to the Quran, was created from a single soul, but then diversified into races and tribes, for, as the Quran states, "He created you [humanity] from a single soul" (39:6). The single origin of humanity implies the profound unity within diversity of human nature, and therefore religion based on the message of Divine Oneness could not have been only meant for or available to a segment of humanity. The multiplicity of races, nations, and tribes necessitates the diversity of revelations. Therefore, the Quran, on the one hand, asserts that "To every people [We have sent] a messenger" (10:48), and, on the other hand, "For each [people] We have appointed a Divine Law and a way. Had God willed, He could have made you one community. But that He may try you by that which He hath given you. So vie with one another in good works. Unto God ye will all return, and He will then inform you concerning that wherein ye differed" (5:48). According to these and other verses, not only is the multiplicity of religions necessary, but it is also a reflection of the richness of the Divine Nature and is willed by God.

Religion *(dīn)*, revelation *(waḥy)*, and prophecy *(nubuwwah)* have a clear meaning in the context of the Islamic worldview and therefore need to be carefully defined in the modern context, where all of these terms have become ambiguous in ordinary discourse. The closest word to the English term "religion" in Arabic is *dīn*, which is said by many to have been derived from the root meaning "to obey, submit, and humble oneself before God." *Al-dīn* means religion in the vastest sense as the sacred norm into which the whole of life is to be molded. It is the total way of life grounded in teachings that have issued from God.

These teachings reach humanity through revelation, which means the direct conveying of a message from Heaven (revelation being understood apart from all the psychological entanglements it has acquired in much of modern Western religious thought). Revelation, moreover, must not be confused with inspiration *(ilhām),* which is possible for all human beings.

Islam sees revelation not as incarnation in the Hindu or Christian sense, but as the descent of the Word of God in the form of sacred scripture to a prophet. In fact, the Quran uses the term "Book" *(kitāb)* not only for the Quran, but also for all other sacred books and the totality of revelations. The Quran considers all revelations to be contained in that "archetypal book," or *Umm al-kitāb* (literally, "the Mother Book"), and the sacred scriptures to be related in conveying the same basic message of the primordial religion of unity in different languages and contexts. As the Quran states, "We never sent a messenger save with the language of his people" (14:4). Even when the Quran states that "the religion with God is *al-islām*" (3:19) or similar statements, *al-islām* refers to that universal surrender to the One and that primordial religion contained in the heart of all heavenly inspired religions, not just to Islam in its more particular sense. There is, moreover, a criterion of truth and falsehood as far as religions are concerned, and the Quran's confirmation of the universality of revelation does not mean that everything that has passed as religion yesterday or does so today is authentic. Throughout history there have been false prophets and religions, to which Christ also referred, as well as religions that have decayed or deviated from their original form.

Islam sees itself as heir to this long chain of prophets going back to Adam and believes all of them, considered to be 124,000 according to tradition, to be also its own. It does not believe, however, that it has inherited their teachings through temporal and historical transmission, for a prophet owes nothing to anyone and receives everything from Heaven, but it does believe that its message bears the finality of a seal. Islam sees itself as at once the primordial religion, a return to the original religion of oneness, and the final religion; the Quran itself calls the Prophet of Islam the "Seal of Prophets." And, in fact, fourteen hundred years of history have confirmed Islam's claim, for during all that time there has not been another plenary manifestation of the Truth like the ones that brought about the births of Buddhism and Christianity, not to speak of the earlier major religions. The two characteristics of primordiality and finality have bestowed upon Islam its trait of universality and the capability to absorb intellectually and culturally so much that came before it. It has also made spiritually alive the prophetic presences that preceded it, so that, for example, such figures as Abraham, Moses, and Christ play a much greater role in the spiritual universe of Islam than Abraham and Moses do in the Christian universe.

While speaking of the finality of the Islamic revelation for this cycle of human history, which will last until the eschatological events at the end of historic time, something must be said, from the Islamic point of view, about the "order" and "economy" of revelation. Muslims believe that each revelation takes place through the Divine Will, but also on the basis of a spiritual economy and is not by any means ad hoc. Each revelation fulfills a major function in human history seen from the religious point of view. For example, around the sixth to fifth century B.C. which also marks the transition from mythological time to historic time, a qualitative change took place in the march of time, which for Islam, as for Hinduism, is not simply linear. This is the period when the myths of Homer and Hesiod recede as Greek history flowers and the stories of mythical Persian dynasties are left behind as the Persian Empire takes shape. From the human point of view, this qualitative change in the terrestrial life of humanity required new dispensations from Heaven, and from the metaphysical perspective, these new dispensations themselves marked the new chapter that was to begin in human history.

This period, which philosophers such as Karl Jaspers have called the Axial Age, was witness to the appearance of Confucius and Lao-Tze in China and the new crystallization of the primal Chinese tradition into Confucianism and Taoism, and the appearance of Shintoism in Japan and the beginning of the terrestrial life of the solar emperors, who marked the beginning of historical Japanese civilization. This age was also witness to the life of the Buddha, whose teaching spread throughout India and Tibet and soon transformed the religious life of East and Southeast Asia. At nearly the same time, we see the rise of Zoroaster, who established Zoroastrianism in Persia and whose teachings greatly influenced later religious life in western Asia. Finally, around the same time we have the rise of Pythagoras and Pythagoreanism, which was central to the spiritual life of ancient Greece and from which Platonism was born. This remarkable cluster of figures, which also includes some of the Hebrew prophets, figures whom Muslims would call prophets, transformed the religious life of humanity, although the still living and viable religions of the earlier period such as Judaism and Hinduism survived. Moreover, this list of figures does not exhaust all the notable sages and prophets of the Axial Age.

One would think that the cycle of revelation would have been terminated in the Axial Age. But the decadence of the

Greek and Roman religions around the Mediterranean Basin and the weakening of the northern European religions created a vacuum that only a new revelation could fill. Therefore Christianity was revealed by God. Although originally a Semitic religion, providentially it soon became, to some extent, Hellenized, and Christ was transformed almost into an "Aryan" solar hero for the Europeans, who were destined to find the path of salvation through this new dispensation from Heaven. It certainly was no accident that in Europe Christianity remained strong and unified, while in the eastern Mediterranean and North Africa, destined to become part of the future "Abode of Islam," it splintered into numerous small denominations fighting among themselves as well as against Byzantium.

This latter situation, added to the inner weakness of Zoroastrianism in the Persian Empire and certain other religions elsewhere, created another vacuum to be filled, this time by a new Semitic religion—Islam. Islam, like Judaism, remained faithful to its Semitic origin, but, like Christianity, was not confined to a particular ethnic group. Islam thus came to reassert the full doctrine of Divine Oneness on a universal scale after the Axial Age and the appearance of Christianity, placing in a sense the last golden brick in that golden wall that is revelation. With it, the structure of the wall became complete, and, as far as Muslims are concerned, although small religious movements may take place here and there, there is to be no plenary revelation after Islam according to the Divine Providence and the spiritual economy of God's plans for present-day humanity. When asked how they know such a truth, Muslims point to the Quran itself and the fact that no previous revelation had ever made such an explicit claim. Being the final religion of this cycle, Islam is not only closely related to its sister monotheisms, Judaism and Christianity, but also possesses an inward link to the religions of the Axial Age as well as to Hinduism. It is this link that made it easier for Islam than for Christianity to incorporate so much of the wisdom of Hinduism and of the religions of the Axial Age, from Buddhism and Pythagoreanism to Zoroastrianism and even later to Confucianism, within its sapiential perspective.

Paradoxically, the insistence of Islam upon God as the One and the Absolute has had as its concomitant the acceptance of multiplicity of prophets and revelations, and no sacred scripture is more universalist in its understanding of religion than the Quran, whose perspective concerning the universality of revelation may be called "vertical triumphalism." In contrast, in Christianity, because of the emphasis on the Triune God, God the One is seen more in terms of the relationality of the three Hypostases, what one might call "Divine Relativity"; the vision of the manifestation of the Divine then became confined to the unique Son and Incarnation, in whom the light of all previous prophets was absorbed. In Christianity the vision is that of the Triune God and a unique message of salvation and savior, hence *extra ecclesiam nulla salus* (no salvation outside the church), whereas in Islam there is the One God and many prophets. Here is to be found the major difference between how Muslims have viewed Jews and Christians over the centuries and how Christians have regarded Jews and Muslims as well as followers of other religions. For Muslims, the Quran completes the message of previous sacred texts without in any way denigrating their significance. In fact, the Torah and the Gospels are mentioned by name as sacred scriptures along with the Quran in the text of the Quran. Likewise, although the Prophet terminates the long chain of prophecy, the earlier prophets lose none of their spiritual significance. Rather, they appear in the Islamic firmament as stars, while the Prophet is like the moon in that Islamic sky.

THE QURAN

The sacred scripture of Islam, known in Arabic by many names, of which the most famous is *al-Qur'ān*, "the Recitation," is considered by all Muslims, no matter to which school they belong, as the verbatim revelation of God's Word made to descend into the heart, soul, and mind of the Prophet of Islam through the agency of the archangel of revelation, Gabriel, or Jibra'īl in Arabic. Both the words and meaning of the text are considered to be sacred, as is everything else connected with it, such as the chanting of its verses or the calligraphy of its phrases. Muslims are born with verses of the Book, which Muslims call the Noble Quran, read into their ears, live throughout their lives hearing its verses and also repeating certain of its chapters during daily prayers, are married with the accompaniment of Quranic recitations, and die hearing it chanted beside them.

The Quran (also known as the Koran in English) is the central theophany of Islam, the fundamental source of its metaphysics, cosmology, theology, law, ethics, sacred history, and general worldview. In a way the soul of the traditional Muslim is like a mosaic made up of phrases of the Quran, which are repeated throughout life, such as the *basmalah,* "In the Name of God, the Infinitely Good, the All-Merciful," with which all legitimate acts begin and are consecrated; *alḥamduli'Llāh,* "Praise be to God," with which one terminates an act or event in the attitude of gratefulness; *inshā'a'Llāh,* "If God wills," which accompanies every utterance concerning the future, for the future is in God's Hands and nothing takes place save through His Will. Even the daily greeting of Muslims, *al-salāmu ʿalaykum*, "Peace be upon you," which the Prophet taught to his companions as the greeting of the people of paradise, comes from the Quran. As some Western scholars of Islam have noted, there is perhaps no single book that is as influential in any religion as the Quran is in Islam.

To fully understand the significance of the Quran, a Westerner with a Christian background should realize that, although the Quran can in a sense be compared to the Old and New Testaments, a more profound comparison would be with Christ himself. In Christianity both the spirit and body of Christ are sacred, and he is considered the Word of God. The Quran is likewise for Muslims the Word of God *(kalimat Allāh)*, and both its inner meaning, or spirit, and its body, or outer form, the text in the Arabic language in which it was revealed, are sacred to Muslims. Arabic is the sacred language of Islam and Quranic Arabic plays a role in Islam analogous to the role of the body of Christ in Christianity. Moreover, as Christians consume bread and wine as symbols of the flesh and blood of Christ, Muslims pronounce, using the same organ of the body, that is, the mouth, the Word of God in the daily prayers. The rationalist and agnostic methods of higher criticism applied by certain Western scholars to the text of the Quran, which was not compiled over a long period of time like the Old and the New Testaments, is as painful and as much a blasphemy to Muslims as it would be to believing Christians if some Muslim archeologists claimed to have discovered some physical remain of Christ and were using DNA analysis to determine whether he was born miraculously or was the son of Joseph.

In any case, for Muslims themselves, Sunni and Shīʿite alike, there is but a single text of the Quran consisting of 114 chapters of over 6,000 verses revealed to the Prophet of Islam in Mecca and Medina over the twenty-three years of his prophetic mission. As verses were received and then uttered by him, they would be memorized by companions, who were Arabs with prodigious memories. The verses were also written down by scribes. The order of the chapters of the Quran was also given by the Prophet through Divine command. During the caliphate of the third caliph, ʿUthmān, some twenty years after the death of the Prophet, as many of those who had memorized the Quran were dying in various battles, the complete text of the Quran was copied in several manuscripts and sent to the four corners of the Islamic world. Later copies are based on this early definitive collection.

It is said in Islam that God gives to each prophet a miracle corresponding to what was important in his time. Since magic was so significant in Egypt, God gave Moses the power to turn his staff into a serpent. Since medicine was such an important art at the time of Christ, God gave him the miracle of raising the dead to life. And since poetic eloquence was the most prized of all virtues for pre-Islamic Arabs, God revealed through the Prophet by far the most eloquent of all Arabic works. In fact, the greatest miracle of Islam is said to be the eloquence of the Quran. Its eloquence not only moved the heart and soul of those Arabs of the seventh century who first heard it, but also moves to tears Muslim believers throughout the world today, even those whose mother tongue is not Arabic, although Arabic is the language of daily prayers for all Muslims, Arab and non-Arab alike. The grace, or *barakah* (corresponding both etymologically and in meaning to the Hebrew *barak*), of the text transcends its mental message and moves souls toward God in much the same way that hearing Gregorian chant in Latin would for centuries in the West deeply affect even those who did not understand the Latin words. Of course, the same can be said for the Latin Mass itself, whose beautiful liturgy was of the deepest significance for some fifteen hundred years even for those Catholics who did not know Latin.

The Quran has many names, each revealing an aspect of its reality. It is *al-Qur'ān,* or "recitation," which also means "gathering" or "concentration." It is *al-Furqān,* or "discernment," because it provides the criteria for discerning between truth and falsehood, goodness and evil, beauty and ugliness. It is *Umm al-kitāb,* the archetypal book containing the root of all knowledge, and it is *al-Hudā,* the guide for the journey of men and women toward God. For Muslims, the Quran is the source of all knowledge both outward and inward, the foundation of the Law, the final guide for ethical behavior, and a net with which the Divine Fisherman ensnares the human soul and brings it back to Unity.

The Quran contains several grand themes. First of all, it deals with the nature of reality, with the Divine Reality and Its relation to the realm of relativity. Second, the Quran says much about the natural world, and in a sense the Islamic sector of the cosmos participates in the Quranic revelation. Then the Quran contains many pages on sacred history, but the episodes of this history are recounted more for their significance as lessons for the inner life of the soul than as historical accounts of ages past. Sacred history in the Quran contains, above all, moral and spiritual lessons for us here and now.

The Quran also deals with laws for the individual and society and is the most important source of Islamic Law, or the *Sharī'ah.* Furthermore, the Quran comes back again and again to the question of ethics, of good and evil, of the significance of living a virtuous life. Finally, the Quran speaks, especially in its last chapters, in majestic language about eschatological events, about the end of this world, about the Day of Judgment, paradise, purgatory, and hell. The language of the Quran, especially in dealing with eschatological realities, is concrete and symbolic, not abstract, or descriptive in the ordinary sense, which would in any case be impossible when one is dealing with realities our earthly imaginations cannot grasp. This trait has caused many outsiders to criticize the Quran for its sensuous description of the delights of paradise as if they were simply a sublimation of earthly joys and pleasures. In reality every joy and delight here below, especially sexuality, which is sacred for Islam, is the reflection of a paradisal prototype, not vice versa.

According to the Prophet and many of the earliest authorities such as ʿAlī and Jaʿfar al-Ṣādiq, the Quran has many levels of meaning, of which the highest is known to God alone. In the same way that God is both the Outward *(al-Ẓāhir)* and the Inward *(al-Bāṭin)*, His Book also has an outward and an inward dimension or, in fact, several levels of inner meaning. Throughout Islamic history, Quranic commentaries have been written from both points of view, the outward and the inward. The first is called *tafsīr* and the second *ta'wīl*. Works of both categories are crucial for the understanding of the text of the Quran, each word and letter of which is like a living being with many levels of significance, including a numerical symbolism, which is studied in the science called *jafr*, corresponding to Jewish and Christian Kabbala.

The chapters *(sūrahs)* and verses *(āyahs)* of the Quran are both the path and the guidepost in the Muslim's earthly journey. The root of everything Islamic, from metaphysics and theology to law and ethics to the sciences and arts, is to be found in it. Every movement that has begun in Islamic history, whether religious, intellectual, social, or political, has sought legitimization in the Quran, and the permanent flow of the daily life of traditional Muslims unaffected by such movements has also been marked in the deepest sense by the presence of the Quran. Jurists have sought to interpret its legal verses and Sufis its inner meaning. Philosophers have drawn from its philosophical utterances and theologians have debated its assertions about the nature of God's Attributes and His relation to the world. Today, as when it was revealed, the Quran remains the central reality of Islam and the heart of Muslim life in both its individual and social aspects.

THE PROPHET OF ISLAM

The Prophet of Islam, to whom we shall henceforth refer simply as the Prophet, is for the West the most misunderstood reality within the Islamic universe. For over a millennium he has been maligned in various European sources as an apostate, a pretender, and even the Antichrist, and one has had to wait well over a thousand years until the twentieth century to see fair treatments of him appear in European languages. Until recently, Christians usually compared him, of course very unfavorably, to Christ, assuming that he holds the same position in Islam as Christ does in Christianity. Westerners therefore called Islam Mohammadanism until a few decades ago, a term detested by Muslims, and concentrated their attacks against him in order to vilify Islam. Even those who admitted to his remarkable achievements in this world refused to accept him as a prophet. Christian attacks against him were, in fact, the most painful and divisive element in Islam's relationship with Christianity over the centuries. Even today the general misunderstanding of the Prophet in the West remains a major obstacle to mutual understanding. In modern times certain Western writers opposed to Christianity tried to use the Prophet as an instrument in their attacks on Christianity without any real appreciation or understanding of the Prophet himself. Rarely does one find in earlier Western history a figure such as the German poet Goethe, who harbored deep respect and even love for the Prophet.

To understand the heart of Islam it is, therefore, essential to understand the significance of the Prophet from the point of view of traditional Muslims—not that of either Muslim modernists who neglect his spiritual dimension or the so-called puritan reformers who for other reasons belittle his significance in the total religious economy of Islam. The Quran asserts clearly that the Prophet was a man and not divine, but also adds that God chose him as His final messenger, the "Seal of Prophets," that he was given the most exalted and noble character, and that he was chosen as a model for Muslims to emulate as mentioned in the verse, "Verily you have in the Messenger of God an excellent exemplar for him who looks to God and the Last Day and remembers God often" (32:21). This verse is the basis for the emulation of the *Sunnah,* or wonts (in the sense of actions and deeds) of the Prophet, that is central to the whole of Islam. For Muslims, the Prophet is a mortal man *(bashar),* but also God's most perfect creature, or what the Sufis, the mystics of Islam, call the Universal Man *(al-insān al-kāmil).* As a Sufi poem recited often throughout the Islamic world asserts,

> Muḥammad is a man, but not like other men.
> Rather, he is a ruby and other men are like stones.

The Prophet was born in Mecca in the "Year of the Elephant," that is, 570 C.E., into an aristocratic branch of a major tribe of Mecca known as the Quraysh. His own family descended from Hāshim, and so he and his descendants are known as Hāshimites, which was a branch of the Quraysh. His father, 'Abd Allāh, died before he was born and his mother, Āminah, also died when Muḥammad, whose most famous name means "the most praised one," was very young, leaving him an orphan. He was brought up in the household of his uncle Abū Ṭālib, the father of 'Alī, the fourth Sunni caliph and the first Imām of Shī'ism. The young Muḥammad also spent some time with the Bedouins in the desert to master Arabic eloquence and to learn their ways, which had been the custom of the people of Mecca from ancient times. From his early days he was known for his honesty and sincerity and given the title of al-Amīn, "the Trusted One." He also had a strong contemplative tendency, which caused him to retreat often into the desert for prayer. Although the Meccans at that time practiced a crass form of idolatry, there were among them those who still followed the primordial monotheism of Abraham and are referred to in the Quran as the *ḥunafā'*, the primordialists. The Prophet was one such person and believed in the one God even before being chosen as prophet.

As a young man Muḥammad began to travel with caravans to Syria, and Muslims believe that it was during one of these trips that a Christian monk, Baḥīrah, predicted that he would become a prophet. Because of his honesty and earnestness, which had become famous, he attracted the attention of a wealthy businesswoman of Mecca, Khadījah, who was fifteen years his senior, but who proposed marriage and asked him to manage her business affairs. Muḥammad accepted and had a very happy marriage, from which issued four daughters, the most famous of whom is Fāṭimah. She later married 'Alī and is the mother of all the descendants of the Prophet, who are called *sayyids* or *sharīfs* and who have played an extraordinary role in Islamic history. The Prophet had a monogamous marriage until Khadījah died when he was fifty years old. It was only in the last years of his life that he contracted other marriages, mostly for the political purpose of unifying the various tribes of Arabia.

When Muḥammad was forty years old and praying in a cave called al-Ḥirā' near Mecca, the archangel Gabriel came to him with the first verses of the revelation that constitutes the beginning of Surah 96, "The Clot." Thus began his prophetic mission, which was to be carried out in the most difficult situation conceivable, for the message was one of uncompromising monotheism in a city that was the center of Arabian idolatry. The Ka'bah, or the House of God, which stands at the center of Mecca and is the most holy site in Islam, was built originally, according to Muslim belief, by Adam himself and rebuilt by Abraham. But this primordial sanctuary had now become filled with the idols of various tribes who would regularly visit Mecca for the purpose of pilgrimage. Mecca had therefore also become a major center for trade, and much of the power and wealth of Meccans derived from the presence of the Ka'bah in their city. The message of the Prophet struck therefore at the heart of not only the religion, but also the source of power and wealth of the people of his own city, including his family.

At first only Khadījah, 'Alī, and the Prophet's old friend Abū Bakr accepted the message that was revealed to him. Gradually, however, a number of others, including such eminent personalities as 'Umar ibn al-Khaṭṭāb, who was later to become the second caliph after Abū Bakr, and

'Uthmān ibn 'Affān, the future third caliph, embraced Islam. The very success of the Prophet's mission made the opposition to him and his followers more severe every day. There were several attempts on his life until, in the year 622 C.E., after agreements made with emissaries sent from the city of Yathrib to the north to Mecca, he migrated by Divine command to that city along with his followers. That migration, called *al-hijrah* in Arabic, marks the major turning point in Islamic history, when Islam was transformed from a small group of devotees to a full-fledged community. Yathrib became known as *Madīnat al-nabī*, the City of the Prophet, and is known to this day as Medina. Here the first Islamic society, which has remained the ideal model for all later Islamic societies, was founded.

Shortly before the migration, an event of supreme spiritual and religious significance took place in the Prophet's life, an event that is also mentioned in the Quran. According to Islamic tradition, he was taken on what is called the Nocturnal Journey, or *al-mi'rāj,* on a supernatural horse, called al-Burāq, by Gabriel from Mecca to Jerusalem. Then, from the place where the mosque of the Dome of the Rock is now located, he was taken through all of the heavens, that is, all the higher states of being, to the Divine Presence Itself, meeting on the journey earlier prophets such as Moses and Jesus. The *mi'rāj* is the prototype of all spiritual wayfaring and realization in Islam, and its architecture even served as a model for Dante's *Divine Comedy*. The experiences of this celestial journey, moreover, constitute the inner reality of the Islamic daily prayers and also the bringing to completion the performance of their outward form.

It was during this journey that the Prophet reached the Divine Presence, beyond even the paradisal states at the station that marks the boundary of universal existence;

beyond this station, which the Quran calls the Lote Tree of the Uttermost End, there is only the hidden mystery of God known to Himself alone. It was in this most exalted state that the Prophet received the revelation that contains what many consider to be the heart of the credo of Islam: "The Messenger believeth, and the faithful believe, in what has been revealed unto him from his Lord. Each one believeth in God and His angels and His books and His messengers: we make no distinction between any of His messengers. And they say: we hear and we obey: grant us, Thou our Lord, Thy forgiveness; unto Thee is the ultimate becoming" (2:285).[3]

Jerusalem had been the first direction that Muslims faced when praying *(qiblah)*, before it was replaced by Mecca by Divine order, and is also considered to be the site of the eschatological events at the end of time according to Islamic tradition. But the Nocturnal Journey made Jerusalem even more significant for Muslims. In fact, the three holy cities of Islam, namely, Mecca, Medina, and Jerusalem, are inextricably intertwined with the life of the Prophet.

In Medina the nascent community was confronted immediately with attacks from the Meccans, and several wars called *maghāzī* were fought in which the Muslims prevailed usually against unbelievable odds. Finally, the message of Islam spread throughout Arabia. The Prophet returned in triumph to Mecca, forgiving all those who had done so much to harm him and his followers. He purified the Ka'bah of the idols in and on top of it and then performed, along with other rites, circumambulations of the House of God, following the footsteps of Abraham, a pilgrimage called *ḥajj*, which continues to this day, being one of the "pillars," or fundamental elements, of the religion. But he did not remain in the city of his birth and upbringing.

Rather, he returned to Medina, where he died in 632 after three days of illness. He was buried in his own apartment, which was adjacent to the mosque he had built. Called the Mosque of the Prophet, or Masjid al-nabī, it is the original model of all later mosques and is visited to this day by millions of Muslim pilgrims every year from all over the world.

The Prophet died having unified Arabia, ended the prevalent violence, and created peace among tribes that had been fighting each other since time immemorial. With few means, a man who had been an orphan and who had suffered in countless ways, laid the foundations for a new religious society and civilization that was soon to make its mark upon a large portion of the world and begin a new chapter in human history. This summary account of the life of the Prophet brings into focus the way in which Muslims view the life of the founder of their religion. In order to understand Islam, it is essential to grasp the significance of this account for Muslims and not to accept blindly what earlier revisionist Christian polemicists or contemporary agnostic historians may have written in the West about him.

To comprehend the significance of the Prophet in Islam, it is necessary to remember that the great founders of religions are of two types. The first constitutes the category of those figures who preach detachment from the world and a spiritual life that does not become entangled with ordinary worldly matters with all their ambiguities and complexities. Supreme examples of this type are found in Christ and the Buddha, both of whom founded what were originally small spiritual communities divorced from and not integrated into the political, social, and economic conditions of the larger society. Christ who said that his kingdom was not of this world did not marry and was not the leader and ruler of a whole human society, and the Buddha left the married life of a prince to devote himself to the monastic life and the attainment of illumination.

The second type is exemplified by Moses, David, and Solomon in the Abrahamic world and by Rama and Krishna in Hinduism. Such figures, whether seen as prophets or avatars, entered into the complexity of the ordinary human order to transform and sanctify it. The Hebrew prophets as well as some avataric figures from Hinduism were also political leaders and rulers of a human community. They were married and had children and therefore appear to those who have been brought up gazing upon the dazzling spiritual perfection of Christ or the Buddha as being too immersed in the life of the world and therefore less perfect. Such a judgment neglects the truth that once Christianity and Buddhism became religions of a whole society, they too had to deal with the earthly realities of human society, with justice, war and peace, and the question of family and sexual relations.

In any case, the Prophet must be seen as belonging to the second category. His contemplativeness was inward, while outwardly he had to face nearly every possible human situation. He experienced being an orphan, living the life of a merchant, suffering persecution. He grieved deeply the loss of his beloved wife Khadījah and his two-year-old son Ibrāhīm, but he also knew the happiness of family life and of final triumph in the world. He, who loved solitude and contemplation, had to deal with the affairs of men and women, with all their frailties and shortcomings. He had to rule over a whole society and to sit as judge in cases of one party's complaints against another. One might say that his mission was to sanctify all of life and to create an equilibrium in human life that could serve as the basis for surrender and effacement before the Divine Truth.

In every religion all the virtues of its adherents derive from those existing in the founder of the religion. In the same way that no Christian can claim to have any virtue that was not possessed to the utmost extent by Christ, no Muslim can have any virtue that was not possessed in the most eminent degree by the Prophet. More specifically, the Prophet exemplifies the virtues of humility; nobility, magnanimity and charity; and truthfulness and sincerity. For Muslims, the Prophet is the perfect model of total humility before God and neighbor; nobility and magnanimity of soul, which means to be strict with oneself but generous, charitable, and forgiving to others; and finally, perfect sincerity, which means to be totally truthful to oneself and to God. This crowning Islamic virtue requires the melting of our ego before God, for, as a Sufi saying asserts, "He whose soul melteth not away like snow in the hand of religion [that is, the Truth], in his hand religion like snow away doth melt."[4]

Love for the Prophet is incumbent upon all Muslims and in fact constitutes a basic aspect of Islamic religious life. It might be said that this love is the key for the love of God, for in order to love God, God must first love us, and God does not love a person who does not love His messenger. The Prophet is also held in the greatest esteem and respect. He has many names, such as Aḥmad ("the most praiseworthy of those who praise God"), 'Abd Allāh ("servant of God"), Abu'l-Qāsim ("Father of Qāsim"), and al-Amīn ("the Trusted One"), as well as Muḥammad. Whenever any of these names are mentioned, they are followed with the formulaic phrase, "May peace and blessings be upon him." It is considered a sign of disrespect to mention his name or the name of any of the other prophets without invoking the benediction of peace upon them.

The invocation of benediction upon the Prophet is so central for Muslims that it might be said to be the only act that is performed by both God and human beings, for, as the Quran says, "Verily, God and His angels shower blessings upon the Prophet. O ye who have faith! Ask blessings on him and salute him with a worthy salutation" (33:56).

The love and respect for the Prophet also extends to other prophets who remain spiritually alive in the Islamic universe. In fact, Muslims do not consider the fact that the message of the Prophet was conclusive to mean that it was also exclusive. The Prophet is for them both the person they love and admire as God's most perfect creature and the continuation of the long chain of prophets to whom he is inwardly connected. A pious Muslim would never think of praising the Prophet while denigrating the prophets who came before him, particularly those mentioned in the Quran. In the metaphysical sense, the Prophet is both a manifestation of the Logos and the Logos itself, both the beginning of the prophetic cycle and its end, and, being its end and seal, he contains from an essential and inward point of view the whole prophetic function within himself. It is in this sense that Maḥmūd Shabistarī sang of the Prophet, using his esoteric name Aḥmad, in his *Gulshan-i rāz* ("The Secret Garden of Divine Mysteries"):

> Since the number hundred has come, ninety is also
> with us.
> The name of Aḥmad is the name of all the prophets.

The love for the Prophet, therefore, far from diminishing respect for other prophets, has only increased the admiration of Muslims for the prophets who preceded the Prophet of Islam and for whom he himself held the greatest respect, as reflected in the many traditions, or sayings, transmitted from him.

These sayings, called in the plural *aḥādīth,* were assembled after his death and, after much critical study, collected in canonical collections by both Sunni and Shī'ite scholars. They form, after the Quran, the most important source of everything Islamic and constitute, in fact, the first commentary upon the Quran. Technically, the *Ḥadīth* is part of the *Sunnah,* which means all the doings or wonts of the Prophet. The *Sunnah* is the model upon which Muslims have based their lives, including the rituals ordained by the Quran. Along with the teachings of the Quran, the *Sunnah* is the primary cause for the unity so observable among Muslims from so many diverse ethnic groups and cultures. As for the *Ḥadīth,* some deal with the most sublime spiritual truths and others with everyday aspects of life, such as how to carry out an economic transaction justly or how to deal fairly with one's family. They include such sayings as:

> "No person is a true believer unless he desires for his brother that which he desires for himself."
>
> "Illumine your hearts by hunger, and strive to conquer your ego by hunger and thirst; continue to knock at the gates of Paradise by hunger."
>
> "To honor an old person is to show respect for God."
>
> "There are heavenly rewards for every act of kindness to a live animal."
>
> "God is beautiful and He loves beauty."
>
> "Charity is a duty for every Muslim. He who has not the means thereto, let him do a good act or abstain from an evil one. That is his charity."

"When the bier of anyone passes by you, whether Jew, Christian, or Muslim, rise to your feet."

"God is pure and loves purity and cleanliness."

"The best *jihād* is the conquest of the self."

"Heaven lies at the feet of mothers."

"The key to Paradise is prayer."

"God saith, 'I fulfill the faith of whosoever puts his faith in Me, and I am with him, and near him, when he remembers Me.'"

The spiritual reality of the Prophet is ever present in Islamic society through the living character of his *Sunnah* and the authority of his *Ḥadīth*. It is moreover experienced through the grace that emanates from his spiritual reality and is called "Muḥammadan *barakah*," a grace that is ever present in the life of Sufism, in the litanies chanted in honor of the Prophet, in the visitation to holy sites throughout the Islamic world, which are like so many extensions of Medina, and in the heart of all Muslims for whom the love of the Prophet is both the necessary concomitant and means of access to the love of God. This love for the Prophet also entails love and respect for other messengers, to which the Quran refers so frequently. Even the Islamic definition of faith *(al-īmān)* states the necessity of having faith in God, His angels, and His *messengers,* not only His *messenger.* As the Quran states, "O ye who believe! Believe in God and His messenger and the Scripture which He has revealed unto His messenger and the Scripture which He revealed before. Whosoever disbelieves in God, His angels and His Scriptures and His messengers and the Last Day, he verily has wandered far away" (4:136). It is not only disbelief in the *messenger,* but in all of God's *messengers* that leads a person away from the path of correct belief and faithfulness. But, of course, to be a Muslim requires specifically the acceptance of the messengership and prophethood of Muḥammad; hence the second testification *(shahādah)* of Islam, *Muḥammadun rasūl Allāh* ("Muḥammad is the Messenger of God"). Through this pronouncement along with the first *shahādah* a person formally becomes a Muslim. The first *shahādah, Lā ilāha illa'Llāh* ("There is no god but God") is by itself in fact universal testimony to the acceptance of religion as such, to *al-dīn,* which lies at the heart not only of Islam, but of all the authentic religions revealed before the descent of the Quran.

ISLAM'S ATTITUDE TOWARD OTHER RELIGIONS IN HISTORY

In light of what has been said of the Islamic conception of revelation and religious diversity, it is important to mention that before modern times Islam was the only revealed religion to have had direct contact with nearly all the major religions of the world. It had met Judaism and Christianity in its birthplace in Arabia and afterward in Palestine, Syria, and Egypt; the Iranian religions such as Zoroastrianism and Manichaeism after its conquest of Persia in the seventh century; Hinduism and Buddhism in eastern Persia and India shortly thereafter; the Chinese religions through the Silk Route as well as through Muslim merchants who traveled to Canton and other Chinese ports; the African religions soon after the spread of Islam into Black Africa some fourteen hundred years ago; and Siberian Shamanism in the form of the archaic religions of the Turkic and Mongolian peoples as they descended into the Islamic world. Centuries ago Zoroaster and the Buddha were common household names among Muslims of the eastern lands of the Islamic world, especially Persia. Indian Muslims had come to know of Krishna and Rama a thousand years ago. The Persian polymath al-Bīrunī had composed a major work on India in the eleventh century, one that is still a valuable source of knowledge for medieval Hinduism. Furthermore, numerous works of classical Hinduism and some of Buddhism were translated into Persian centuries ago, including the Upanishads and the Bhagavad Gita. Chinese Muslim scholars knew the Confucian classics and many considered Confucius and Lao-Tze prophets.

The global nature of the religious knowledge of a learned Muslim sitting in Isfahan in the fourteenth century was very different from that of a scholastic thinker in Paris or Bologna of the same period. On the basis of the Quranic doctrine of religious universality and the vast historical experiences of a global nature, Islamic civilization developed a cosmopolitan and worldwide religious perspective unmatched before the modern period in any other religion. This global vision is still part and parcel of the worldview of traditional Muslims, of those who have not abandoned their universal vision as a result of the onslaught of modernism or reactions to this onslaught in the form of what has come to be called "fundamentalism."

Within this global religious context, it is, of course, the Jewish and Christian traditions with which Islam has the greatest affinity. The Hebrew prophets and Christ are deeply respected by Muslims. The Virgin Mary is considered by the Quran to hold the most exalted spiritual position among women. A chapter of the Quran is named after her, and she is the only woman mentioned by name in Islam's sacred scripture. Moreover, the miraculous birth of Christ from a virgin mother is recognized in the Quran. Respect for such teachings is so strong among Muslims that today, in interreligious dialogues with Christians and Jews, Muslims are often left defending traditional Jewish and Christian doctrines such as the miraculous birth of Christ before modernist interpreters who would reduce them to metaphors and the sacred history of the Hebrew prophets to at best inspired stories.

The sacred figures of Judaism and Christianity are often mentioned in the Quran and even in prayers said on various occasions. The tombs of the Hebrew prophets, who are also Islamic prophets, are revered and visited in pilgrimage by Muslims to this day. One need only recall the holiness for Muslims of the tomb of Abraham in al-Khalīl, or Hebron, in Palestine, of that of Joshua in Jordan, and of Moses' resting place on Mt. Nebo, also in Jordan. Some Muslims have occasionally criticized intellectually and also engaged militarily Jews and Christians, but they have not criticized the Jewish prophets or Christ (even if certain theological differences with followers of Judaism and Christianity did exist), at least not those who have heeded the call of the Quran and understood its message. Islam sees itself as the third of the Abrahamic religions, which are bound together by countless theological, ethical, and eschatological beliefs even though they are marked by differences willed by God.

To speak of the Judeo-Christian tradition against which Islam is pitted as the "other" is an injustice to the message of Abraham and also theologically false, no matter how convenient it might be for some people. There is as much difference between Judaism and Christianity as there is between Christianity and Islam. In certain domains Judaism is closer to Islam than it is to Christianity: it has a sacred language, Hebrew, like Arabic in Islam, and it has a sacred law, the *Halakhah,* corresponding to the *Sharīʿah.*

Furthermore, they share an opposition to all forms of idolatry and to the creation of iconic sacred art, which would allow an image of the Divinity to be painted or sculpted. In certain other ways Islam is closer to Christianity: both emphasize the immortality of the soul, eschatological realities, and the accent on the inner life. Then there are those basic principles upon which all three religions agree: the Oneness of God, prophecy, sacred scripture, much of sacred history, and basic ethical norms such as the sanctity of life, reverence for the laws of God, humane treatment of others, honesty in all human dealings, kindness toward the neighbor, the application of justice, and so forth. Islam is an inalienable and inseparable part of the Abrahamic family of religions and considers itself to be closely linked with the two monotheistic religions that preceded it. Islam envisages itself the complement of those religions and the final expression of Abrahamic monotheism, confirming the teachings of Judaism and Christianity, but rejecting any form of exclusivism.

WHO IS A BELIEVER AND WHO IS AN INFIDEL?

With this framework in mind, it will be easier to understand the categorization in Islam of people into believers *(mu'mins)* and what has been translated in the West as "infidels" or "nonbelievers" *(kāfirs),* which means literally "those who cover over the truth." Every religion has a way of distinguishing itself from the other religions. Judaism speaks of Jews and Gentiles, and Christianity of the faithful and the heathens or pagans. Each of these categorizations has both a theological and a popular and historical root related to the self-understanding as well as the history of that religion. In the case of Islam, the distinction is based more on the question of faith, or *īmān,* and less on the more general term *islām.* In the Quran faith implies a higher level of participation in the religion, as we shall discuss in the next chapter, and even today only those who take their religion very seriously and are virtuous are called *mu'min* (or possessors of *īmān*). And yet the Quran does not limit the term *mu'min* only to those who follow the Islamic religion; it includes the faithful of Islam along with followers of other religions, as is evidenced by the Quranic assertion, "Verily, those who have faith [in what is revealed to the Prophet] and those who are Jews and Christians and Sabaeans—whosoever has faith in God and the Last Day and does right—surely their reward is with their Lord, and no fear shall overcome them and neither shall they grieve" (2:62). In this verse as well as verse 69 of Surah 5 ("The Table Spread"), which nearly repeats the same message, recognition of other religions is extended even beyond Judaism, Christianity, and Sabaeanism to include "whosoever has faith in God," and the possibility of salvation is also made explicitly universal. Likewise, the boundary between the Muslim faithful and the faithful of other religions is lifted. One could therefore say that in the most universal sense whoever has faith and accepts the One God, or the Supreme Principle, is a believer, or *mu'min,* and whoever does not is an infidel, or a *kāfir,* whatever the nominal and external ethnic and even religious identification of that person might be.

As a result of this explicit universality of the Quranic text, the use of the terms "believer" or "faithful" and "infidel" or "nonbeliever" is much more complicated than what we find in Christianity. In Islam there is, first of all, the Sufi metaphysical view of absolute Truth, which is seen to be beyond all duality, even beyond the dichotomy of *īmān* and *kufr*, or faith and infidelity; yet, to reach that transcendent Truth beyond all duality one must begin with faith and start from the formal foundations of Islam, which distinguishes itself clearly from *kufr*. The esoteric understanding of *kufr* and *īmān*, so prevalent in classical Sufi poetry, especially among the Persian poets such as Rūmī, Shabistarī, and Ḥāfiẓ must not, therefore, be confused with the prevalent idea in certain Western circles that one can reach the absolute Truth by simply avoiding the world of faith as well as infidelity. On the levels of external religious forms, *īmān* has to do with truth and *kufr* with falsehood. This dichotomy is not destroyed by the exhortation of the Sufis to go beyond *kufr* and *īmān*, which means to reach *tawḥīd*, or oneness beyond all oppositions and dichotomies.

On the formal and popular plane, traditional Muslims have often used the category of "believer" or "faithful" for Muslims as well as followers of other religions, especially Christians and Jews. But there have been also historical periods in which the term "faithful" was reserved for Muslims and *kāfir*, or "infidel," was used for non-Muslims, as in the Ottoman Empire, where Europeans were called *kuffār*, infidels. The situation is, however, made even more complicated by the fact that throughout Islamic history certain Muslim groups have called other Muslim groups infidels, some even going to the extent of treating them in practice as enemies. For example, during early Islamic history the Khawārij, who opposed both the Sunnis and Shī'ites as infidels, attacked both groups physically and militarily. Later, Ismā'īlīs were considered *kuffār* by many Sunni scholars, and even in mainstream Islam over the centuries some Sunni and Twelve-Imām Shī'ite scholars have called each other *kāfir.* In the eighteenth century the Wahhābī movement, which began in Najd in Arabia, considered orthodox Sunnis and Shīʿites both not to be genuine Muslims, and often cast the anathema of being infidels, or what is called *takfīr,* upon them, while many Ottoman Ḥanafī scholars considered the Wahhābīs themselves to be *kuffār.*

The prevalent image in the West that all Muslims are united as the faithful against the infidels—even if some well-known Christian preachers repeat to their flocks this assertion made by some extremists within the Islamic world—is simply not true. There have always been those who have spoken of the necessity of the unity of Muslims as the faithful, and in a certain sense that unity has been always there despite diversity on many levels. But the whole question of who is a believer, or a person of faith, and who is an unbeliever, or infidel, requires a much more nuanced answer than is usually given in generally available sources.

Moreover, the term *kāfir* has both a theological and judicial definition and a popular political and social definition, and the two should not be confused. In the conscience of many devout Muslims, a pious Christian or Jew is still seen as a believer, while an agnostic with an Arabic or Persian name is seen as a *kāfir.* And the anathema of *kufr,* far from involving only outsiders, has also concerned various groups within the Islamic world itself. Today, even while some Muslims hold "infidels" responsible for the onslaught of a secularist culture from the West, they also use the same characterization for those within the Islamic world itself who, while still formally Muslim, accept and preach secularist ideas that negate the very foundations of the Islamic revelation. As a matter of fact, secularism is the common enemy of all the Abrahamic traditions, and the erosion of moral authority in secular societies that we observe today poses as many problems for Jews and Christians as it does for Muslims.

ISLAM AND RELIGIOUS PLURALISM TODAY

Muslims today continue to experience the presence of other religions in their midst as they have done over the centuries. In the middle part of the Islamic world there are Christian minorities, the largest being in Egypt, and still some Jews, especially in Iran and Turkey, although most of the Jews from Arab countries migrated to Israel after 1948. There are still Zoroastrians in Iran, and Muslims live with Hindus in India, of course, but also in Bangladesh, Nepal, Malaysia, and Indonesia, and with Buddhists in Sri Lanka, Thailand, Ladakh, Burma, China, and elsewhere. They also live with Confucians and Taoists not in only China, but also in Malaysia and Indonesia. By and large, through most periods of Islamic history, the relation between Muslims and religious minorities living in their midst has been peaceful. Exceptions have arisen when severe political issues, such as the partition of Palestine or India, have altered ordinary relations between Muslims and followers of other religions. Today, despite some abuses here and there issuing from so-called fundamentalist currents in various Islamic countries, religious minorities in the Islamic world usually fare better than Muslim minorities do in other lands, except in America and some Western countries, where they have been able to practice their religion until now without manifest or hidden restrictions. All one has to do is to compare the situation of the Christian minorities of Syria, Iraq, and Iran, three states not known for their leaning toward the West, with Muslim minorities in China, the Philippines, India, and the Russian Caucasus, not to speak of the Balkans, where the horror inflicted by Christian Serbs upon Muslim Bosnians and Kosovars is still fresh in everyone's memory.

The peaceful presence in the Islamic world of various religious minorities, especially Christians, has been upset to a large extent in recent times by Western missionary activity, which has caused severe reaction not only among Muslims, but also among Hindus, Buddhists, and others. This question of Christian missionary activity (of the Western churches, not Orthodoxy) is a complicated matter requiring an extensive separate treatment, but it must be mentioned briefly here. Suffice it to say that, as far as the Islamic world is concerned, this activity was from the beginning of the modern period combined with colonialism, and many Western Christian missionaries have preached as much secularized Western culture as Christianity. Many of them have tried and still try to propagate Christianity not through the teachings of Christ alone, but mostly by the appeal of material aid such as rice and medicine, given in the name of Christian charity, but with the goal of conversion. Many of their schools have been happy if they could wean the Muslim students away from firm belief in Islam, even if they could not make them Christian. It is not accidental that some of the most virulent anti-Western secularized Arab political leaders of the past decades have been graduates of American schools in the Middle East first established by missionaries, schools where these students were religiously and culturally uprooted.

To understand current Islamic reactions to Christian missionary activity in many countries, one should ask how the people of Texas and Oklahoma, where many American evangelists come from, would respond to the following scenario. Suppose that, with vast oil money from the

Islamic world, Islamic schools were to be established in those states. Because of their prestige, these schools attracted the children of the most powerful and well-to-do families, and these future leaders, in attending these schools, underwent a systematic process of cultural Arabization even if they did not participate in the encouraged formal conversion to Islam.

Western missionary activity is not like that of medieval Christian preachers of the Gospels, or like the Orthodox missionaries among the Inuits of Canada, who would adopt the language of the Inuits and even their dress. Most modern Western missionary activity throughout Asia and Africa has meant, above all, Westernization and globalization combined with the cult of consumerism, all in the name of Christianity. Were there not to be such a powerful political, economic, and even military pressure behind the presence of these missionaries, then their presence would be in a sense like that of Tibetan Buddhists or Muslims in Canada or the United States and would not pose a danger to the very existence of local religions and cultures. But the situation is otherwise, and therefore Christian missionary activity, especially in such places as Indonesia, Pakistan, and sub-Saharan Africa, plays a very important role in creating tension between Islam and Christianity and indirectly the West, which gives material and political support to these missionaries even if, as in France, the state is avowedly secularist.

Of course, this identification with modern Western secularist and now consumerist culture has not always been the case with all missionaries. The French Catholic Père de Foucault lived for a long time among Muslim North Africans as a humble witness to Christ and was greatly respected by his Muslim neighbors, as were a number of other monks and priests. There have also been humble Protestants who came to Muslims to represent a presence of Christ's message without aggressive proselytizing through material enticement of the poor. Such exceptions have certainly existed. Nevertheless, Western Christian missionary activity, supported as it is directly or indirectly by all the might of the West, poses a major problem for contemporary Muslims' dealings with Western Christianity, in contrast to local forms of Christianity with which Muslims have lived usually in peace for centuries. One need only recall in this context that while Baghdad was being bombed during the Persian Gulf War, no Iraqi Muslims attacked any local Iraqi Christians walking down the street, whereas the reverse has not been true since the tragic September 11 terrorist acts; a number of American and European Muslims have been attacked and harassed as a result of the religious, racial, and ethnic xenophobia that has been created in certain circles by that great tragedy.

In speaking of missionary activity, it is necessary to say something about Islamic teachings concerning apostasy *(irtidād)*, which has been criticized by missionary circles and others in the West. According to classical interpretations of the *Sharīʿah*, the punishment for apostasy for a Muslim is death, and this is interpreted by many Westerners to mean the lack of freedom of conscience in Islam. To clarify this issue, first of all, a few words about conversion. The Quran says, "There is no compulsion in religion" (2:256), and in most periods of Islamic history there was no forced conversion of the "People of the Book." In fact, forced conversion is an affront to God and the dignity of the human conscience created by Him. Arabia at the time of the Quranic revelation was an exception. There the pagan Arabs who practiced a most crass form of polytheism were given the choice of either becoming Muslims or battling against them. It was very similar to the choice offered by Christian to European "pagans" once Christianity gained power on that continent. But even in Arabia, the Jews and Christians were not forced to become Muslims.

The *Sharīʿite* ruling on apostasy may therefore seem strange in light of Islam's attitude toward other heavenly inspired religions. The reason for such a ruling must be sought in the fact that attachment to Islam was related before modern times to being a member of the Islamic state as well as community, and therefore apostasy was seen as treason against the state, not just religious conversion. Today when the state is no longer Islamic in the traditional sense in most Islamic countries, many religious scholars have spoken against capital punishment for apostasy. Moreover, in practice, although the law is still "on the books," in many places it is hardly ever applied, as can be seen by the presence of several million Christians converted from Islam by Western missionaries in recent times in such countries as Indonesia, Pakistan, and several West African nations. In practice this law is somewhat like laws against adultery that are still "on the books" in England, but not applied. Sectarian fighting between Muslims and newly converted Christians still occurs in Indonesia, Pakistan, Nigeria, the Sudan, and a few other places, but these have more to do with local political, economic, and social issues than with the traditional *Sharīʿite* ruling about apostasy.

The traditional *Sharīʿite* ruling, which is now being amended by some legal authorities and for the most part ignored because of changed conditions, must be understood not in the context of the modern West, where religion has been to a large extent marginalized and pushed away from the public arena, but in the framework of the

Christian West. One only has to think what would have happened to Christians in medieval France or seventeenth-century Spain if they had converted to Islam. In any case, the question of apostasy raised so often by those who ask about Islam's relation to other religions must be understood in both its classical context and the present-day situation, when it is largely overlooked because of changed conditions and is, in fact, being reinterpreted by a number of important Islamic legal experts.

Another issue often raised in the West when discussing Islam's relation to other religions is that Islam does not allow the presence of non-Muslims in a certain area around Mecca while Christianity allows non-Christians even into the Vatican. Now, it must be understood that each religion has its own regulations concerning sacred spaces. In Hinduism certain areas in Benares are closed to all non-Hindus, and Muslims respected those rules even when they ruled over that city and did not force their way into the Monkey Temple or other sacred sites. Like Hinduism and several other religions, Islam has a sacred space around Mecca whose boundaries were designated by the Prophet himself and where non-Muslims are not allowed.

That has never meant that the rest of the Islamic world has been closed to the presence of other religions and their houses of worship. Churches dot the skyline of Cairo, Beirut, Damascus, and many other cities, and synagogues are also found everywhere a Jewish community lives from Tehran to Fez. Within the Ottoman Empire in many places in the Balkans where Jews, Christians, and Muslims lived together, synagogues, churches, and mosques were built next to each other. To this day this harmonious presence of different houses of worship is visible in Istanbul itself. Outside of the *ḥarīm,* or sacred precinct, in Arabia, it is the duty of the Muslim state, according to the *Sharīʿah,* to allow the building and maintenance of houses of worship of the "People of the Book," and any order to the contrary is against the tenets of Islamic Law and traditional practice.

Of course, during Islamic history there were occasions when after a major triumph a church was converted into a mosque, as happened with the Hagia Sophia, but the reverse also took place often, as when the Grand Mosque of Cordova was converted into a cathedral. Altogether for Islam, the general norm is the one established by 'Umar, who, when he conquered Jerusalem, ordered the Church of the Holy Sepulchre to be honored and protected as a church. Otherwise, most of the churches in the Islamic world that later became mosques were those abandoned by Christian worshipers, somewhat like what one sees in some cities in Great Britain these days.

On the intellectual plane, there is a great deal of interest in the Islamic world today in religious dialogue, the impetus for which originated in Christian circles mostly after World War II. In many countries, such as Morocco, Egypt, Jordan, Syria, Lebanon, Iran, Malaysia, and Indonesia, religious dialogue has even been encouraged by governments as well as by individuals and religious organizations. Numerous conferences have been held in many parts of the world with Protestants, Catholics, and more recently Orthodox Christians; with Hindus in India and Indonesia; and with Buddhists and Confucians in Malaysia. Because of the Palestinian-Israeli problem, the dialogue with Judaism has been somewhat more difficult, but even that has also continued to some extent in both the Middle East and the West. In these dialogues scholars from many different schools of thought have participated, both those within the Islamic world and those Muslims living in the West. There have been some exclusivists who have opposed such dialogues, as one sees also among Christians and Jews, but the activity of religious dialogue has gone on for decades in the Islamic world and is now an important part of the current Islamic religious and intellectual landscape.

Even on the more theoretical and philosophical level, what has come to be known as religious pluralism has become a matter of great interest and a major intellectual challenge in many Islamic countries today, including some of those called "fundamentalist" in the West. There is no country in the Islamic world in which there is greater interest in the theological and philosophical questions involved in the issue of religious pluralism than Iran. There works of such famous Protestant and Catholic writers on the subject as John Hick and Hans Küng have been translated and are being discussed even in the public media; there the views of traditionalist metaphysicians such as Frithjof Schuon, who speaks of the "transcendent unity of religions," a view that is also my own, are part and parcel of the general intellectual discourse. The same keen interest is also to be found in countries as different as Turkey, Pakistan, and Malaysia.

Faced with the danger of loss of identity and the enfeeblement of religion as a result of the onslaught of modernism with its secularist bias, some Muslims, many very active and vocal, espouse a radical exclusivist point of view when it comes to the question of the relation of Islam to other religions. But for the vast majority of Muslims, the Quranic doctrine of the universality of revelation and the plurality of prophets under the One God still resonates deeply in their hearts and souls, and they remain ever mindful of the many verses of the Quran concerning the reality of One God *and* the multiplicity of revelations sent by

Him. When they think of their beloved Prophet, they are mindful of these words of God:

> We inspire thee [Muḥammad] as We inspired Noah and the prophets after him, as We inspired Abraham and Ishmael and Isaac and Jacob and the tribes, and Jesus and Job and Jonah and Aaron and Solomon, and as We imparted unto David the Psalms;
>
> And messengers We have mentioned unto thee before and messengers We have not mentioned unto thee; and God spoke directly to Moses;
>
> Messengers of good news and warning; in order that mankind might have no argument against God after the messengers. God is Mighty, and Wise. (4:163–65)

Two

THE SPECTRUM OF ISLAM

Sunnism, Shīʿism, and Sufism and Traditional, Modernist, and "Fundamentalist" Interpretations of Islam Today

O, mankind! Verily We have created you male and female, and have made you nations and tribes that ye may know each other.

(Quran, XLIX:13)

Differences between the scholars of my community are a mercy from God.

Ḥadīth

ISLAMIC PATTERNS

Often in the West Islam is depicted as a monolith, and little attention is paid to the rich diversity within both the religion and civilization of Islam. Recent events, however, have made the Islamic world the focus of much attention. Although the attempt by the media to deal more with Islam is laudable, what is presented is usually highly selective and politically charged, dominated by the Arab-Israeli conflict and extremism manifesting itself in threats or acts of terror. Therefore, despite greater interest in covering matters pertaining to Islam, the reductionist message associated with extremism continues to dominate the scene, hiding from the Western public the great diversity of the Islamic world and the multiple interpretations of the Islamic religion.

The vast world of Islam is actually like a Persian medallion carpet; it has incredible diversity and complexity, yet it is dominated by a unity into which all the complex geometric and arabesque patterns are integrated. This complexity can be better understood if one views it as the superimposition of a number of patterns upon the plane of the carpet. In the vast world of Islam also, one can gain a better grasp of the whole by separating the patterns and seeing how each is related to vertical and horizontal dimensions of the religion of Islam itself as well as to cultural, ethnic, and linguistic factors. Then reuniting the patterns and seeing how they all fit together yields a vision of the total spectrum of Islam, in which unity leads to diversity and diversity is integrated into unity.

FACTORS THAT CREATE UNITY

Before turning to the components of the Islamic spectrum and the question of diversity, let us first ask which factors have created and sustain unity in the Islamic world. Despite political fragmentation, theological differences, and ethnic distinctions, there is a strong sense of the unity of the Islamic community *(ummah)* and a constant desire for greater political unity within the "Abode of Islam" *(dār al-islām)* in the hearts of all Muslims, and there is, of course, a visible unity in Islamic civilization.

The central factor in the creation of unity among Muslims is the Quran. For all Muslims, it is the very Word of God, with the same text, which is chanted as well as read and written, and the same message for all Muslims, although interpretations of that message differ among various Muslim groups and there are levels of meaning to the text. Then there are the *Sunnah* and *Ḥadīth* of the Prophet, which are very powerful unifying factors, although again there are local variations of interpretation of certain facts and features of the Prophet's life, actions, and words. Despite these variations in the understanding of the twin sources of the Islamic religion, that is, the Quran and the *Sunnah* (along with the *Ḥadīth*), there are three central doctrines upon which all schools of Islam agree, namely *tawḥīd*, or Divine Oneness, *nubuwwah,* or prophecy, and *ma'ād,* or eschatology, to which we shall turn in Chapter 6. Only very small groups here and there have deviated from these basic principles, which are the source of Islam's sapiential and practical teachings and whose unifying power can hardly be overestimated. Those who have deviated from these basic doctrines have sometimes brought about civil and religious crises within the community and sometimes even violence.

Another unifying factor is Islamic Law, or the *Sharīʿah,* which is interpreted according to different schools but the basic elements of which are the same throughout the Islamic world, especially as they concern the rites of the religion. These rites, which consist of the five daily prayers performed in Arabic whether one is in Malaysia or Bosnia, the annual pilgrimage *(ḥajj)* made from all parts of the Islamic world, the fast of the month of Ramaḍān carried out by all healthy adult Muslims throughout the seven climes, the tithe paid to the poor, and other religious acts, bind Muslims together wherever they might be. Over the ages the ethical norms related to the *Sharīʿah,* the injunctions of the Quran and *Sunnah,* and the spiritual etiquette, or *adab,* associated with ethics and based on the Prophetic model have also acted as powerful integrating forces. To these must be added the presence of Sufi orders, which cut across confessional and ethnic boundaries and which, basing themselves by definition on the Unity that transcends all multiplicity, have been a major factor in the integration of Islamic society. Finally, on the plane of forms, one must mention Islamic art, from the chanting of the Quran to geometric patterns found on articles and structures, an art that, despite local differences, has its own unique genius and has played a very important role in bringing about unity on the physical plane while permitting local variations and cultural diversity.

SOURCES OF DIVERSITY: THE HIERARCHICAL LEVELS OF MEANING AND INTERPRETATION OF THE TRADITION

To understand the sources of diversity in the Islamic world, one must first of all turn to the hierarchy within the religion of Islam itself. The total religion called Islam may be said to consist of the levels of *islām, īmān,* and *iḥsān,* or surrender, faith, and spiritual beauty. The Quran refers often to the *muslim,* the possessor of surrender, the *mu'min,* the possessor of faith, and the *muḥsin,* the possessor of virtue. Although the Quran emphasizes that all Muslims stand equally before God, it also insists that human beings are distinguished in rank according to their knowledge of the truth and virtue, as in the verses, "Are those who know equal with those who know not?" (39:9), to which the Quran gives the resounding answer of no, and, "Verily, those of you most close to God are those who are the best in conduct" (59:13). These verses refer to degrees of perfection of believers, as one sees also in Christianity, and do not imply in any way exclusion, ostracism, or support for violence against certain groups.

Later Islamic sages, especially the Sufis, have also spoken of the hierarchy of the *Sharīʿah,* or the Divine Law, the *Ṭarīqah,* or the spiritual path, the *Ḥaqīqah,* or the Divine Truth, which is the origin of both. Islam is then envisaged as a circle whose center is the *Ḥaqīqah.* The radii of the circle are the *ṭuruq* (plural of *Ṭarīqah*), later identified with the Sufi orders, and the circumference is the *Sharīʿah.* Each Muslim is like a point on the circumference, whose totality composes the Islamic community, or *ummah.* To reach the *Ḥaqīqah,* one must first stand on the circumference, that is, practice the *Sharīʿah,* and then follow the *Ṭarīqah,* or Path to God, whose end is the Center, God Himself, or the *Ḥaqīqah.*

In a famous tradition of the Prophet known as the *ḥadīth* of Gabriel, this primary vertical structure and hierarchy, which does not in any way obviate the reality that each

Muslim stands as his or her own priest before God, is made evident:

> 'Umar said, "One day when we were sitting with the Messenger of God there came unto us a man whose clothes were of exceeding whiteness and whose hair was of exceeding blackness, nor were there any signs of travel upon him, although none of us knew him. He sat down knee unto knee opposite the Prophet, upon whose thighs he placed the palms of his hands, saying: 'O Muḥammad, tell me what is the surrender *(islām)*.' The Messenger of God answered him saying: 'The surrender is to testify that there is no god but God and that Muḥammad is God's Messenger, to perform the prayer, bestow alms, fast Ramaḍān and make, if thou canst, the pilgrimage to the Holy House.' He said: 'Thou hast spoken truly,' and we were amazed that having questioned him he should corroborate him. Then he said: 'Tell me what is faith *(īmān)*.' He answered: 'To believe in God and His Angels and His Books and His Messengers and the Last Day, and to believe that no good or evil cometh but by His Providence.' 'Thou hast spoken truly,' he said, and then: 'Tell me what is excellence *(iḥsān)*.' He answered: 'To worship God as if thou sawest Him, for if thou seest Him not, yet seeth He thee.' 'Thou hast spoken truly,' he said. . . . Then the stranger went away, and I stayed a while after he had gone; and the Prophet said to me: 'O, 'Umar, knowest thou the questioner, who he was?' I said: 'God and His Messenger know best.' He said: 'It was Gabriel. He came unto you to teach you your religion.'"[1]

It is clear from this *ḥadīth* clarifying *dīn,* or religion, for Muslims that *islām* encompasses what is expected of all Muslims in the acceptance and performance of the "pillars" *(arkān)* of Islam, with which we shall deal later. *Īmān,* or faith, involves not only belief in the ordinary sense in God, His angels, messengers, His revealed books, and the eschatological (end-time) realities, but also knowledge of these matters, and it was into this dimension of the Islamic tradition that intellectual disciplines such as theology and traditional philosophy were integrated. As for *iḥsān,* it is obvious that not everyone can worship God as if they saw Him. This is the station of the saintly, and *iḥsān,* which means both "virtue" and "beauty," is associated with the spiritual path that leads to sanctity and is considered practically a definition of Sufism.

Not everyone who is a *muslim* is a *mu'min* and not everyone who is a *mu'min* is a *muḥsin,* but a *muḥsin* must also be a *mu'min* and a *mu'min* a *muslim.* Reference to this hierarchical distinction is also made in some sources as the exoteric, or outward *(ẓāhir),* and esoteric, or inward *(bāṭin),* dimensions of the tradition. In any case, throughout Islamic history there have been the ordinary believers, or *muslims,* those of intense piety, or *mu'mins,* and those who have sought God here and now, or *muḥsins,* about whom the Quran says, "God loves the *muḥsinīn*" (3:133, and many other verses). *Iḥsān* later became crystallized almost completely but not exclusively in Sufism, which can still be found throughout the Islamic world. Serious attachment to Sufism also requires attachment to the *Sharī'ah,* and therefore a person who is a Sufi must also be the follower of this or that school of Law. Some *Sharī'ite* Muslims may reject Sufism, especially today among both modernized and so-called fundamentalist or reformist circles, but the Sufis show the greatest attachment to the *Sharīʿah*, whose inner significance they seek to reach. And they must of necessity follow one of its schools.

It is meaningless to ask, as many Western scholars and especially anthropologists have done, whether a particular Muslim is a Sunni or a Sufi, or for that matter a Shīʿite or a Sufi. A Sunni or a Shīʿite can be a Sufi or not a Sufi, but the situation is not one of alternatives, because these dimensions of the religion are not situated on the same level of reality. That is why the presence of Sufism has never been a cause for division in traditional Islamic society. In contrast, it has been a cause of integration and the return to that inner unity whose attainment is the goal of Islam. The first division in the structure of the religion must, in fact, be sought not in the difference between *Sharīʿite* Islam and Sufism, but in the separation of Sunnism and Shīʿism from each other in the first century of Islamic history. The Sunni-Shīʿite division is the most important in the formal structure of Islam, although even this division does not destroy the unity of Islam and both share the unifying elements already mentioned. Moreover, Sufism, representing the inner dimension of the religion, transcends this dichotomy. Not only are there Sunnis as well as Shīʿites who are Sufis, but Shīʿism and Sufism also share together the original inner message of the Prophet and the power of spiritual and initiatic guidance *(walāyah/wilāyah),* so that the situation is somewhat more complex than stated. But for the present discussion it suffices to say that Sufism, or the *Ṭarīqah,* belongs to the inner dimension of Islam and transcends *Sharīʿite* differences, and Sunnism and Shīʿism mark a division within Islam on the formal and legal level.

While on the subject of Sufism, it must be recalled here that Sufism has had the greatest role in the spread of

Islam itself, in addition to its vital function in the preservation and purification of ethical life, the creation of the arts, and the exposition of unitive knowledge *(ma'rifah)* and metaphysics within Islamic society. From the eleventh and twelfth centuries onward, Sufism became organized in orders usually named after their founders; older ones, such as the Rifā'iyyah and Qādiriyyah, which still survive, were followed by many later ones, such as the Shādhiliyyah, the Khalwatiyyah, the Mawlawiyyah, the Chishtiyyah, the Naqshbandiyyah, and the Ni'matullahiyyah. Some of the orders have died out over time and occasionally new ones are created, but they all rely on the continuity of the "initiatic" chain, or *silsilah,* which goes back to the Prophet. There is hardly an Islamic country in which Sufi orders are not to be found, and since the beginning of the twentieth century some orders, beginning with the Shādhiliyyah, have spread into Europe and America. In some countries, such as Senegal and the Sudan, the Sufi orders are so popular that people's identification on the *Sharī'ite* level is often combined with their *Ṭarīqah* affiliation. Such a situation is found, however, only in Sunnism and not in Shī'ism, unless one identifies the Ismā'īlī branch of Shī'ism as a *Ṭarīqah* in itself, as many Ismā'īlīs themselves tend to do.

It is important to recall here the fact that, in contrast to the claim of those who only look at the quantitative aspects of things and consider the esoteric element of religion to be marginal and peripheral, the esoteric dimension actually lies at the heart of religion and is the source of both its endurance and renewal. We observe this truth not only in Islam, but also in the Kabbalistic and Hasidic traditions in Judaism and various mystical currents in Christianity. In Islam itself, Sufism has been over the centuries the hidden heart that has renewed the religion intellectually, spiritually, and ethically and has played the greatest role in its spread and in its relation with other religions.

SUNNISM AND SHĪ'ISM AND THEIR BRANCHES

Today about 87 percent of all Muslims are Sunnis and about 13 percent are Shī'ite. The Sunni majority within Islam is the largest in comparison with any denomination in other religions, such as Catholicism within Christianity and Mahāyāna within Buddhism. But the Shī'ite population is located almost completely in the heartland of Islam, that is, in the area between Egypt and India. Such countries as Iran, Iraq, Azerbaijan, Bahrain, and Islamic Lebanon have majority Shī'ite populations, and India, Pakistan, Afghanistan, Syria, Saudi Arabia, the Persian Gulf states, and East Africa have notable Shī'ite minorities. Both intellectually and historically, Shī'ism has played a much greater role in the Islamic world than its number might warrant, and the accord or discord between Sunnism and Shī'ism today is one of the most important factors in contemporary Islamic society.

The word *sunni* in Arabic comes from the term *ahl al-sunnah wa'l-jamā'ah,* that is, people who followed the *Sunnah* of the Prophet and the majority, while Shī'ism comes from the Arabic term *shī'at 'Alī,* meaning partisans of 'Alī ibn Abī Ṭālib. After the death of the Prophet, while 'Alī, his son-in-law and first cousin, and the rest of the family were burying him, the rest of the community gathered in Medina and chose Abū Bakr as the Prophet's successor, not in his prophetic function but as ruler of the newly established Islamic community. He was thereby given the title of *khalīfah rasūl Allāh,* or the vicegerent of the Messenger of God, from which comes the title caliph, taken not only by the first four caliphs, who are called the "rightly guided" *(rāshidūn),* but also by later Muslim rulers of the Umayyad, 'Abbāsid, and Fāṭimid dynasties and even by the Ottomans. A number of people thought that 'Alī should have become the Prophet's successor and rallied around him, forming the first nucleus of Shī'ism. 'Alī himself refused to oppose Abu Bakr and in fact worked closely with him and his two successors, 'Umar and 'Uthmān, until he himself became the fourth of the "rightly guided" caliphs of Sunni Islam. It was only after his death at the hands of a member of the Khawārij, an extremist group that rejected the claims of both Mu'āwiyyah, who had contested the caliphate of 'Alī, and 'Alī himself, that Shī'ism became an organized religio-political movement in Iraq.

The major point of contention between Sunnism and Shī'ism was not only the question of who should succeed the Prophet, but the question of what the qualifications of such a person had to be. For Sunnism, the function of the caliph was to protect the borders of Islam, keep security and peace, appoint judges, and so forth. For the Shī'ites, such a person also had to have the deepest knowledge of Islamic Law as well as esoteric knowledge of the Quran and Prophetic teachings. He could therefore not be elected, but had to be chosen by the Prophet through Divine command. The Shī'ites believe that this investiture did in fact occur at the pool of water called Ghadīr Khumm when the Prophet was returning to Medina from pilgrimage to Mecca. According to Shī'ites, the person chosen by him was 'Alī, whom they consider their first Imām, using this term in the special sense of someone who bears the Muḥammadan Light *(al-nūr al-muḥammadī)* and the power of initiation within himself and who is master of both the exoteric and the esoteric sciences. Otherwise the term *imām,* coming from the root meaning "standing before or in front," is used in general for the person who leads the daily prayers, and in Sunni Islam also as an honorific title given to great religious scholars such as, for example, Imām al-Ghazzālī, one of the foremost theologians and Sufis in Islamic history. Sunni authors have also occasionally referred to the caliph as *imām,* but all of these meanings must be distinguished from the specific Shī'ite usage of the term.

The understanding of the term *imām* therefore differs greatly in Sunnism and Shī'ism. In Sunni Islam the term has many uses, but it is never used in the mystical and esoteric sense given to it in Shī'ism. In Shī'ism, the Imām, like the prophets, is inerrant *(ma'ṣūm)* and protected from sin by God. He possesses perfect knowledge of both the Law and the Way, both the outer and inner meaning of the Quran. He also possesses the power of initiation *(walāyah/wilāyah)* and is the spiritual guide par excellence, like the Sufi masters within their orders. In fact, the first eight Shī'ite Imāms are also central spiritual authorities or poles of Sufism and appear in the initiatic chain of nearly every Sufi order. 'Alī, who is the representative par excellence of Islamic esoteric teachings, is not only the first Imām of Shī'ism, but also at the origin of the initiatic chain of nearly all Sufi orders. There are in fact many Sunnis, such as the majority of Egyptians, almost all of whom are Sunnis, who have the same love and respect for the Shī'ite Imāms and the *Ahl al-bayt,* that is, members of the family of the Prophet with whom the Imāms and Shī'ism itself are associated, as do Persian or Iraqi Shī'ites.

As far as Sunnism is concerned, its followers are divided according to the schools of Law *(madhhab)* they follow. In the eighth and ninth centuries the schools of *fiqh,* or jurisprudence, were codified by the doctors of the Law. Some of these codifications or schools died out, but four have survived during the past millennium and constitute the main body of traditional Sunnism. They are the Ḥanafī, Mālikī, Shāfi'ī, and Ḥanbalī.

Ḥanafism was founded by a Persian, Imām Abū Ḥanīfah (d. 768), who was a student of Imām Ja'far al-Ṣādiq (d.757), the sixth Imām of Shī'ism and founder of Twelve-Imām Shī'ite Law, which is called Ja'farī Law. Imām Abū Ḥanīfah sought to create possibilities for the integration of local practices into the Law as much as possible. His school held great attraction from the beginning for Turks as well as Muslims of the Indian subcontinent. Today the Ḥanafī School has the largest number of followers in the Sunni world, including most Sunni Turks, the Turkic people of Caucasia and Central Asia, European Muslims, and the Muslims of the Indian subcontinent. As for the Sunni part of Afghanistan, its people are, like the Sunnis of Pakistan, mostly Ḥanafī, and this is one of the elements that especially links the eastern part of Afghanistan to Pakistan.

Mālikism, founded by Imām Mālik ibn Anas (d. 795), is based mostly on the practice of Medina and is very conservative in its approach to the Law. There have been some Mālikīs in the Arab East and especially in Egypt, but the heart of Mālikism is North Africa. In fact, the whole of Islamic North and West Africa outside of Egypt is solidly Mālikī, and this legal homogeneity has made an important contribution to the cultural unity of the area, which in traditional Islamic geography is called al-Maghrib, or the West, the name that is now used for the "Far West" of the Islamic world, that is, Morocco.

The Shāfi'ī School was founded by a student of Imām Abū Ḥanīfah, Imām Muḥammad al-Shāfi'ī (d. 820). It is he who completed and perfected the methods of jurisprudence in Islamic Law. In many ways, of the different Sunni schools of Law, his school is the closest to the Ja'farī School. Buried in Cairo, he is greatly loved and admired by Egyptians, nearly all of whom are Shāfi'īs, as are many others south of Egypt as well as most of the Malays in Southeast Asia, whether they are in Indonesia, Malaysia, Singapore, or Thailand.

The Ḥanbalī School, founded by Imām Aḥmad ibn Ḥanbal (d. 855) from Baghdad, based itself solely on the Quran and *Ḥadīth* and gave a very strict interpretation of the *Sharī'ah*. Although in days of old it had many followers in Iraq, Persia, and other lands, in recent times its adherents have been confined mostly to Syria. Wahhābism, which is dominant in Saudi Arabia, is an offshoot of Ḥanbalism, but must not be simply identified with it. Wahhābism, which arose as a reformist movement in the eighteenth century in Najd in southern Arabia, opposed the later refinements of Islamic culture in the form of philosophy and theology as well as the arts; in the domain of religion itself it strongly opposed both Sufism and Shī'ism, the visit to the tombs of saints, and intercession by saints before God for an individual believer. It was opposed not only by Shī'ites, but also by orthodox Sunnis, and in the nineteenth century the Ottoman caliph even sent an army to defeat the movement. But through an alliance made between the Wahhābī scholars and the House of Sa'ūd, the movement was kept alive in Najd until the beginning of the twentieth century, when it began to consolidate political power. After World War I it captured Hijaz, where Mecca and Medina are located, and created the Kingdom of Saudi Arabia. As a result of this historical process, Wahhābism became accepted throughout Saudi Arabia as the official interpretation of Islam. Despite its opposition to mainstream Sunni Islam, Shīʿite, and Sufism, however, Wahhābism was not in itself always violent, although it was quite exoteric and exclusivist in its interpretation of Islam. Its influence remained, however, confined to Saudi Arabia until the increased wealth in the kingdom due to income from oil made it possible for Wahhābī schools and mosques to be established in many other areas of the world. But even then its influence remained limited, and today the vast majority of Sunnis cannot in any way be described as Wahhābī, not to speak of Shīʿites, who have always opposed Wahhābism. Within Arabia itself during the past two decades there has been a notable opening in certain religious circles toward other schools of Islam, both Sunni and Shīʿite, although the influence of Wahhābism is still dominant.

The four founders of the traditional schools of Sunni Law mentioned above are highly respected and revered by all Sunnis. Converting from one school to another takes place occasionally, and in modern times some governments have drawn from various schools, including the Shīʿism, to create civil laws in their countries. The difference between the Sunni schools of Law and the Jaʿfarī or other Shīʿite schools of Law is minor, especially when it comes to the practice of rites. In certain fields, such as laws of inheritance or the legality of temporary marriage, there are, however, notable differences.

As for Shīʿism, although one could distinguish the various schools from each other on the basis of their legal orientation, a more telling criterion for distinction, used by Muslims themselves as well as by Western scholars, is the position each branch of Shīʿism takes on the Imāms. After ʿAlī, his son Ḥasan became Imām. He lived a quiet, politically inactive life in Medina disseminating knowledge of the

Quran, but his brother Ḥusayn, who became the third Imām, arose against Yazīd, the son of Mu'āwiyyah, who had opposed 'Alī and who had founded the Umayyad caliphate with its capital in Damascus. Ḥusayn was invited to go to Iraq by the people of the Iraqi city of Kufa, who promised to support him. And so in the year 680 he set out with his family and many followers from Medina for Iraq. Before reaching Kufa, however, he was met by the army of Yazīd in Karbalā', where he and all the male members of the family of the Prophet, save Zayn al-'Ābidīn, who was ill, were killed. Ḥusayn's body was interred in Karbalā' and his head brought to Damascus, but Yazīd, afraid of the reactions that might follow, tried to distance himself from the incident and exiled Zaynab, the sister of Ḥusayn, to Egypt with the head of her brother. According to Sunni tradition, she buried the head at a site that became the heart of what was later to become the city known as al-Qāhirah, or Cairo. This tragic event crystallized the Shī'ite movement in Iraq and later elsewhere, especially in Persia, and finally led to the downfall of the Umayyads. To this day the tragedy of Karbalā' is commemorated on the tenth of Muḥarram in many countries, especially Iran, Iraq, the Indo-Pakistani subcontinent, and Lebanon, and these events are the most notable popular religious ceremonies in Islam after the annual pilgrimage, or *ḥajj*. Recollection of vast religious processions, sermons, and passion plays of Muḥarram, which dominated the life of Tehran during my childhood spent in that city, are still indelibly etched in my memory.

All other Imāms of Shī'ism were descendants of Ḥusayn through his one son who survived, Zayn al-'Ābidīn al-Sajjād, who became the fourth Imām. The main branch of Shī'ism, which includes the vast majority of Shī'ites, is called Ithnā 'ashariyyah, or Twelve-Imām Shī'ism, which is dominant in Iran and is a majority in Iraq, Azerbaijan, Bahrain, and among the Muslims of Lebanon. The Twelvers accept a chain of Imāms descending from the fourth, including his son, Muḥammad al-Bāqir, the fifth Imām, and his son, Ja'far al-Ṣādiq, the sixth Imām, down to the Twelfth, Muḥammad al-Mahdī, whom they believe to have been given a mysteriously long life by God, but who is in occultation *(ghaybah)*. He is alive like Elijah, who was taken to Heaven alive according to Jewish belief. But the Twelfth Imām is also the secret master of this world and can appear to those who are in the appropriate spiritual state to see him. He will appear publicly before the end of time, when inequity and oppression have become dominant, to reestablish justice and peace on earth, and he will prepare for the second coming of Christ, an event in which Muslims have as firm a belief as Christians. This eschatological expectation is therefore called Mahdīism and is by no means confined to Shī'ism. Sunnism also contains such teachings, the difference being that Shī'ites claim to know here and now who the Mahdī is, whereas Sunnis expect a figure with such a name to appear in the future.

Apocalyptic thought, although present in Islam, does not, however, play the same role there as it does in contemporary Christianity, especially among certain televangelists in America who have commercialized their contentious interpretations of the Book of Revelation and other Christian sources on the basis of an exclusivism that is utterly astounding. In the Islamic world, although the idea of the coming of the Mahdī exists, there is much less public talk about it, especially on television, and there is little emphasis on creating an exclusive club of those who will be saved while the rest will be damned. Although in Black Africa there have been a few Mahdīist leaders with followers willing to die for them, in the heartland of Islam phenomena such as Waco and Jonestown have not existed, except for the one episode in Mecca in 1980 when a person claiming to be the Mahdī entered the Holy Mosque with his followers and was finally killed when government forces attacked the group inside the mosque.

The second most important branch of Shīʿism is Ismāʿīlism, which separated from the main body of Shīʿism over the question of the identity of the seventh Imām. The sixth Imām, Jaʿfar al-Ṣādiq, had chosen, by Divine command according to Shīʿite belief, his son Ismāʿīl as the seventh Imām, but Ismāʿīl died while his father was still alive. Subsequently, Imām Mūsā al-Kāẓim was chosen as the seventh Imām, but a number within the Shīʿite community refused to accept this investiture and continued to consider Ismāʿīl their imām, hence the name Ismāʿīlism. For some time their imāms were not present in public, until suddenly in the tenth century the Ismāʿīlīs arose in Tunisia to declare themselves rulers and were able to extend their domination to Egypt, much of the rest of North Africa, and even as far as Syria. They established the Fāṭimid caliphate, which vied with and opposed the Sunni ʿAbbāsid caliphate, which had its capital in Baghdad. They made Cairo their capital and built it into a great center of the sciences and the arts. Al-Azhar University, over a thousand years old and the most important seat of Sunni learning in the Islamic world today, was built by the Fāṭimids, whose rulers were also Ismāʿīlī imāms.

Fāṭimid Ismāʿīlism was its most moderate form, but other more radical movements followed from it. The Fāṭimid caliph Mustanṣir bi'Llāh had transferred the investiture of the imamate from his older son, Nizār, to his younger son, Mustaʿlī. Upon his death in 1094, some Ismāʿīlīs followed Nizār and others Mustaʿlī. The Mustaʿlīs, or followers of Mustaʿlī, continued the moderate teachings of the earlier Fāṭimids, but those who followed Nizār became more radical. In Iran the Nizārīs created fort cities on top of mountains, of which the most famous was Alamūt. The Persian Ismā'īlī Ḥasan Ṣabbāḥ had a major role to play in the creation of these forts and the propagation of the Nizārī cause. In 1164 the Ismā'īlī imām of the time, Ḥasan, declared the "Great Resurrection" and proclaimed that henceforth only the spiritual and esoteric aspect of Islam mattered and the legal and formal aspect was to be put aside. Nizārī Ismā'īlism became a radical and revolutionary force until finally defeated by the Mongols. It is said that Ismā'īlī devotees, who would sacrifice their lives as martyrs and were called *fadā'iyān,* assassinated their Sunni opponents who were oppressing them. The English word "assassin," in fact, comes most likely from the name Ḥasan, although some Western scholars have claimed that it derives from *ḥashīsh,* which the assassins are said by their enemies to have taken before committing acts of assassination.

The revolutionary character of Ismā'īlism died down after the Mongol invasion in the thirteenth century, and in Persia itself most Ismā'īlīs went underground. Meanwhile, the Musta'līs were flourishing in the Yemen. There was also a third group of Ismā'īlīs, who had settled in Sindh and Gujrat in India in early Islamic history and also converted some Hindus to Ismā'īlism. This community was split later and the major group came to be known as the Sat Panth (True Path). This branch of Ismā'īlism was very eclectic in its practices, incorporating many Hindu themes. Its religious poetry, called the *Ginān,* has verses in which the major figures of Islamic sacred history such as 'Alī are compared to and even identified with various Hindu avatars. By the nineteenth century the Persian and Yemeni branches of Ismā'īlism, known as the Ṭayyibiyyah, were also centered in India, especially with the migration of the Aga Khan from

Persia to India. One now has primarily two branches of Ismā'īlism, the Aga Khanid and the Bohras, both having their concentration of followers in India and to some extent Pakistan. But there are also notable Ismā'īlī communities in Central Asia, Persia, Syria, East Africa, and Canada, to which many Ismā'īlīs from East Africa migrated after the political tragedies of the 1960s and 1970s.

No one outside of the Ismā'īlī community knows the exact number of Ismā'īlīs, although, since their imām is alive and functioning as the head of the community, they are well organized and have a strong global network that embraces the whole community. Although their number is relatively small in comparison to the Ithnā 'ashariyyah, Ismā'īlīs have played an important role in Islamic history, intellectually, artistically, and politically, and constitute, despite their relatively small number, a notable part of the Islamic spectrum.

Finally, the third branch of Shī'ism, the Zaydī, chose Zayd, the son of the fourth Imām, as its leader. The Zaydīs represent a moderate form of Shī'ism and, in contrast to the Ismā'īlīs, do not emphasize the esoteric over the exoteric dimension of the religion. They had many followers in Persia and the Arab East in the tenth century, but gradually they receded to the Yemen, where they constitute almost half the population today and where they ruled for a thousand years until 1962, following the Egyptian invasion of the Yemen. Zaydīism has its own school of law and theology as well as a political philosophy according to which any Muslim who is pious and learned and can defend the country and preserve peace and security can be accepted as imām and ruler.

Although the Zaydīs and Ismā'īlīs number in the few millions, Twelve-Imām Shī'ism has some 150 million followers. The history of its early expansion was less connected to political institutions than to the spread of its teachings by individual adherents. In fact, its political expression came later than both Zaydīism and Ismā'īlism. It was not until 1499 that the Safavids established themselves as rulers of Persia, which included not only present-day Iran, but also Afghanistan as well as parts of Pakistan, Caucasia, and Central Asia. They established Twelve-Imām Shī'ism as the state religion and gave support to Shī'ism elsewhere, especially in Iraq, over which they ruled for some time before losing it to the Ottomans. There were also local dynasties in India that were Twelve-Imām Shī'ite. Consequently, the number of Twelve-Imām Shī'ites rose considerably during the past few centuries and today it constitutes the vast majority of Shī'ites throughout the world.

RELIGIOUS SECTS WITHIN THE ISLAMIC WORLD

There is a *ḥadīth* of the Prophet according to which his community would become divided into seventy-two groups, of which only one would possess the Truth, but this saying pertains more to theological *(kalām)* differences rather than to *Sharī'ite* ones. In practice there are far fewer sects in Islam than there are in Christianity, which has experienced continuous fragmentation and division within Protestantism since the Reformation. First of all, Sunnism and majority Shī'ism must be understood as the orthodox mainstream and not as sects as this term is used in English. In the context of Islam, the term "sect" *(firqah)* can be used in its classic sense to refer to small groups entertaining particular theological views that deviate from the general norm, or one can use this term in its current English usage to mean "a dissenting denomination" or "a schismatic group holding to a distinctive doctrine," but apply it to the case of Islam. The classic meaning has to be put aside in a work such as this because the discussion of *firaq* (plural of *firqah*) in classical Islamic thought would require delving into minutiae of Islamic theology and sacred history with which we cannot be concerned here. It is, however, important, in order to understand all the details of the tapestry of the present-day Islamic world, to mention some of the more important small religious groups that qualify as sects as this term is currently understood in English.

There are, first of all, the remnants of the early Khawārij, who existed in the seventh century and opposed both Sunnism and Shī'ism. At that time they were a revolutionary and violent movement with some following among the nomads. Later they settled down into established communities. Today they are to be found mostly in southern Algeria and Oman and are known as 'Ibādīs. They have their own school of law and although they began as a sect, today they are closer to the mainstream than other sects.

Before modern times, most of the sects in Islam issued from extreme forms of Shī'ism deviating in the direction of the divinization of 'Alī or some other personage or in emphasizing some esoteric teachings without the appropriate exoteric ones. To this day there is a sect known as the 'Alīallāhī in Iraq and Iran that divinizes 'Alī. The Druze, who live in southern Lebanon and Syria as well as northern Israel, broke away from Fāṭimid Ismā'īlism and consider the seventh Fāṭimid caliph, al-Ḥākim bi'Llāh, to be a divine incarnation. In Turkey there are the 'Alawīs (not to be confused with the 'Alawīs of Syria or with the 'Alawī Sufi orders). The Turkish 'Alawīs, who live mostly in central Anatolia, are remnants of Shī'ites who, after the rise of the Safavids and the Ottoman opposition to them, became isolated and oppressed, forgetting many of the tenets of traditional Shīʿism. The ʿAlawīs of Syria, also known as Nuṣayrīs, who now hold political power in the country, were originally a pre-Islamic religious sect with roots in Gnosticism and Babylonian religions. They have survived by describing themselves as a school of Shīʿism and have, in the past few decades, been trying to gain more Shīʿite legitimacy.

There are other small communities of this kind in the Islamic world, such as the Yazīdīs of Iraq, the inhabitants of Kāfirestan in northern Afghanistan, and the Sabaeans of Iraq and Iran. Like the Nuṣayrīs, they are remnants of pre-Islamic religions and cannot properly be called Islamic sects. There are also groups of this kind among Muslims of Black Africa. It must be emphasized, however, that the number of all these and similar sects is quite small. They came to play a more prominent role only when they became a factor in the balance of power in local situations, as one sees in the case of the Druze in Lebanon as well as in Israel, or in the exceptional case of the ʿAlawīs of Syria, a small sect that has been able to take hold of the reins of power. The case of the Taliban in Afghanistan presents another example of an extremist minority group that was able to dominate the country for several years.

In the early nineteenth century, one of the responses to the domination of the Islamic world by colonial powers was a wave of Mahdīism that swept over many Muslim lands. In certain areas it produced local Mahdīs with considerable religious and political influence, as one sees in the case of ʿUthmān Dan Fadio, who changed the religious landscape of West Africa, or the Mahdī of the Sudan, whose followers play an important role in that country to this day. But such movements did not give rise to new sects. Movements that did, however, create sects include Bābism in Persia and the Aḥmadiyyah movement in the Punjab, the former issuing from a Shīʿite and the latter from a Sunni background. In Persia there had developed already in the eighteenth century the Shaykhī movement, which was a very pious form of Shīʿism with extreme emphasis on reverence for the Imāms and an "anti-intellectual" attitude in theology and law. The movement remained, however, still within the fold of Twelve-Imām Shīʿism. From its background there arose in the early decades of the nineteenth century the Bābī movement, whose founder, Sayyid Muḥammad Bāb, claimed to be the *bāb,* or "gate," to the Mahdī. One of the Bāb's students, Bahā' Allāh, went further and declared himself not only the Mahdī, but a new prophet and founder of Bahā'ism, which also exists in the West today, but which, although based on a Shīʿite background, cannot be called Islamic. Rather, it is a modernist religious movement seeking to attach iself to certain of the prophetic and universalist principles of Islam, but not in the way that Muslims understand those principles.

The Aḥmadiyyah movement, founded by Ghulām Aḥmad in what is now Pakistan, was in many ways a reaction to English missionary activity in India. Its founder claimed for himself a new Divine dispensation, if not an out-and-out prophetic mission. He established for the first time in Islam missionary activity along the lines of the Christian version. Supported to a large extent for political reasons by the British, the Aḥmadiyyah established the first major mosque in Britain, which still stands, and sent many missionaries to Africa as well as Europe. In practice the Aḥmadiyyah, in contrast to Bahā'īs, follow Islamic practices, but their theological views are rejected by the mainstream Islamic community, especially their view that Christ migrated to and died in India and Ghulām Aḥmad's subtle challenge to the finality of the prophethood of the Prophet of Islam. Since its inception, the status of the Aḥmadiyyah has been somewhat ambiguous. Some Muslims have accepted them as an Islamic sect, although deviant in some ways, while others have declared that they are not Muslims. In any case their status vis-à-vis Islam is different from that of Bahā'ism, which separated itself clearly from Islam and cannot be considered in any way as a sect or branch of Islam.

INTELLECTUAL AND THEOLOGICAL DIVERSITY

In addition to those variations delineating Sunnism and Shī'ism and the numerous sects, there have existed since the beginning of Islamic history, within the mainstream, different theologies and philosophies that have contributed to diversity within the Islamic world, even within a particular school of Law. When one thinks of Islam, it is important to remember that, on the intellectual and theological levels, as well as on the juridical one, Islam is not a monolithic structure, but displays remarkable diversity, the elements of which are bound together by the doctrine of *tawḥīd*, or unity. Over the centuries, Islam has created one of the richest intellectual traditions of the world, favorably comparable in its depth and diversity to those of India, China, and the Christian West. In medieval times, in fact, many Jewish and Christian theological and philosophical schools in Europe were created as a result of the influence of and in response to Islamic philosophical and theological teachings.

To discuss in depth all the different theological and philosophical schools or even the most important ones would not be possible here. What is important in the present context is to at least mention the best-known schools and point out that even on some of the most important central religious issues—the meaning of Divine Unity especially in relation to multiplicity, the nature of God's Names and Qualities, the relation between faith and works in human salvation, predestination and free will, revelation and reason, the relation between God's Mercy and His Justice, and questions of eschatology, not to mention political philosophy—there have existed numerous views, sometimes opposed to each other.

In theology, which in Islam is called *'ilm al-kalām* or simply *kalām,* there developed in the Sunni world in the eighth century, first of all, the Mu'tazilite school, which favored extensive use of reason in the interpretation of religious matters, a position to which certain strict literalist interpreters of the Quran and *Sunnah,* such as the Ḥanbalīs, were opposed. In fact, the Ḥanbalīs have remained opposed to all forms of *kalām* until today, as has their Wahhābī offshoot. To this day the teaching of any form of *kalām* is forbidden in religious universities in Saudi Arabia.

In the tenth century a new school of *kalām* called the Ash'arite arose in Baghdad with the aim of creating a middle ground on many questions, such as the use of reason in religious matters. Ash'arism, which many orientalists have identified with Islamic theological orthodoxy as such, spread quickly among the Shāfi'īs and reached its peak in many ways with al-Ghazzālī, who did, however, hold some non-Ash'arite views, and with Fakhr al-Dīn al-Rāzī, in the eleventh and twelfth centuries. Gradually Ash'arism spread among the Ḥanafīs and Mālikīs as well and became the most widely held school of *kalām* in the Sunni world until the contemporary period. But there were also other Sunni schools of *kalām* that held sway in certain localities, such as

Māturīdism in Khurasan and Central Asia and Ṭahāwism in Egypt. Since the late nineteenth century, certain Muslim "reformers" such as Muḥammad 'Abduh of Egypt have sought to revive Mu'tazilism, because it made greater use of reason rather than relying predominately on the tenets of the revelation.

In Shī'ism also, *kalām* has had a long history. Ismā'īlī *kalām*, which began to be developed from the eighth century onward, was closely allied to Ismā'īlī philosophy and took greater interest in what in the West would be called mystical theology than Sunni schools of *kalām*. As for Twelve-Imām Shī'ite *kalām*, it developed along more intellectual lines than Ash'arite *kalām* and received its systematic formulation in the thirteenth century in the hands of Naṣīr al-Dīn Ṭūsī, who was also one of the greatest philosophers, mathematicians, and astronomers of Islam. The Zaydīs adopted more or less Mu'tazilite *kalām*, which therefore survived in the Yemen long after it had become eclipsed by Ash'arism after the eleventh century in the intellectual centers of the heartland of the Islamic world in the Arab East and Persia.

Islamic philosophy was developed by Islamic thinkers rooted in the Quranic revelation and meditating upon translations of Greek and Syriac texts into Arabic. The result was the integration of ideas drawn mostly from Pythagoreanism, Platonism, Aristotelianism, Neoplatonism, Hermeticism, and to some extent Stoicism into the Quranic worldview and the creation of new philosophical perspectives. Various schools were developed, starting with the Peripatetic *(mashshā'ī)* and Ismā'īlī from the ninth century onward. This early period produced such famous philosophers as al-Kindī, al-Fārābī, Ibn Sīnā (Avicenna), and Ibn Rushd (Averroës), whose influence on the medieval West was immense. One cannot conceive of either the Christian philosophy of the Middle Ages and such figures as Albert the Great, St. Thomas, and Duns Scotus or medieval Jewish philosophy as represented by such masters as Ibn Gabirol and Maimonides (who wrote his most famous work, *The Guide of the Perplexed*, first in Arabic), without consideration of the influence of early Islamic philosophy and to some extent *kalām* upon them.

Although the influence of Islamic philosophy upon the West came more or less to an end in the thirteenth century with the translation of Averroës and earlier Islamic philosophers into Latin, Islamic philosophy itself not only did not come to an end, but was revived in the eastern lands of Islam and especially Persia. In the twelfth century Suhrawardī founded a new school of philosophy called the School of Illumination *(ishrāq)* and in the seventeenth century Ṣadr al-Dīn Shīrāzī created a major synthesis of philosophy, doctrinal Sufism or gnosis in the sense of illuminative and unitive knowledge *('irfān)*, and theology in a new school he called "the transcendent theosophy" *(al-ḥikmat al-muta'āliyah)*. Both of these schools are still very much alive and have played a major role in the intellectual life of Persia, India, and as far as the school of *ishrāq* is concerned, to some extent, Ottoman Turkey.

Another major school that developed in the later history of Islam is doctrinal Sufism, or gnosis, associated with, more than anyone else, the name of the thirteenth-century Andalusian Sufi Muḥyī al-Dīn ibn 'Arabī, the most influential intellectual figure in Islam during the past seven centuries. His teachings spread from Sumatra and China to Mali and Mauritania, and his school produced numerous major thinkers and poets in nearly every Islamic land.

All of these schools of *kalām*, philosophy, and gnosis along with the philosophy of law, methods of Quranic commentary, and the study of other transmitted sciences with which we cannot deal here, as well as various schools of the sciences from medicine to astronomy, all of which are so important for both Islam and the development of science in the West, had both their adherents and opponents, and all of them must be seen as so many strands in the total tapestry of the Islamic intellectual tradition. Although they were all concerned with either the intellectual aspects of the religion, the cosmos in light of the truths of revelation, or purely theoretical knowledge, they often also exercised either direct or indirect influence on the popular level. In any case, their diversity must be considered when studying the spectrum of Islam in its totality. Their very existence also demonstrates the remarkably open universe of intellectual discourse within the framework of the Islamic tradition, an openness that marked many periods of Islamic history yet did not lead to rebellion against the sacred framework established by Islam, as was to happen in Christianity in the West after the Middle Ages.

THE QUESTION OF ORTHODOXY AND HETERODOXY

The question of orthodoxy in any religion is of the utmost importance, for the very word means "correctness of belief or doctrine." If there is truth, there is also error, and if nothing is false, then there is no truth. As the Quran says, "The truth has come and falsehood has perished" (17:81). Orthodoxy means possession of religious truth, and orthopraxy, the correct manner of practicing and reaching the truth. In the context of the totality of the Islamic tradition and in light of what has been said of the spectrum of Islam, orthodoxy and orthopraxy can be understood as the state of being on the "straight path" *(al-ṣirāṭ al-mustaqīm);* Islam itself is sometimes called the "religion of the straight path."

There is no magisterium in Islam, as there is in Catholicism, to determine the correctness of doctrine, and on the level of belief and doctrine Islam has been less stringent than Catholicism in determining what is orthodox. Usually acceptance of the testifications of faith, that is, "There is no god but God" and "Muḥammad is His Messenger," has sufficed, even if opposition has been made to other beliefs and interpretations of a particular person or group. Like Judaism, Islam has insisted more on the importance of orthopraxy than orthodoxy. Although it has been lenient on the level of orthodoxy as long as the principle of *tawḥīd* and the messengership of the Prophet have been accepted, it has been more stringent on the level of practice of the daily prayers, fasting, pilgrimage, and so forth; in observing dietary laws such as abstention from pork and alcoholic drinks; and in following moral laws dealing with sexual relations, theft, murder, and so on.

As to what plays the role of the magisterium in Islam, the best response is the *ummah,* or the Islamic community itself, and for Shīʿism the guidance of the Imām. Throughout Islamic history, the consensus of the community has decided in the long run what new interpretations of the Quran and *Sunnah* on the level of both thought and action are permissible and what is to be rejected. But this action by the community must always remain subservient to the teachings of God's Word and those of His Prophet. At that level any innovation *(bidʿah)* has always been seen as a major sin and deviation from the "straight path," but the strong rejection of *bidʿah* in its technical religious sense has never meant opposition to adaptation and application of the immutable principles of Islam to new conditions and situations, as has happened often throughout Islamic history.

With these definitions in mind, we can now turn to the spectrum of Islam and pose the question "What constitutes orthodox Islam?" In most Western studies, orthodoxy is limited to its exoteric aspect, and when Islam is considered, the four Sunni schools of Law alone are considered orthodox. But this appraisal is totally inadequate. There is an exoteric orthodoxy and orthopraxy and there is an esoteric orthodoxy and orthopraxy. Traditional and orthodox Sufism is not only part of Islamic orthodoxy, but is its heart and must not be seen as analogous to various mystical and occult manifestations in postmedieval Christianity that are called heterodox. Sufism is as much a part of Islamic orthodoxy as Franciscan or Dominican spirituality was part of Catholic orthodoxy in the Middle Ages.

To understand the position of Shīʿism within the Islamic tradition, one must compare it not to Protestantism, which arose many centuries after the foundation of Christianity as a protest against Catholicism, but to Eastern Orthodoxy, which has been there from the beginning. Although Catholicism and Orthodoxy have been at odds with each other for nearly one thousand years, both belong to the totality of Christian orthodoxy. The same holds true for Sunnism and mainstream Shīʿism of the Twelve-Imām School. One might say that in the middle of the spectrum of Islam as far as orthodoxy and heterodoxy are concerned stand Sunnism and Twelve-Imām Shīʿism. On the side of Sunnism leaning in the direction of extremism stand the Khawārij and similar groups, and on the side of Shīʿism after the Zaydīs and moderate Ismāʿīlīs stand those called Shīʿite extremists *(ghulāt)*, including eclectic forms of Ismāʿīlism and the various sects described above. Certainly on the formal and exoteric level all the four schools of Sunni Law, Twelve-Imām Shīʿism, Zaydīism, as well as those at the two sides of the central bands of the spectrum, whether they be Ismāʿīlīs or ʿIbādīs, as long as they practice the *Sharīʿah,* belong to the category of Islamic orthodoxy, as does of course all normative Sufism that bases itself on the practice of *Sharīʿite* injunctions. In fact, because of the centrality of orthopraxy one could say that Muslims who practice the *Sharīʿah* belong also to Islamic orthodoxy as long as they do not flout the major doctrines of the faith such as the Prophet being the seal of prophecy, as do the Aḥmadiyyah.

The use of such terms as "heterodox" and "sect" must be weighed closely in light of the nature and structure of the Islamic tradition. One should never refer to Shīʿism as a whole as a sect, any more than one would call the Greek Orthodox Church a sect. Nor should one call Sufism heterodox, unless one is pointing to a particular figure or group which has adopted either beliefs or practices that are indeed heterodox as judged by the consensus, or *ijmāʿ*, of the mainstream community on the basis of the Quran and the *Sunnah,* but such a phenomenon pales into insignificance when compared with the vast reality of Sufism. Authentic esoterism, far from being heterodox, lies at the heart of orthodoxy and orthopraxy in their most universal sense.

CULTURAL ZONES IN ISLAMIC CIVILIZATION

People often speak of Arabic, Persian, or Turkish Islam as if they were three Islams. In reality there is only one Islam, but with local coloring related to the ethnic, linguistic, and cultural traits of the different peoples who became part of the Islamic community. Wherever Islam went, it did not seek to level the existing cultural structures to the ground, but to preserve and transform them as long as they did not oppose the spirit and form of the Islamic revelation. The result was the creation of a single Islamic identity. The vast area of the "Abode of Islam" *(dār al-islām)* therefore came to display remarkable diversity on the human plane while reflecting everywhere the one message of the Quran revealed through the Prophet. This cultural and ethnic diversification must therefore be added to all of the factors already mentioned to make clearer the patterns that, superimposed upon each other, have created the great diversity in unity found in Islam.

The first cultural zone in the Islamic world is the Arabic zone, which stretches from Iraq and the Persian Gulf to Mauritania and before 1492 into the southern part of the Iberian Peninsula. Needless to say, in contrast to what many in the West think, the Arab world is not by any means synonymous with the Islamic world. In fact, Arab Muslims constitute less than a fifth of all Muslims, being around 220 million in number, but since the Quran was revealed to the Arab Prophet of Islam and the first Islamic society was established in Arabia, the Arabic zone of the "Abode of Islam" is the oldest part of the Islamic community and remains central to it. One of the great mysteries of early Islamic history is that as the Arab armies came out of Arabia, the lands that they conquered to the north and the west became both Islamicized and Arabized. The word "Arab" is a linguistic and not an ethnic term when used in a phrase like "the Arab world." There was also much Arab migration into this world, but what made it decisively Arab was the adoption of the Arabic language from Morocco to Iraq. Even a country with such an unparalleled ancient past as Egypt became Arab and in fact remains to this day the center of Arabic culture. In contrast, the people of the Persian Empire under the Sassanids, who were conquered by the Arabs in the seventh century, became Muslim, but they did not adopt the Arabic language. Rather, they developed Persian on the basis of earlier Iranian languages and retained a distinct cultural zone of their own. Iraq was the only exception. Although the seat of the Sassanid capital, it became Arab and in fact the center of the ʿAbbāsid caliphate, but it always retained strong Persian elements.

It is interesting to compare this development with the spread of Christianity into Europe. Through becoming Christian, Europe also became to some extent a part of the Abrahamic world, but remained less Semiticized than the non-Arab Muslims who embraced Islam, because through St. Paul Christianity itself had already become less "Semitic" before spreading into Europe. That is why the Christianization of Europe was not accompanied by the spread of Aramaic or some other Semitic language in the same way that Arabic spread in the Near East and Africa and also among Persians and Indians, who belonged to the same linguistic and racial stock as the Europeans. Not only were the Gospels written in Greek and not Aramaic, which Christ spoke, but also the Bible itself was translated early into Latin as the Vulgate and became linguistically severed from its origin. Latin became the closest in its role as the language of religion and learning in the West to what Arabic was in the Islamic world, with the major difference that Arabic is *the sacred* language of Islam as Hebrew is that of Judaism, whereas Latin is a *liturgical* language of Christianity along with several other liturgical languages such as Greek and Slavonic. The Arabization of what is now the Arab world and the significance of Arabic among non-Arab Muslims cannot therefore be equated with the Christianization of Europe and the role of Latin in the medieval West, although there are some interesting parallels to be drawn between the two worlds.

The Arabic zone, characterized by the use of Arabic as not only the language of religion, which is common to all Muslims, but also as the language of daily life, is further divided into an eastern and a western part, with the line of demarcation being in the middle of Libya. The western lands, called in classical Arabic al-Maghrib, that is, "the West," are further divided into the "near West," including western Libya, Tunisia, and most of Algeria, and "the far West," including western Algeria, Morocco, Mauritania, and in earlier periods of Islamic history al-Andalus, or Muslim Iberia. Also within the western zone are important non-Arab groups, the most important being the Berber, who inhabit mostly the Atlas Mountains and who have their own distinct language.

The second zone of Islamic culture, whose people were the second ethnic group to embrace Islam and to participate with the Arabs in building classical Islamic civilization, is the Persian zone, consisting of present-day Iran, Afghanistan, and Tajikistan (with certain cities in Uzbekistan). The dominant language of the people of all these countries is Persian, known locally by three different names, Fārsī, Darī, and Tājik, all of which are the same language; the differences between them are no greater than differences between the English of Australia, England, and Texas. This zone also included southern Caucasia, the old Khorasan, Transoxiana, and parts of what is today Pakistan before the migration south of Turkic people from the tenth and eleventh centuries and subsequent ethnic and geopolitical changes. The people of this zone are predominantly of the Iranian race, which is a branch of the Aryan or Indo-

Iranian-European peoples, and Persian is related to the Indo-European languages as are other Iranian languages spoken in this zone, such as Kurdish, Baluchi, and Pashtu. This zone has a population of some 100 million people, but its influence is felt strongly beyond its borders in other zones of Islamic culture in Asia from the Turkic and the Indian to the Chinese.

The first Persian to embrace Islam was Salmān-i Fārsī, a slave whom the Prophet caused to become free, making him a member of his "Household." From the beginning the Persians were deeply respectful of the "Family of the Prophet" and many of the descendants of the Prophet, including the eighth Imām, 'Alī al-Riḍā, are buried in Persia. But it would be false to think that the Persians were always Shī'ites and the Arabs Sunnis. Shī'ism began among Arabs and in the tenth century much of the Arab east was Shī'ite, while Khorasan, a major Persian province, was the seat of Sunni thought. It is only after the establishment of the Safavids that Persia became predominantly Shī'ite and this majority increased when Afghanistan, a part of Baluchistan, and much of Central Asia, which were predominantly Sunni, were separated from Persia, and Iran in its present form was created. As far as Afghanistan is concerned, during the Safavid period until the eighteenth century it was part of Persia. Then the leader of the Afghan tribes defeated the Safavids and killed the last Safavid king. Shortly thereafter Nādir Shāh, the last oriental conqueror, recaptured lands all the way to Delhi, including what is today Afghanistan. After his death, however, eastern Afghanistan became independent, and in the nineteenth century finally, under British pressure, Persia relinquished its claim on Herat and western Afghanistan, and thereafter Afghanistan as we now know it came into being.

The third zone of Islamic culture is that of Black Africa. Among the entourage of the Prophet, in addition to Salmān, there was another famous companion who was not Arab. He was Bilāl ibn Rabah al-Ḥabashī, the muezzin or caller to prayer of the Prophet, who was a Black African. His presence symbolized the rapid spread of Islam among the Blacks and the creation of the Black African zone of Islamic culture, encompassing a vast area from the highlands of Ethiopia, where Islam spread already in the seventh century, to Mali and Senegal. The descendants of Bilāl are said to have migrated to Mali, forming the Mandinka clan Keita, which helped create the Mali Empire. Some of the companions of the Prophet also migrated to Chad and established Islam there a generation after the Prophet. Altogether Islam spread in Black Africa mostly through trade, and such tribes as the Sanhaja, who themselves embraced Islam early, became intermediaries between Arab Muslims to the north and Black Africans. By the eleventh century a powerful Islamic kingdom was established in Ghana, and by the fourteenth century the Mali Empire, which was Muslim, was one of the richest in the world; its most famous ruler, Mansa Mūsā, one of the most notable rulers in the whole of the Islamic world.

In East Africa, which received Islam earlier than West Africa, the process of Islamization took a different path and was influenced greatly by the migration of both Arabs and Persians into the coastal areas of West Africa. By the twelfth century a Swahili kingdom was established with its capital in Kilwa, and from the mixture of Arabic, Persian, and Bantu the new Swahili language, perhaps the most important Islamic language of Muslim Black Africa, was born. But in contrast to the Arab and Persian worlds, where one language dominates, the Black African zone of Islamic culture consists of many subzones with very distinct languages ranging from Hausa and Fulani to Somali. Some of these languages are also spoken by Christians and are culturally signficant for African Christianity.

Although the north of the African continent was already Arab a century after the rise of Islam, the area called classically the Sudan, which included the steppes and the grasslands from present-day Sudan to Senegal, also became to a large extent Muslim over a millennium ago. It is, however, only since the nineteenth century that Islam has begun to penetrate inland into the forest regions south of the classical Sudan. There are of course also intermediate regions between the Arabic north and Black Africa where the two zones become intermingled, such as present-day Sudan, Eritrea, and Somalia. The zone of Black African Islamic culture with a population of well over 150 million people is bewilderingly diverse and presents a remarkable panorama of ethnic and cultural diversity within the local unity of Black African culture and the universal unity of Islam itself.

The fourth zone of Islamic culture is the Turkic zone, embracing all the people who speak one of the Altaic languages, of which the most important is Turkish, but which also include Adhari (Azeri), Chechen, Uighur, Uzbek, Kirghiz, and Turkeman. The Turkic people, who were originally nomadic, migrated south from the Altai Mountains to conquer Central Asia from the Persians, changing its ethnic nature but remaining culturally very close to the Persian world. By the time they had entered the Persia of that historical period, they had already embraced Islam and in fact became its great champions. Not only did they defeat local Persian rulers such as the Samanids, but they soon pushed westward toward Anatolia, defeating the Byzantine army at the Battle of Manzikert (Malazgirt in Turkish) in 1071. This was one of the pivotal battles of Islamic history. It opened the Anatolian pasturelands to the

Turkic nomads and led to the Turkification of Anatolia, the establishment of the Ottoman Empire, and finally to the conquest of Constantinople in 1453. The Turks were powerful militarily and ruled over many Muslim lands, including Persia and Egypt, and their role in later Islamic history can hardly be exaggerated. Today the Turkic peoples, composed of more than 150 million people, are spread from Macedonia to Siberia and all the way to Vladivostok and are geographically the most widespread ethnic and cultural group within the Islamic world. There are notable Turkic groups also within other areas that are not majority Turkic, including Persia, Afghanistan, Egypt, Jordan, Syria, and Russia, which has important Turkic minorities who are remnants of people conquered during the expansion of the Russian Empire under the czars.

The fifth major zone of Islamic culture is that of the Indian subcontinent. Already in the first decade of the eighth century, the army of Muḥammad ibn Qāsim had conquered Sindh, and thus began the penetration of Islam into the subcontinent during the next few centuries, but Islam spread throughout India mostly through Sufi orders. There were also invasions by various Turkic rulers into India, and from the eleventh century onward and until the British colonization of India Muslim rulers dominated over much of India, especially the north, where the Moghuls established a major empire in the sixteenth century. Indian Islam is ethnically mostly homogeneous, with some Persian and Turkic elements added to the local Indian population, but it is culturally and linguistically very diverse. For nearly a thousand years the intellectual and literary language of Indian Muslims was Persian, but several local languages, such as Sindhi, Gujrati, Punjabi, and Bengali, also gained some prominence as Islamic languages. Gradually, from the sixteenth and seventeenth centuries, a new language was born of the wedding of the Indian languages and Persian with Turkic elements added and became known as Urdu. Written in the Arabic-Persian script, Urdu became, like Swahili, Ottoman Turkish, and several other Islamic languages, a major language of Islamic discourse and was later adopted as the official language of Pakistan. The Indian zone of Islamic culture includes Pakistan, Bangladesh, Muslims of India and Nepal, and the deeply rooted Islamic community of Sri Lanka. There are some 400 million Muslims in this region, more than in any other. The reason for this vast population is the rapid rise of the general population in all of India since the nineteenth century, including both Hindus and Muslims, and the fact that more than one-fourth of Indians had embraced Islam, which was able to provide providentially a path of salvation for those who could no longer function within the world of traditional Hinduism. They have created some of the greatest works of Islamic art and culture, and although ruled often by Turkic dynasties, they have been very close in cultural matters to the Persian world until modern times.

The sixth zone of Islamic culture embraces the Malay world in Southeast Asia. Islamicized by Arab traders from the Persian Gulf and the Arabian Sea and also by merchants and Sufis from India from the thirteenth century onward, Malay Islam displays again much ethnic homogeneity and possesses local traits all its own. Influenced deeply from the beginning by Sufism, which played a major role in the spread of Islam into that world, Malay Islam has usually reflected a mild and gentle aspect also in conformity with the predominant ethnic characteristics of the people. Dominated by Malay and Javanese languages, Malay Islam embraces Indonesia, Malaysia, Brunei, and sizable minorities in Thailand as well as the Philippines and smaller minorities in Cambodia and Vietnam. Altogether there are over 220 million Muslims in this zone, and although this part of the Islamic world is a relative newcomer to the "Abode of Islam," its adherents are known for their close attachment to Mecca and Medina and love for the Prophetic traditions. As is the case with Africa and India, Malay Islam is highly influenced and colored operatively and intellectually by Sufism.

Besides these six major zones of Islamic culture, a few smaller ones must also be mentioned. One is Chinese Islam, whose origin goes back to the seventh century, when soon after the advent of Islam Muslim merchants settled in Chinese ports such as Canton. There has been a continuous presence of Islam in China since that time, but mostly in Sinkiang, which Muslim geographers call Eastern Turkistan. The Islamic population of China includes both people of Turkic origin, such as the Uigurs, and native Chinese called Hui. Even among the Hans there are some Muslims. The number of Muslims in China remains a great mystery and figures from 25 to 100 million have been mentioned. There is a distinct Chinese Islamic architecture and calligraphy as well as a whole intellectual tradition closely allied to Persian Sufism. The Islamic intellectual tradition in China began to express itself in classical Chinese rather than Persian and Arabic only from the seventeenth century onward.

Then there are the European Muslims—not Turkish enclaves found in Bulgaria, Greece, and Macedonia, but European ethnic groups—that have been Muslims for half a millennium. The most important among these groups are the Albanians, found throughout Albania, Kosovo, and Macedonia, and Bosnians, found mostly in Bosnia but to some extent also in Croatia and Serbia. These groups are ethnically of European stock, and the understanding of their culture is important for a better comprehension of both the spectrum of Islam in its totality and the rapport between Islam and the West in today's Europe.

Finally, there are the new Islamic communities in Europe and America, including both immigrants and converts (or what many Muslims prefer to call reverts, that is, those who have gone back or reverted to the primordial religion, which is identified here with Islam). These include several million North Africans in France, some 3 million Turks and a sizable number of Kurds in Germany, some 2 million mostly from the Indian subcontinent in Great Britain, and smaller but nevertheless sizable populations in other European countries. In America there are both immigrants, mostly from the Arab East, Iran, and the subcontinent, and converts, primarily among African Americans but also some among whites. The spread of Islam among African Americans began with Elijah Muhammad, who created the Nation of Islam, which espouses reverse racism against whites. This movement later split into two groups and most of its members, along with other African American Muslims, soon joined the mainstream of Islam. In this process the role of El-Hajj Malik El-Shabazz, better known as Malcolm X, was of particular significance. There are some 25 million Muslims in Europe, some 6 million (although some have claimed other figures ranging from 5 to 7 million) in America, half a million in Canada, and perhaps over 2 million in South America. To view the spectrum of Islam globally, it is necessary to consider also these Islamic communities in the West, especially since they play such an important role as a bridge between the "Abode of Islam" *(dār al-islām)*, from which they come, and the West, which is their home.

These zones of Islamic culture described briefly here display a bewildering array of ethnicities, languages, forms of

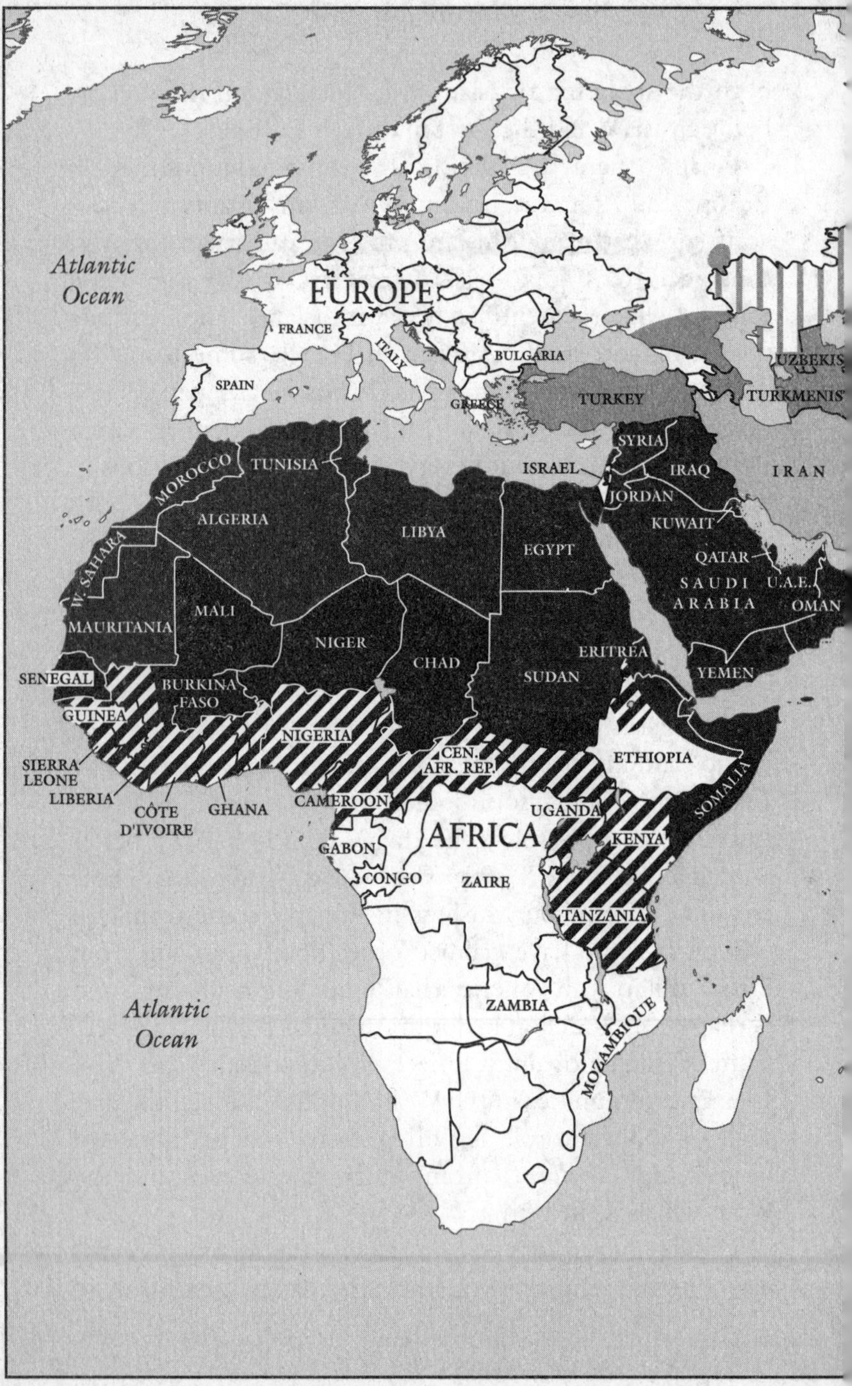

Atlantic Ocean
EUROPE
FRANCE
SPAIN
ITALY
BULGARIA
GREECE
TURKEY
UZBEKIS
TURKMENIS
SYRIA
ISRAEL
IRAQ
IRAN
JORDAN
KUWAIT
QATAR
SAUDI ARABIA
U.A.E.
OMAN
YEMEN
TUNISIA
MOROCCO
ALGERIA
LIBYA
EGYPT
W. SAHARA
MAURITANIA
MALI
NIGER
CHAD
SUDAN
ERITREA
SENEGAL
BURKINA FASO
GUINEA
NIGERIA
SIERRA LEONE
LIBERIA
CÔTE D'IVOIRE
GHANA
CAMEROON
CEN. AFR. REP.
ETHIOPIA
SOMALIA
UGANDA
KENYA
AFRICA
GABON
CONGO
ZAIRE
TANZANIA
ZAMBIA
MOZAMBIQUE
Atlantic Ocean

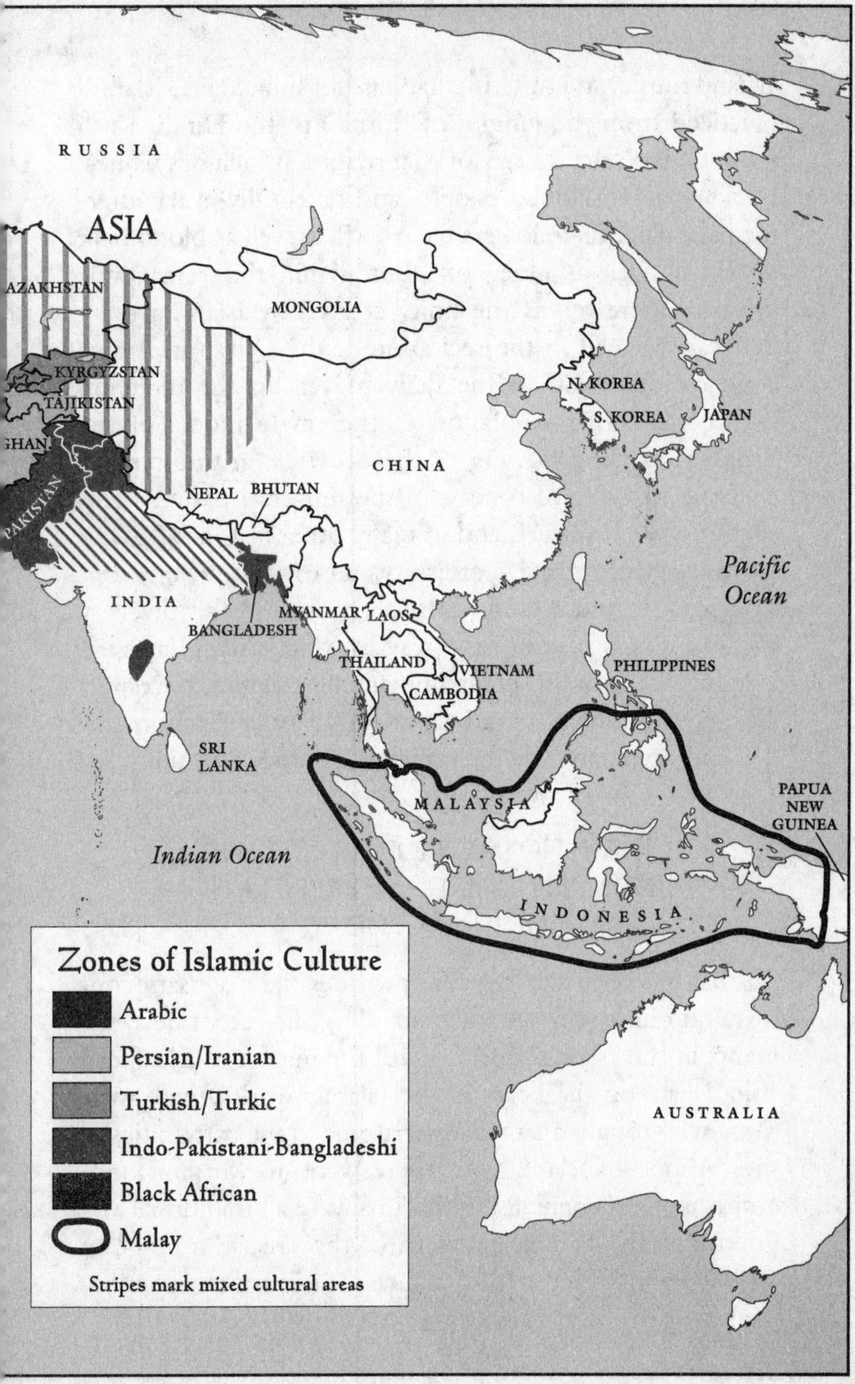

RUSSIA
ASIA
AZAKHSTAN
MONGOLIA
KYRGYZSTAN
TAJIKISTAN
GHAN.
PAKISTAN
N. KOREA
S. KOREA
JAPAN
CHINA
NEPAL
BHUTAN
Pacific Ocean
INDIA
MYANMAR
LAOS
BANGLADESH
THAILAND
VIETNAM
PHILIPPINES
CAMBODIA
SRI LANKA
MALAYSIA
PAPUA NEW GUINEA
Indian Ocean
INDONESIA
AUSTRALIA
Zones of Islamic Culture
Arabic
Persian/Iranian
Turkish/Turkic
Indo-Pakistani-Bangladeshi
Black African
Malay
Stripes mark mixed cultural areas

art and music, and differing habitats for human life. Islam is practiced from the jungles of Borneo to the Hindu Kush mountains to the deserts of Mauritania. It includes whites, blacks, yellow-skinned people, and practically every intermediary type. Its followers have black as well as blond hair, brown as well as blue eyes. But within this remarkable diversity there reigns the unity created by Islam, a unity that can be seen in the recitation of the Quran in Arabic from east to west, in the daily prayers in the direction of Mecca, in the emulation of the single model of the Prophet, in the following of the *Sharīʿah,* in the spiritual perfume of the Sufi orders, in the universal patterns and rhythms of Islamic art, and in many other factors. Unity in Islam has never meant uniformity and has always embraced diversity. To understand both this unity and this diversity within unity is to grasp the way in which Islam has been able to encompass so many human collectivities, to respect God-given differences and yet create a vast civilization unified and dominated by the principle of *tawḥīd,* or unity.

TRADITIONAL, MODERNIST, AND "FUNDAMENTALIST" INTERPRETATIONS OF ISLAM TODAY

All that has been said thus far provides the necessary context and framework for understanding the recent developments in the Islamic world. Until the impact of European colonialism on the heart of the Islamic world, there were those who fought against Western rule in the extremities of the "Abode of Islam," but there were no Muslim modernists or fundamentalists. Muslims were all traditional and fitted into the complex pattern of the spectrum of Islam outlined above. But with the advent of European domination of the heartland of Islam, represented by the Napoleonic invasion of Egypt in 1798, the period of diverse reactions and interpretations leading to the contemporary period began.

The European encroachment upon the Islamic world had actually begun over two and a half centuries earlier with the Portuguese and later Dutch and British domination of the Indian Ocean, which had been a major economic lifeline for Islamic civilization. There had also been European invasions of North Africa, the decisive defeat of the Ottoman navy in the Battle of Lepanto in 1571, which cut the Ottomans off from the western Mediterranean, and the defeat of the Ottomans in their siege of Vienna in 1683, which marked the beginning of the waning of their power. But none of these events, nor the Dutch colonization of the East Indies, nor British penetration into India, moved the minds and souls of Muslims as did the conquest of Egypt. That event awakened Muslims to a challenge without precedence in their history.

The Quran states, "If God aideth you, no one shall overcome you" (3:159). In the eyes of Muslims, twelve centuries of Islamic history had demonstrated the legitimacy of their claim and the truth of their call. God had been "on their side" and aided them over all those centuries, notwithstanding the defeat of Muslims in Spain and the destruction of the Tartar kingdom by the Russians, because these were at the margins of the world of Islam and lack of internal unity was considered as the reason for these defeats. Otherwise, wherever Islam had gone, it had become victorious; even the powerful Mongols had soon embraced Islam. But these Europeans, whom Muslims had neglected for so long and considered their cultural inferiors, were now dominating the Islamic world and there was no possibility of their accepting Islam as the Turks or Mongols had. They claimed themselves to be superior and were so proud of their own culture that they showed no interest in anything else. This situation created a crisis of cosmic proportions with eschatological overtones.

Several attitudes could have been taken in face of this crisis, and in fact every one of them was adopted by one group or another. One view held that Muslims had become weak because they had strayed from the original message of the faith and had become corrupted by luxury and deviations. This was the position of the so-called puritanical reformists, of whom the most famous, the eighteenth-century Muḥammad ibn ʿAbd al-Wahhāb from Najd, lived in fact before the Napoleonic invasion of Egypt at the end of the eighteenth century, but whose message sought to respond to causes for Muslim weakness. Although his message remained mostly in Arabia, this type of puritanical reformism, which was usually against Sufism, Shīʿism, Islamic philosophy and theology, and the refinement of classical Islamic cities as demonstrated in the arts, became known as the Salafiyyah, that is, those who follow the early predecessors, or *salaf*, disregarding the thirteen or fourteen centuries of development of the Islamic tradition from its Quranic and Prophetic roots.

A second possibility was to turn to eschatological *ḥadīths* concerning the end of the world, when, it was said, oppression would reign everywhere and Muslims would become weakened and dominated by others. As a result of this focus, a wave of Mahdiism swept across some areas of the Islamic world in the early nineteenth century, ranging from the Brelvi movement in the northwestern province of present-day Pakistan; to the movements of Ghulam Aḥmad and the Bāb already mentioned; to uprisings by major figures in West Africa, of whom the most significant, although his career began somewhat earlier, was 'Uthmān Dan Fadio, the founder of the Sokoto Caliphate, whose influence spread even to the Caribbean; to the Mahdīist movement of the Sudan, which inflicted the only defeat on the British army in the nineteenth century. As with every millennialist movement, this Mahdīist wave gradually died down, in this case by the second half of the nineteenth century.

The third possibility was to say, in the manner of European modernists, that the regulations of Islam were for the seventh century and times had changed; therefore religion had to be reformed and modernized. The modernists began in Egypt, the most famous of whom were Jamāl al-Dīn al-Afghānī, who was of Persian origin, and Muḥammad 'Abduh. They also appeared in Ottoman Turkey, especially within the Young Turk movement; in India, with such figures as Sir Sayyid Aḥmad Khān; and in Persia, which produced several other figures besides al-Afghānī, whose effect was, however, more local. These modernists varied in their degree of modernism and approach, but in general they were great admirers of the West and of rationalism, nationalism, and modern science. The most philosophical of all of them was Muḥammad Iqbāl, who belongs to the end of this first period of response to the West, which lasted until World War II. When Western scholars speak of Islamic reformers, they have mostly such figures in mind, along with the so-called puritanical reformers. From the ranks of the modernists rose nationalists and liberal thinkers, men who sought to modernize Islamic society, on the one hand, and fight against the West in the name of national independence, on the other. The colonial wars fought against Western powers for national independence by such figures as Ataturk, Sukarno, Bourgiba, and others were carried out in the name of nationalism, not Islam. Consequently, when Western powers left their colonies, at least outwardly, in many areas they left behind them ruling groups who were Muslim in name, but whose thinking was more like that of the colonizers they had replaced.

There were, of course, also groups of fighters for independence who were not modernists at all, but traditional Muslims, often associated with various Sufi orders. They usually carried out military resistance to preserve their homelands with a degree of nobility and magnanimity that deeply impressed their European enemies. One can cite as a supreme example of this type Amīr ʿAbd al-Qādir, the great Algerian freedom fighter and Sufi sage; his opponent, a French general, wrote back to Paris saying that fighting against the Amīr was like confronting one of the prophets of the Old Testament. Another notable example is Imām Shāmil, who fought for years in Caucasia against Russian encroachment. The example of the saintly nature of these men and the manner in which they treated their enemies as well as noncombatants, no matter what the other side was doing, is of the utmost importance for Muslims as well as Westerners to remember in the present-day situation.

Most of the Islamic world in the period between, let us say, 1800 and World War II did not react in any of the three manners described above. They were the traditional Muslims for whom the life of the *Sharīʿah* as well as the *Ṭarīqah* continued in its time-honored manner. There were, of course, continuous renewals from within that must not, however, be confused with reform in its modern sense. Many great scholars of Law continued to appear and Sufism was rejuvenated in several areas, especially in the Maghrib and West and East Africa, as we see in the rise of the Tijāniyyah and Sanūsiyyah orders as well as the appearance of such great masters as Shaykh al-Darqāwī, Shaykh Aḥmad al-ʿAlawī, and Shaykh Salāmah al-Raḍī, all of whom revived the Shādhiliyyah Order. Nevertheless, the *modus vivendi* of traditional Muslims was not reaction, but continuation of the traditional Islamic modes of life and thought.

After World War II most Islamic countries had become politically free, except for Algeria, which gained its independence in 1962 after a war that cost a million lives, and Muslim areas within the Communist world. The general population of Muslims had expected that with political independence would come cultural, social, and economic independence as well. When the reverse occurred, that is, when with the advent of political independence Westernized classes began ruling over a deeply pious public, as can be seen in countries as different as Turkey, Iran, Egypt, and Pakistan, major reactions set in that can be seen throughout the Islamic world to this day.

The old modernist and liberal schools of thought became discredited, as did the modernists as a political class, which had failed to solve any of the major problems that society faced in addition to suffering humiliating defeats, especially in the several Arab-Israeli wars. Nevertheless, modernism continued, often with a new Marxist component, and remained powerful because it controlled and still controls the state apparatus in most Muslim lands. But its intellectual and social power began to wane and weaken nearly everywhere except in Turkey, where Ataturk's secularism remains strong, held in place by the force of the army. Iran was the first country in which a political revolution removed the modernist government in favor of an Islamic one. A process of internal Islamization also took place, gradually and without revolutionary upheaval, in

Pakistan, Afghanistan, Malaysia, the Sudan, Jordan, Egypt, and some other countries, and that process continues.

As for what is called "fundamentalism," the earlier form of it as found in Saudi Arabia became transformed in many ways. By the 1960s there was a general malaise in the Islamic world caused by the simple emulation of a West, which, according to its leading thinkers, did not know where it was going itself. Many people, even among the modernized classes, turned back to Islam to find solutions to the existential problems posed by life itself and more particularly the actual situation of Muslims. The desire of the vast majority of people was to be left alone to solve the problems of the Islamic world, to preserve the religion of Islam, including the revival of the *Sharī'ah,* and to rebuild Islamic civilization, but the dominant civilization of the West hardly allowed such a thing to take place. Many organizations were nevertheless established to pursue these ends by peaceful means, chief among them the Ikhwān al-Muslimīn, or Muslim Brotherhood, founded in Egypt in the 1920s by Ḥasan al-Bannā', and the Jamā'at-i islāmī, founded by Mawlānā Mawdūdī in 1941, both of which remain powerful to this day.

In the past few decades this desire to preserve religion, re-Islamicize Islamic society, and reconstruct Islamic civilization has drawn a vast spectrum of people into its fold, all of whom are now branded indiscriminately in the West as "fundamentalist." The majority of such people, however, pursue nonviolent means to achieve their goals, as do most Christian, Jewish, or Hindu "fundamentalists." But there are also those who take recourse to violent action, nearly always when they are trying to defend their homeland, as in Palestine, Chechnya, Kashmir, Kosovo, or the southern Philippines, or sometimes in exasperation to defend their faith and traditional cultural values, as one sees in occasional violent eruptions in Indonesia, Pakistan, and elsewhere. But to act Islamically is to act in defense. Those who inflict harm upon the innocent, no matter how just their cause might be, are going against the clear teachings of the Quran and the *Sharīʿah* concerning peace and war (to which we turn later in Chapter 6). In any case, the unfortunate use of the term "fundamentalism," drawn originally from American Protestantism, for Islam cannot now be avoided, but it is of the utmost importance to realize that it embraces very different phenomena and must not be confused with the demonizing usage of the term in the Western media.

Disappointment among Muslims with the lack of true freedom after the attainment of political freedom after World War II also led to a new wave of Mahdīism, as seen in the coming of Ayatollah Khomeini to power in Iran at the time of the Iranian Revolution of 1979 (which was a major event in modern history and which definitely possessed eschatological overtones), the taking over of the Grand Mosque in Mecca in 1980, and the appearance of Mahdī-like figures in Nigeria during the last two decades. There is no doubt that there is again a presence of Mahdīism in the air throughout the Islamic world, as there are millennialist expectations among both Jews and Christians today.

As for traditional Islam, in contrast to the first phase of the encounter with the West, from the 1960s onward it began to manifest itself in the public intellectual arena and to challenge both the modernists and the so-called fundamentalists. Scholars deeply rooted in the Islamic tradition but also well acquainted with the West began to defend the integral Islamic tradition, the *Ṭarīqah* as well as the

Sharī'ah, the intellectual disciplines as well as the traditional arts. At the same time they began in-depth criticism not of Christianity or Judaism, but of secularist modernism, which was first incubated and grew in the West, but later spread to other continents. Such scholars base themselves on the universality of revelation stated in the Quran and seek to reject the substitution of the "kingdom of man" for the "Kingdom of God" as posited by modern secularism. Their criticisms of the modern world have drawn much from Western critics of modernism, rationalism, and scientism, including not only such traditionalists as René Guénon, Frithjof Schuon, Titus Burckhardt, and Martin Lings, but also such well-known European and American critics of the modernist project, including modern science and technology, as Jacques Ellul, Ivan Illich, and Theodore Roszak. The traditional Islamic response began with those trained in Western-style educational organizations, but during the past two decades has come to also include figures from among the class of religious scholars, or *'ulamā',* and traditional Sufis. These scholars and leaders seek to preserve the rhythm of traditional Islamic life as well as its intellectual and spiritual traditions and find natural allies in Judaism and Christianity in confronting the challenges of modern secularism as well as globalization.

The great majority of Muslims today still belong to the traditionalist category and must be distinguished from both secularist modernizers and "fundamentalists," as the latter term is now used in the Western media. In fact, it would be the greatest error to fail to distinguish the traditionalists from the "fundamentalists" and to include anyone who wishes to preserve the traditional Islamic way of life and thought in the "fundamentalist" category. It would be as if in contemporary Catholicism one were to call Padre Pio and Mother Teresa "fundamentalists" because they insisted on preserving traditional Catholic teachings. It is essential to realize that the notion of extremism implies a center, or median, of the spectrum; phenomena are judged "extreme" according to their distance, on either side, from this designated center. Unfortunately in the Western media today, that center is usually defined as the modernizing elements in Islamic society, and it is forgotten that modernism is itself one of the most fanatical, dogmatic, and extremist ideologies that history has ever seen. It seeks to destroy every other point of view and is completely intolerant toward any *Weltanschauung* that opposes it, whether it is that of the Native Americans, whose whole world was forcibly crushed by it, or Hinduism, Buddhism, or Islam, or for that matter traditional Christianity or Judaism. Orthodox Jews have as much difficulty resisting the constant assault of modern secularism upon their worldview and religious practices as do Hindus or Muslims. If one is going to speak of "fundamentalism" in religions, then one must include "secularist fundamentalism," which is no less virulently proselytizing and aggressive toward anything standing in its way than the most fanatical form of religious "fundamentalism."

In the case of Islam, there are today certainly religious extremists of different kinds, but they do not define the mainstream, or center, of Islam. That center belongs to traditional Islam. And that center is the one against which one should view fanatical religious extremism, on the one side, and the rabid secularist modernism found in most Islamic countries, but especially in such places as Turkey, Tunisia, and Algeria, on the other. Traditional Islam is not opposed to what the West wishes to do within its own borders, but to the corrosive influences emanating from modern and postmodern Western culture, now associated so much with what is called globalization, that threaten Islamic values, just as they threaten Christian and Jewish values in the West itself. But the philosophy of defense of traditional Islam has always been to keep within the boundaries of Islamic teachings. Its method of combat has been and remains primarily intellectual and spiritual, and when it has been forced to take recourse to physical action in the form of defense of its home and shelter, its models have been the Amīr 'Abd al-Qādirs and Imām Shāmils, not the Reign of Terror of the French Revolution or homegrown models of Che Guevara.

To understand events in the Islamic world today, even the most outrageous and evil actions carried out in the name of Islam, it is necessary to have a context within which to place these actions, in the same way that Westerners are able to place Jonestown, Waco, bombs by the Irish Republican Army, Serbian ethnic cleansing, or the killings carried out by Baruch Goldstein or Rabbi Kahane's group in context and not to identify them simply with Christianity or Judaism as such. This context can only be provided by looking at the vast spectrum of Islam outlined above. Yes, there are those in the Islamic world today who have taken recourse to military action and violence using modern technology with the supposed aim of ameliorating real or imaginary wrongs and injustices. Considering the history of the recent past, it is hardly surprising that such extremist illicit and morally reprehensible actions by a few using the name of Islam should take place, especially when injustices and suppressions within Islamic societies are added to external ones. Nor does asking why despicable actions take place in the name of Islam by the few and coming to understand the background of these actions in any way condone or excuse them.

The vast majority of Muslims still breathe in a universe in which the Name of God is associated above all with Compassion and Mercy, and they turn to Him in patience even in the midst of the worst tribulations. If it seems that more violence is associated with Islam than with other religions today, it is not due to the fact that there has been no violence elsewhere—think of the Korean and Vietnam wars, the atrocities committed by the Serbs, and the genocide in Rwanda and Burundi. The reason is that Islam is still very strong in Islamic society. Because Islam so pervades the lives of Muslims, all actions, including violent ones, are carried out in the name of Islam, especially since other ideologies such as nationalism and socialism have become so bankrupt. Yet this identification is itself paradoxical because traditional Islam is as much on the side of peace and accord as are traditional Judaism and Christianity. Despite such phenomena, however, if one looks at the extensive panorama of the Islamic spectrum summarized below, it becomes evident

The Spectrum of Islam

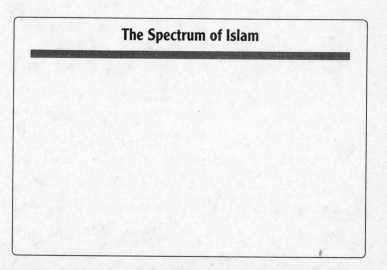

that for the vast majority of Muslims, the traditional norms based on peace and openness to others, norms that have governed their lives over the centuries and are opposed to both secularist modernism and "fundamentalism," are of central concern. And after the dust settles in this tumultuous period of both Islamic and global history, it will be the voice of traditional Islam that will have the final say in the Islamic world.

Three

DIVINE AND HUMAN LAWS

And now We have set thee (O Muḥammad)
on a clear road (Shar‘) *of Our Commandment;*
so follow it, and follow not the whim
of those who know not.

Quran 45:18

It is the Law of God which has taken
course aforetime. Thou wilt not find
any change in the Law of God.

Quran 48:23

THE PHILOSOPHY OF LAW IN ISLAM

One of the most difficult aspects of Islam to understand for modern Westerners is the "philosophy of law," which provides the conceptual foundation for the *Sharīʿah* (literally, "road" or "path"), or Divine Law, in Islam. Since Christ did not promulgate a law like those of the prophets of the Old Testament and the Prophet of Islam, but rather came to break the letter of the law in the name of the Spirit, religious law in the West developed in a very different manner than it did in Islam. Even during the Middle Ages, when Western society was thoroughly Christian, everyday laws were drawn from Roman sources or common law. These sources were clearly distinguished from Divine Law, which in the Christian context involved spiritual principles and not ordinary laws dealing with society in general. Moreover, Christian theologians developed an elaborate doctrine of natural law, which does not have an exact counterpart in Islam, although there are striking developments worthy of comparison in this domain within the two traditions.

Originally, natural law meant a system of rights or justice common to all human beings and derived from nature. St. Thomas Aquinas provided the greatest elaboration of this concept, stating that eternal law exists in God's mind and is known to us only in part through revelation and in part through reason. For St. Thomas, the law of nature is the "participation of the eternal law in the rational creature." Human law, based on precepts that human beings can derive by their own reason, must be a particular application of that law. Now, although Muslim theologians also debated among themselves whether our God-given reason can know the good without revelation, they did not develop a theory of natural law such as one finds in Thomism. Their view was closer to that of John Duns Scotus and Francisco Suarez, who believed that the Divine Will, rather than reason, was the source of law. In any case, even in the Middle Ages there were differences between the Islamic and certain of the predominantly Catholic schools of theology concerning the philosophy of law.

From the Renaissance onward laws became more and more secularized in the West, and they came to be seen as ever-changing regulations devised and defined by society to be made and discarded as circumstances dictate. And with the rise of parliamentary democracy, these laws came to be made and abrogated by the representatives of the people. Within the context of such a background, it is easy to see why the understanding of the Islamic, and more generally the Semitic, concept of law, which is associated with the Will of God and is meant to determine society rather than be determined by it, poses such a problem for modern Westerners.

Yet such a view should not be so difficult to understand in the West if one only turns to Jewish Law and the Old Testament, which is of course also a part of Christian sacred scripture. In the Old Testament is stated a clear theology that determines the meaning of law for human society. According to it, God is the Transcendent Reality Who is all powerful and sovereign over human beings. He is the only ultimate sanction of law, and the laws of human society are the embodiments of His Will. In the Bible, law is designated as God's commandments (*mitsvah;* as in Deut. 11:13), teaching or instruction (*torah;* Gen. 26:5), utterance (*davar;* Deut. 4:13), and norm (*mishpot;* Exod. 21:1), along with other expressions. Violation of law is seen not only as an offense against society, but also as a moral sin and a violation of God's order to humanity, for which human beings are accountable to God (Gen. 20:6; Lev. 19–20, 22). The Bible makes no distinction between religious and secular offense against the law, and the law is seen as a norm by which not only men and women, but all beings must abide (Gen. 2:11–17; 9:1–7). For the rabbis, there was no distinction between *fas,* God-given laws, and *lex,* human laws, as claimed by the Romans; all laws were seen as expressions of God's Will.

Now, this whole understanding of the meaning of law in the Bible corresponds very much to that of the Quran. If modern Westerners were only to grasp what the Old Testament says about law or how contemporary traditional Jews comprehend and practice Talmudic Law, it would be much easier to understand the "philosophy of law" in Islam. For Muslims also, God as the supreme and transcendent Sovereign has revealed His Laws through His prophets. The *Sharīʿah* is the concrete embodiment of the Divine Will, and in its most universal sense it embraces the whole of creation; what we call laws of nature are "the *Sharīʿah*" of various orders of corporeal reality. There is no distinction between the religious and secular realms, although the existence of non-*Sharīʿite* laws are recognized in practice, as we shall see later.

In the Islamic perspective, Divine Law is to be implemented to regulate society and the actions of its members rather than society dictating what laws should be. The injunctions of Divine Law are permanent, but the principles can also be applied to new circumstances as they arise. But the basic thesis is one of trying to make the human order conform to the Divine norm, not vice-versa. To speak of the *Sharī'ah* as being simply the laws of the seventh century fixed in time and not relevant today would be like telling Christians that the injunctions of Christ to love one's neighbor and not commit adultery were simply laws of the Palestine of two thousand years ago and not relevant today, or telling Jews not to keep Sabbath because this is simply an outmoded practice of three thousand years ago. Modern secularists might advance these arguments, but it is difficult to understand how Jews or Christians who still follow their religious tradition could do so. As far as Christianity is concerned, how Christians hold the spiritual teachings of Christ to be immutable can be a key for the understanding of how Muslims regard the *Sharī'ah*. As for Jews, such an understanding should be even easier, because the Islamic understanding of Divine Law is so similar to that found in Judaism, and the *Sharī'ah* and *Halakhah* hold very similar positions in the two religions, respectively.

As in Judaism, for Islam Divine Law is more central than theological thought to the religious life. One can be a very serious Muslim without interest in *kalām*, or Islamic theology, but one cannot be a serious Christian without interest in Christian theology unless one is a mystic or pietist. One could, in fact, say that what theology is to Christianity, the *Sharī'ah*, or Divine Law, is to Islam. To be a Muslim is to accept the validity of the *Sharī'ah*, even if one is too weak to practice all of its injunctions, and to understand the *Sharī'ah* is to gain knowledge of the formal religious structure of Islam. Even those who have sought to go beyond the formal level, through the *Ṭarīqah* to the absolute Truth, which transcends all forms, have never ceased to revere the *Sharī'ah* and to practice it. The greatest philosophers of Islam from Avicenna to Averroës practiced the

Sharīʿah; so did the greatest saints and mystics, such as Ibn ʿArabī, who wrote that his heart was the temple for idols and house for the Torah, the Gospels, and the Quran, but who never broke the Divine Law or stopped saying his daily prayers, promulgated by the *Sharīʿah,* until his death. The transcending of the Law in Islam in the direction of the Spirit has never been through the flouting of the Law, through breaking or denying its formal structure, but by transcending it from within. If there have been exceptions for those crazed by the love of God and in a paranormal state of consciousness, they have been there as exceptions to prove the rule. To speak of Islam on the level of individual practice and social norms is to speak of the *Sharīʿah,* which has provided over the centuries guidelines for those who have wanted or wish today to live according to God's Will in its Islamic form. When we hear in the Lord's Prayer uttered by Christ "Thy Will be done on earth as it is in Heaven," for the Muslim His Will is expressed in the *Sharīʿah,* and to live according to this Will on earth is, first of all, to practice the injunctions of the Divine Law. It is on the basis of this practice, meant for all Muslims, that the saintly can then surrender their whole will to the Will of God.

God, then, is the supreme Legislator *(al-Shāriʿ).* Through His Laws, before which according to Islam all men and women are equal, human life is sanctified. The Divine Law embraces every aspect of life and removes the distinction between sacred and profane or religious and secular. Since God is the creator of all things, there is no legitimate domain of life to which His Will or His Laws do not apply. Even the most ordinary acts of life carried out according to the *Sharīʿah* are sanctified, and persons of faith who live a life according to the Divine Law live a life immersed in grace, or what in Arabic is called *barakah*. Their life gains meaning, and they move through the journey of life certain that they are following a road *(sharʿ)* designated by God, a road that leads to salvation and felicity in the ultimate encounter with Him. To live according to the *Sharīʿah* in both form and inner meaning is to live an ethical life in the fullest sense.

THE SOURCES OF THE *SHARĪʿAH* AND THE METHODOLOGY OF ISLAMIC JURISPRUDENCE

The most important source of the *Sharīʿah* is the Quran, which some scholars claim to be the only basic source; all other sources serve only to elucidate and elaborate the roots and principles contained in the Sacred Text. There are some 350 legal verses, or what Western law calls *juris corpus*, in the Quran. Some of them deal with specific legal issues and penalties for illicit and illegal acts. A large number deal with the principles of the acts of worship and in some cases the details of such actions. Another group of verses deals with commercial and economic issues. In addition, many verses deal with the questions of justice, equality, evidence in law, legal rights, and so forth. Together these verses constitute only a small part of the Quran, but they are essential as the roots of Islamic Law.

The injunctions of the Quran would not, however, be fully understood without the *Sunnah* and *Ḥadīth* of the Prophet, which constitute its first commentary. The Quran orders Muslims to pray, but how to pray was learned from the model established by the Prophet. After the Quran, therefore, the *Sunnah* and *Ḥadīth* are the second most important source of the *Sharīʿah*. All schools of Law, Sunni and Shīʿite alike, accept these two as the absolutely necessary sources for Islamic Law. It is important to note that it was only after the canonical collections of *Ḥadīth* were assembled in the ninth century that the definitive work on the methodology of jurisprudence was produced by Imām al-Shāfiʿī.

Other *Sharīʿah* sources are accepted by some schools and not by others. They include *qiyās*, or analogy, in its juridical sense, which technically means the extension of a *Sharīʿite* ruling or value from a known and accepted case *(aṣl)* to a new case with the same effective cause, legally speaking. These sources also include *ijmāʿ*, or consensus, which is usually considered to be the consensus on a legal matter of the legal scholars who are specialists in the *Sharīʿah*, but which in Islamic history has also been the consensus of the whole community over a long period, as in the case of the banning of slavery and the acceptance of tobacco as being *ḥalāl*, that is, legally acceptable rather than forbidden. There is, in fact, a *ḥadīth* of the Prophet that asserts: "My community shall never agree on error." Then there is *istiḥsān*, or equity, which differs from equity in Western law in that in the latter equity relies on the concept of natural law, whereas *istiḥsān* relies on the *Sharīʿah*; otherwise, they are similar in that both are concerned with the idea of fairness and conscience in law. Finally, in this brief account one must mention *maṣlaḥah mursalah*, or considerations of public interest that are harmonious with the *Sharīʿah* and the objectives of the Lawgiver.

An important point here is the position within the *Sharīʿah* of human custom and law as distinct from the Divine Law. What in classical texts is called *ʿurf* or *ʿādah*, meaning human custom or habit, is considered valid in the *Sharīʿah* itself if such a custom or habit does not contradict or contravene the *Sharīʿah*. Therefore, human laws not derived from the Divine Law can become integrated into the Islamic legal system as long as they do not oppose the edicts of the *Sharī'ah*. This occurred often throughout Islamic history. Divine Law is referred to as *Shar'*, and human law is referred to as *qānūn* (from the Greek word *kanōn*, which is also the source for the word "canonical" in Western law). Paradoxically, nonreligious law in Islam uses the same term as religious or ecclesiastical law in Christianity. From the point of view of the *Sharī'ah*, to follow the *qānūn* of any country in which one finds oneself is itself commended as long as that *qānūn* or law does not contradict the injunctions of the *Sharī'ah*.

Historically and in contrast to the modern period, there was much harmony between *Shar'* and *qānūn* in the Islamic world, and traditional Muslims did not feel any appreciable tension between Divine Law and human law. This tension is a modern phenomenon that began in the nineteenth and early twentieth centuries with the abrogation of the *Sharī'ah* in certain Muslim countries and the forced implementation of various European legal codes, for example, in Persia, Egypt, Turkey, and North Africa. In these and similar countries, needless to say, the substitution of European laws for the *Sharī'ah* created a tension between private religious life and the public domain and drew the majority of the population further away from their governments, which they began to view as anti-Islamic or at best indifferent to Islam.

In the hierarchy of the sources mentioned above, the Quran stands at the highest level, followed by the *Sunnah* and *Ḥadīth*. An elaborate methodology was developed to deduce rulings from these sources and create the body of Islamic laws. This science of deriving juridical decisions from sources is called the "principles of jurisprudence" *(uṣūl al fiqh)* and is central to Islamic Law. Although *fiqh* itself originally meant "understanding" or "knowledge" in general, gradually it came to be associated with the "science of the law," or jurisprudence, corresponding to what the Romans called *iurisprudentia*. It deals with the body of the law and ways of concluding legal views from the principles and sources of the law. *Fiqh* has, therefore, a more technical legal meaning than the *Sharīʿah,* which includes moral laws and the general framework for the religious life of Islam. *Fiqh,* according to traditional authorities, is knowledge of the practical regulations and rules of the *Sharīʿah* acquired by reference to and detailed study of the sources.

Although the fifth and sixth Shīʿite Imāms, Muḥammad al-Bāqir and Jaʿfar al-Ṣādiq, said much about *fiqh* and its principles, it was Imām al-Shafiʿī who, in his *Risālah* ("Treatise"), established the systematic methodology for deriving laws from the sources. To exercise such an intellectual undertaking is called *ijtihād,* and the person who can give fresh views on matters of law by going back to the sources is called a *mujtahid*. In the Sunni world the "gate of *ijtihād*" closed after the tenth and eleventh centuries, when the major schools were established, whereas in the Shīʿite world it has remained open to this day and in each generation the *mujtahids* have derived the laws from the established principles and sources, which for Shīʿites are the Quran, the *Ḥadīth* of the Prophet, and the teachings of the Imāms.

Through the meticulous following of the methodologies elaborated in *uṣūl al-fiqh,* the major schools of Sunni Law already mentioned, that is, the Ḥanafī, Mālikī, Shāfiʿī, and Ḥanbalī, came into being, as did the Twelve-Imām Jaʿfarī School and the Zaydī, Ismāʿīlī, and ʿIbādī schools. Since the last century, a great debate has taken place in the Sunni world about opening the "gate of *ijtihād*" again, and in both the Sunni and the Shīʿite worlds, fundamental discussions are taking place today about the future development and application of the *Sharīʿah* to Islamic society facing major new challenges, including those issuing from biotechnology and all the problems that it poses for ethics. In this domain the recent responses of Jewish and Christian thinkers are close to Muslim ones, and the followers of the three monotheistic faiths can certainly collaborate together on many issues in the fields of bioethics and environmental ethics.

The *Sharī'ah* can best be understood through the use of the symbol of the tree, mentioned in the Quran: "Seest thou not how God coineth a similitude: A good saying, as a goodly tree, its roots set firm, its branches reaching into heaven" (14:24). This symbol has many levels of meaning, one of which concerns the *Sharī'ah*. Divine Law is like a tree whose roots are sunk firmly in the ground of revelation, but whose branches extend in different directions and have grown in various ways. The firmness of the roots does not mean that the tree is not living. On the contrary, it is the very firmness and immutability of the roots that guarantee the flowing of the sap into the branches and the continuous life of the tree. The *Sharī'ah* has developed in many different cultural and political climates over the centuries. It has harbored many differences of interpretation, and yet it has remained the *Sharī'ah*. Today it is faced with unprecedented challenges both from within the borders of the "Abode of Islam" and from outside, but it remains a living body of law that Muslims consider the concrete embodiment of God's Will for them to follow on the basis of their faith and free will.

TO WHOM DOES THE *SHARĪ'AH* APPLY?

According to all schools of Islamic Law, the injunctions of the *Sharī'ah* of Islam apply to all Muslims, male and female, who have reached the legal age and only to them. All Muslims are in principle equal before the law, whether they are kings or beggars, women or men, black or white, rich or poor. The Quran especially emphasizes that its injunctions concern both men and women in several verses where both sexes are addressed clearly and in a distinct manner, as when it says:

> Verily, men who surrender unto God, and women who surrender, and men who believe and women who believe, and men who obey and women who obey, and men who speak the truth and women who speak the truth . . . and men who give alms and women who give alms, and men who fast and women who fast, and men who guard their modesty and women who guard (their modesty), and men who remember God much and women who remember—God hath prepared for them forgiveness and a vast reward. (33:35)

In a society ruled by the *Sharīʿah* and in which Muslims are the majority, accepted religious minorities are absolved from following the Islamic *Sharīʿah* except in that which concerns public order. According to the Islamic *Sharīʿah* itself, Jews, Christians, and other "People of the Book," which in India included Hindus and in Persia the Zoroastrians, have their own *Sharīʿah,* and therefore their personal and communal affairs should be left to them. This is how the "community system," or *millat* system, of the Ottoman world functioned for many centuries. In the *millat* system the central government, although Islamic, recognized fully the social, economic, and especially religious rights of established minorities, so that there was no danger of the majority destroying the presence or identity of minority groups. Under the Ottomans the rights of Jews and Christians were guaranteed by the state itself. Although there were occasionally social frictions, by and large there was certainly much greater tolerance between various groups than what we have observed in Yugoslavia since its breakup, with all those horrendous acts of ethnic cleansing and genocide that followed.

CATEGORIES OF ACTIONS AND VALUES

According to Islamic Law, the Lawgiver, that is, God, has made a demand upon human beings in five categories: *wājib* or *fard* (obligatory), *mandūb* (recommended), *ḥarām* (forbidden), *makrūh* (abominable), and *mubāḥ* or *ḥalāl* (permissible). Each of these categories possesses nuances and subdivisions into which we cannot go here. Just to cite one example, *wājib* or *fard* can involve the individual *(ʿaynī)* or the collectivity *(kafāʾī)*. The daily prayers are *wājib ʿaynī,* incumbent upon each and every individual, while building orphanages and hospitals is obligatory upon the community as a whole *(wājib kafāʾī)* and not on a particular person.

Obligatory injunctions include the "pillars of Islam," or the rites to which we shall turn later, and taking good care of one's health to the extent possible. They also include supporting one's family, feeding the hungry, and paying the dowry of one's wife. Recommended *(mandūb)* acts are not required, but are pleasing in the eyes of God and bring reward in the Hereafter. Such acts are called acts of rectitude and bring with them reward from God *(thawāb).* They include acts of nonobligatory charity, for example, building a school or mosque, performing extra prayers, and following the example of the Prophet in personal matters recommended but not required by the *Sharīʿah.*

The category of the forbidden *(ḥarām)* includes all acts the commission of which is punishable and the omission of which is rewarded. This includes all the "Thou shalt not" injunctions in the Ten Commandments such as murder, adultery, and theft as well as others such as the eating of pork, the drinking of blood, use of alcoholic beverages, usury, gambling, marrying two sisters at the same time, and looking at the private parts of others (excluding one's spouse). This category covers a wide range from moral and ethical issues to practical dietary matters.

Something is abominable *(makrūh)* if omitting it is better than performing it, and this category is the opposite of what is recommended *(mandūb)*. The person who commits an act that is *makrūh* cannot be punished by law, but the person who avoids the *makrūh* gains merit with God. Something such as divorce, which is permitted but considered to be "the most abominable of permitted things" in the sight of God, is *makrūh*. Another example is the wearing of gold and silk by men. There are also *makrūh* acts in the economic field, such as making an offer to buy something for which another person has already made an offer.

Finally, the permissible, or *mubāḥ*, pertains to any act a person has the equal option of performing or not performing. The most obvious case is that of consumption of food that the Quran and *Sunnah* consider to be permissible to Muslims. Also, a sinful act committed under necessity can become permissible and *mubāḥ*. An example of this would be eating a carcass of a dead animal when one is dying of hunger and has no other means of nourishment. In general any act that does not belong to one of the other four categories is permissible, provided it does not cause harm.

Since many Muslims now live in the West, the term *ḥalāl* has practically entered into everyday English vocabulary. This fact necessitates elucidating somewhat further how the category of *ḥalāl* pertains to dietary regulations, although of course this category is far from limited to these matters. Like Judaism and Hinduism and in contrast to Christianity, Islam has dietary regulations that have a religious basis and are a means of sanctifying everyday life. Islamic dietary laws are not as complicated as those of Hinduism and Judaism, but they share some elements with the latter. Like Jews, Muslims refrain from eating products of the swine, whether flesh or grease derived from the flesh. And also like Jews, they eat only certain animals, such as cows, sheep, birds, and so on, but on condition that they have been killed ritually and in the Name of God. For Christians the sacrifice of Christ removed the necessity of the ritual slaughter of animals in order that their meat might be consumed, but not for Jews and Muslims. What is called kosher meat in Judaism corresponds closely to *ḥalāl* meat in Islam. Muslims also refrain from the use of any alcoholic beverages, not because they are chaotic in their very substance like the flesh of swine (the swine is envisaged by both Judaism and Islam from the point of view of ritual purity for human beings and in light of what it consumes as an animal), but because, as the Quran says, its harmful effects outweigh its positive ones. The Quran speaks of the pure wine the virtuous shall taste in Paradise, and wine as a symbol of realized knowledge of God combined with love for Him plays a central role in Sufi poetry.

Some in the West have claimed that the *Sharīʿite* division of acts into five categories destroys the spontaneity of religious life and reduces it to a mechanical exercise without grace. Nothing could be further from the truth for either Islam or other religions with similar views of Sacred Law, such as Hinduism and Judaism. The *Sharīʿite* categories are so many signposts along the road of life, but men and women still have to travel on this road and in every step there is the tension between the good and the evil tendencies of the soul, between what Simone Weil called gravity and grace. The drama of human existence and the tremendous responsibility that having free will entails for the human being are not in any way diminished by any Sacred Law, but are enacted and lived in each religious universe according to the principles and norms dominating that universe. But the drama within the soul is nevertheless there for all religious beings whether they are Jews, Zoroastrians, Christians, Muslims, Hindus, Buddhists, Taoists, Confucians, or followers of one of the primal religions. The *Sharīʿah* for Muslims neither destroys that drama nor removes human responsibility before God and one's own conscience. Rather, it provides the framework for the religious life of the individual and the community and sanctifies daily life.

THE CONTENT OF THE *SHARĪʿAH:* ACTS OF WORSHIP AND TRANSACTIONS

Traditionally the *Sharīʿah* has been divided into two parts: the *ʿibādāt,* or acts of worship, and the *muʿāmalāt,* or transactions. The heart of the *Sharīʿah* may be said to be the part dealing with the *ʿibādāt.* Even in modern times, when in many lands governments have replaced much of the *Sharīʿah* with European laws, the part dealing with worship continues to be practiced and could not but continue to be the foundation of the religion, or what Muslims themselves call *arkān al-dīn,* the "pillars of the religion." These "pillars" include (besides bearing witness to the two *shahādahs*) the daily prayers *(ṣalāh),* fasting *(ṣawm),* almsgiving *(zakāh),* and pilgrimage *(ḥajj).* As for *jihād,* meaning "exertion in the path of God," to which we shall turn extensively later in this book, it is a necessity for carrying out any act pleasing to God including all the "pillars."

Acts of Worship

Daily Prayers: Of all the Islamic rites, the most important and central are the daily prayers *(ṣalāh),* whose form was revealed by God to the Prophet and was then taught by him to Muslims. This rite is obligatory upon all men and women (except during their menstrual period) from the age of puberty until death. Five times a day, determined by cosmic events and not any mechanical or electronic means, Muslims must make a ritual ablution, which is a purification like the Catholic confession, and then perform the prayers.

The ordinary ablution involves the ritual washing with clean water of the hands, face, arms, feet, and the top of the head. This is in addition to the washing of the anus and the male or female organ after relieving oneself. A total ablution, which involves the washing of the whole body, must be performed after certain states and actions such as sexual intercourse. That is why every Muslim town and city from the seventh century onward has always had public baths, some of which that have survived being outstanding works of art. Before modern times, for many centuries the only towns in Europe that had bathhouses were those that were or had been ruled by Muslims. The ritual ablution, a very important aspect of the Islamic pattern of life, is also closely associated with the importance of cleanliness. Certain verses of the Quran and sayings of the Prophet constitute the Islamic counterpart of the Western adage that cleanliness is related to godliness.

After making the ablution, wearing ritually clean clothing and standing on clean ground, Muslims turn in the direction of Mecca and perform the prayers. These involve the recitation of verses of the Quran and the making of certain bodily movements that integrate the psycho-physical dimension of the human being into its spiritual archetype. In the prayers each person acts as his or her own priest standing directly before God. But when two or more people are present, it is recommended that the prayers be said in assembly with one person, called the imām, leading it. On Fridays the major weekly congregational prayers include a sermon, which often contains an important social and political message as well as an ethical and spiritual one.

The heart of *ṣalāh* is the first chapter of the Quran, called the *Sūrat al-Fātiḥah* (or Opening Chapter), which is repeated in every unit of the canonical prayer. It is the heart of the Quran and contains the message pertaining to the dimensions of the ultimate relation between human beings and God. The *sūrah* is as follows:

> Praise be to God, the Lord of the worlds,
> the Infinitely Good, the All-Merciful,
> Master of the Day of Judgment.
> Thee we worship, and in Thee we seek help.
> Guide us upon the straight path,
> the path of those on whom Thy Grace is,
> not those on whom Thine Anger is,
> nor those who are astray.
>
> (1:2–7)[1]

The life of the practicing Muslim is punctuated ever anew by the daily prayers, which break the hold of profane time upon the soul and bring men and women back to a sacred time marked by the meeting with God and to a sacred space pointing to the supreme center of the Islamic universe, Mecca, where the celestial axis penetrates the plane of earthly existence. The prayers are a rejuvenation for the soul, protection against evil acts, and a shelter for believers amid the storm of the life of this world. They have many levels of meaning, from the most outward to the most esoteric known to and experienced only by the sages and saints who are the friends of God. The canonical prayers were constituted in such a way that all kinds of people with various degrees of understanding and perspicacity can participate in them and be nourished by them according to their own capacity. They are a Divine norm transcending the individual order, and yet they act as the gate for the individual's access to the universal. There are in Islam two other modes of prayer, the prayer of the heart, meant only for those following a spiritual path, or *Ṭarīqah,* and individual prayers *(duʿā)* that Muslims, like Christians, Jews, and others, perform from time to time. The *ṣalāh,* however, is incumbent upon all Muslims, for it is the guarantee of our living in accordance with our theomorphic nature as beings reflecting God's Names and Qualities and the means whereby we stand directly before God to address Him as His vicegerents on earth.

Fasting: Like the daily canonical prayers, fasting *(ṣawm)* is an obligatory rite to be performed during the lunar month of Ramaḍān by all Muslim men and women from the age of puberty until old age. It is a fast from all food, drink, smoke, and sexual activity (also evil thoughts and deeds) from dawn to sunset (and for Shīʿites until dusk). This rite is, however, obligatory only for those who have the physical capability to carry it out. Exceptions are made for the sick and those on a journey (who must make it up later), women in their menstrual period or pregnant or nursing a child, and those who are too weak because of old age. The month of Ramaḍān was the month of the descent of the Quran. In this holiest of Islamic months, Muslims combine physical and psychological purification with an intensification of prayer, recitation of the Quran, and acts of charity. During this month, in almost all Islamic cities, vast amounts of food are provided free for the poor, and the cost of the one meal that one and one's family does not eat each day is given to the needy.

During the fast one puts on, in a sense, the dress of death and distances oneself from the passions that attach one to the world. It is a time for great self-discipline and the practice of the virtues of patience and persistence in hardship for the sake of God. It is also a time to develop greater compassion toward the needy and to realize what it means to suffer from hunger. The Prophet loved fasting, and in a way fasting from food in Islam corresponds to abstaining from sexuality in Christianity, which exists as a religious ideal although only practiced fully by those who observe celibacy. The Founder of Islam fasted on many other days during the year, and there are many who emulate his model to this day. But the only obligatory fast is that of Ramaḍān, which is practiced by the vast majority of Muslims throughout the world to this day.

It is necessary here to say something about the Islamic lunar calendar, which determines the period of fasting as well as other religious rites and ceremonies. In Islam all religious events are based on the lunar calendar, although the solar calendar is used for agricultural and other matters. In fact, the most accurate solar calendar ever devised, more accurate than the Julian or Gregorian calendars, is the Jalālī calendar, devised by the famous mathematician-poet 'Umar Khayyām and others in the twelfth century and still in use in Iran and Afghanistan. This solar calendar divides the year into twelve months, the first six of which have thirty-one days, the next five, thirty days, and the twelfth month, twenty-nine days, except on leap year when it has thirty days. It therefore makes it easier to keep count of how many days are in each month as compared with the Western calendar and is also astronomically more precise. But Islam explicitly bans intercalation, which means adding a number of days to the lunar year to make it the equivalent of the solar year. Consequently, the Islamic lunar calendar moves through the solar calendar completing one cycle every thirty-three years. As a result, Ramaḍān is sometimes in the winter and sometimes in the summer, sometimes during long and hot days and sometimes during short and cool ones. Since Islam is a global community, this injunction banning intercalation, as foreseen in the Quran, guarantees fairness and justice as far as conditions go for fasting, the *ḥajj*, and early morning prayers for people living in different geographical latitudes and in the two different hemispheres of the globe.

Almsgiving: The word for almsgiving, *zakāh,* comes from the root *zky,* meaning "to purify." It is a tithe or alms whose payment is obligatory according to the *Sharīʿah* and is the means of "purifying" what bounties God has given by sharing some of it with the poor and the needy. In traditional Islamic society, this sum was paid to the public treasury. Many projects for public use, such as the creation and maintenance of schools, hospitals, orphanages, and the like, were implemented by use of the sums collected through this religious tax.

Those familiar with Jewish and Christian practices can see obvious similarities in the use of tithing in the three Abrahamic traditions. The word "tithe" comes from the Old English word meaning "tenth," but the practice goes back to Judaism, where Mosaic laws prescribed the paying of tithes for the support of the Levites and temple service. The book of Numbers (18:21) in the Old Testament states, "I have given the children of Levi all the tithes in Israel for an inheritance in return for the work which they perform." The practice was followed later by the Roman Catholic Church and revenues were used for the support of clergy, churches, and the poor. It became enjoined by ecclesiastical law from the sixth century onward and enforced by secular law starting in the eighth century. It provided the main source of funds for the building of the beautiful medieval cathedrals. Martin Luther approved of tithing, while the French Revolution repealed it. In contrast to Catholicism and Protestantism, however, the Orthodox Church did not accept the practice of tithing. As far as the United States is concerned, the practice of tithing was never enforced except by Mormons. Looking at Western Christianity in general, one can therefore see that tithing and *zakāh* are similar, although the amount of the alms or religious tax has not been the same in the three Abrahamic faiths.

In Shī'ite Islam in addition to *zakāh,* there is also another obligatory religious tax called *khums,* meaning one fifth. Moreover, there are many other kinds of almsgiving common to all Muslims, such as *ṣadaqah,* a sum given to the poor in gratefulness to God for the warding off of some danger or the receiving of a special blessing, or *fiṭriyyah,* money given to the poor at the end of the month of Ramaḍān. These forms of almsgiving must not, however, be confused with the *zakāh,* which is obligatory and one of the "pillars" of Islam.

In general, the *Sharī'ah* encourages giving *(īthār)* in the path of God, and Muslims agree completely with the dictum of the Gospels, "It is more blessed to give than to receive." Much of the social and economic life of Islamic society, in fact, continues to be financed through various forms of religious charity. The institution of *waqf,* or religious endowment, whose conditions are set forth in Islamic Law, has played the greatest role in Islamic history in the creation of public facilities, especially schools and hospitals. Today in most Islamic countries the *waqf* is taken over by governments, but traditionally the *waqf* was like the endowments created and sustained by the private sector in America today, except that it was always of a religious character.

Pilgrimage: Thanks to radio and television broadcasts available globally, most of the world has now heard of the Muslim pilgrimage, the *ḥajj,* and most likely seen images of what is perhaps the largest annual religious gathering in the world. The *ḥajj,* which is obligatory at least once in a Muslim's lifetime if he or she has the financial means and is physically able to perform it, involves pilgrimage to Mecca during a particular period in the lunar month of Dhu'l-ḥijjah. The rite retraces the acts of Abraham after he rebuilt the Ka'bah (the cubic structure at the center of Mecca considered by Muslims to be the most ancient sanctuary, built originally by Adam) and follows the model established by the Prophet. It is in a sense an Abrahamic rite within the final expression of monotheism, that is, Islam, which revived and reestablished pure Abrahamic monotheism.

The pilgrim, whether male or female, must wear a special white cloth, called *iḥrām,* before entering the sacred precinct around Mecca, within which only Muslims are allowed, a cloth that is often used later as one's shroud. In becoming *muḥrim,* that is, clothed with this special cloth, men and women must leave the world behind. During the *ḥajj* they must abstain from sexual activity and devote themselves wholly to God, whose House, the Ka'bah, they are visiting. Here all external distinctions are erased; king and peasant are dressed in the same manner. The complicated rites involve among other acts circumambulation around the Ka'bah in a counterclockwise direction with the awareness that one is moving against the march of time and washing away from one's soul all the dross that has accrued within as the result of the flow of time. Through these rites, which include the sacrifice of an animal symbolizing the sacrifice of one's passionate soul before God, the pilgrim returns to the state of primordiality, or the Edenic state in which he or she was created, and God forgives that person's sins if the *ḥajj* is performed with full sincerity and devotion. That is why many older people make the pilgrimage with the hope of dying in the process and therefore leaving this world cleansed of their sins. At the corner of the Ka'bah is to be found the black stone that symbolizes the covenant between human beings and God. All pilgrims seek to kiss and touch it to remind themselves concretely of the primordial covenant they have made with God to accept the state of being human, which means to accept the Lordship of God and surrender to Him.

The *ḥajj* is both the means of purification of the individual and the integration of society. Muslims from all parts of the world are to be seen at the *ḥajj*. Today the over 2 million people who perform it each year come from all quarters of the world and include Arabs, Persians, and Turks as well as Black Africans and Malays, Chinese and Indo-Pakistanis as well as Germans and Americans, black-skinned as well as fair-skinned people, pilgrims with dark eyes as well as blue ones. Nowhere else in the world is the ethnic and racial diversity of the Islamic community unified in the surrender to the One God more evident than in Mecca during the *ḥajj*. Here, exchange of ideas and goods also takes place between Muslims from various parts of the world, and the *ḥajj* has been called by some Western scholars the world's first international scientific congress as well as international economic fair. But more than anything else, through the *ḥajj*, pilgrims are purified and in returning home bring something of the grace, or *barakah,* of the Center to the farthest outreaches of the Islamic world.

With the global population explosion, the problem of accommodating all the pilgrims who wish to make the *ḥajj* has become acute. Although the number of pilgrims has now risen to over 2 million, this is still a small percentage of the 1.2 billion Muslims in the world, not all of whom, however, fulfill the conditions necessary to make the *ḥajj*. The number of those who do qualify annually according to the Divine Law to make the *ḥajj,* however, is much larger than those given permission to perform it. There is therefore a great deal of pressure on most Muslim governments as well as on Saudi Arabia to permit more pilgrims every year, while at the same time the very logistics of such a large gathering and the space limitations make it impossible to continue to increase the number of pilgrims. In view of the limitations, some Muslims make the pilgrimage to Mecca outside of the specified season to benefit from the grace of the visit to the House of God even if it is not during the days specified by Islamic Law.

The *ḥajj,* however, is not the only form of Islamic pilgrimage, but the only one that is obligatory according to the *Sharīʿah* if certain conditions are fulfilled. Today in America, pilgrimage does not play such a central role in the religious life of Protestants, although there are still those who make pilgrimage to Jerusalem. As for Catholics, both in America and Europe there are still those who make pilgrimage to Jerusalem, Lourdes, or Rome, and in Central and South America to local shrines such as that of the Virgin of Guadalupe in Mexico City. In the Middle Ages, however, pilgrimage was much more common in the West, not only to Jerusalem, which served as the excuse for the Crusades, but also to many local sites such as Canterbury in England and Santiago de Compostela in Spain. The importance of pilgrimage in Islam today must be compared more to practices in the earlier eras of Christian history than those today, especially in America.

In the Islamic world, those who make the *ḥajj* also visit the tomb of the Prophet in Medina and before the 1967 Israeli takeover of Jerusalem, they also made pilgrimage in large numbers to this third holy city of Islam. Many local sites of pilgrimage are loci of grace associated with the tombs of descendants of the Prophet and the great saints. All of these sites are so many extensions of Medina and expand the *barakah* of the city of the Prophet and his sacred remains to the various areas of the Islamic world. Some of these sites are the tomb of Aḥmad Bamba in Touba, West Africa; the two Moulay Idrīses in the proximity of Maknes and in Fez; the Mosque of the "Head of Ḥusayn" in Cairo; the tomb of Sayyid Aḥmad Badawī, the patron saint of Egypt, in Tanta; and the "sacred stations" of Zaynab in Cairo and Damascus. The many holy sites in Iraq include the tomb of 'Abd al-Qādir al-Jīlānī and the mausoleums of the Shī'ite Imāms, especially those of 'Alī in Najaf and Ḥusayn in Karbalā'. The mausoleum of Jalāl al-Dīn Rūmī in Konya, Turkey; the holy cities of Mashhad and Qom in Iran; the mausoleum of Khwājah 'Abd Allāh Anṣārī in Herat and that of Bahā' al-Dīn Naqshband near Bukhara; and the tombs of many of the great Sufi saints of the subcontinet of India such as that of Dādājī Ganjbakhsh in Lahore, Niẓām al-Dīn Awliyā' in Delhi, and Mu'īn al-Dīn Chishtī in Ajmer, which are among the greatest sites of religious life in Islam. During annual commemorations of the death of these saints, often hundreds of thousands of people gather at these locations for religious rites and to receive blessings.

It is important to note that these sites of blessing are not limited to the sacred station *(maqām)*, or mausoleum, of males, but include those of females as well. In Cairo, after the Mosque of the "Head of Ḥusayn," the most important sanctuary and center for pilgrims is the *maqām* of the granddaughter of the Prophet, Zaynab, whose other *maqām* in Damascus is in many ways the religious center of the city. Also in Cairo, the mausoleum of Sayyidah Nafīsah, a great scholar, saint, and descendant of the Prophet, is a major religious site. In Iran, after Mashhad, the city of Qom, which is the center of Twelve-Imām Shīʿism, is the most important shrine in Iran because of the tomb of Haḍrat-i Maʿṣūmah, the sister of Imām Riḍā, who is buried in Mashhad. And before the Wahhābīs destroyed the mausoleums of the wife and daughter of the Prophet, Khadījah and Fāṭimah, in the Hijaz, those sites were also major centers for pilgrimage. Naturally, these mausoleums of female saints are visited especially by women, but not exclusively. Both men and women participate in large numbers in pilgrimage to all of these sites, whether they are associated with a male or female saintly figure.

Visits and pilgrimage to the tombs of saints is strongly opposed by Wahhābīs and other puritanical reformers and also discouraged by modernists. The Wahhābī opposition is based on the idea that to visit the tomb of a saint is like idol worship and takes one's attention away from the transcendence of God; modernists have discouraged such pilgrimages in order to secularize social life, but their opposition has never been as severe as that of the Wahhābīs. Still, the practice of pilgrimage to various holy sites remains to this day at the heart of the religious life of the Islamic world. One cannot understand the religious practice of Islam without paying attention to the significance of pilgrimage, which ranges hierarchically from the *ḥajj* and the pilgrimage to Medina to visitation of local sacred sites that exist in most Muslim lands. These "lesser" forms of pilgrimage do not, however, in any way detract from the centrality of the *ḥajj,* but are like so many foretastes and reflections of it. The visit to the "House of God" remains supreme in the mind of Muslims when it comes to pilgrimage, and many visit it even outside the designated season in what is called *ʿumrah.* That is why today, when populations have increased and travel is easier, every day of the year there are numerous pilgrims in Mecca, and in the middle of any night during any season one finds thousands of pilgrims circumambulating around the Kaʿbah and praying before the house rebuilt by Abraham in celebration of the One God who in the Old Testament uttered, "I am That I am."

Besides all these rites promulgated by the *Sharīʿah,* there are also many other religious practices in Islam based on the *Sunnah* of the Prophet and later traditional elaborations thereof. They include ritualized ways of feeding the poor, sessions of special prayers, ritualized sermons, sacrifice of animals whose meat is then distributed among the needy, and many other activities. In the traditional Islamic world, in fact, nearly every necessity of life is sanctified, and the *Sharīʿah* considers even the earning of one's daily bread a religious act. It is the totality of the obligatory rites as well as the recommended ones together with the sacralized forms of many different actions that constitute the Islamic way of life, in which, in principle, there is no distinction between the sacred and the profane and what we now call ordinary or everyday life is integrated into the matrix of the sacred.

Transactions

It is precisely the all-embracing nature of the *Sharīʿah* that has necessitated its dealing with what are called transactions *(muʿāmalāt)*—social, environmental, economic, and political matters such as personal laws, the family, the neighbor, and so forth. Social teachings are dealt with in the next chapter, but here it is necessary to say a few words about the environmental, economic, and political teachings of the *Sharīʿah,* some of which are parts of jurisprudence, or *fiqh,* and others principles to be applied by various generations of Muslims to specific situations in the absence of explicit legal rulings.

Environmental Teachings: The environmental crisis is primarily the consequence of an inner malaise and a whole worldview that gives human beings unlimited power over nature seen as a desacralized reality. This manner of looking at things has resulted in the reduction of nature to only a resource for economic production. As far as dealing with it on the social and legal planes is concerned, however, for Islam environmental matters may be said to be a legal issue already treated in principle in the sources and applications of Islamic Law, whereas in the West law seems to be trying to "catch up" with the problems caused by this crisis. The traditional Islamic worldview is totally opposed to the prevalent modern paradigm of the relation between human beings and nature, which has caused unprecedented harm to the natural environment, has led to the loss of many species, and now threatens the very future of human life on earth. Islam sees men and women as God's vicegerents on earth. Therefore, in the same way that God has power over

His creation but is also its sustainer and protector, human beings must also combine power over nature with responsibility for its protection and sustenance. The Quran is replete with references to nature, and the phenomena of nature are referred to as God's signs and are therefore sacred. In traditional Islamic society human beings lived in remarkable harmony with their natural environment, as can be seen in the urban design of traditional Islamic cities and also in the life in the villages, which, as in other premodern parts of the world, is still based on remarkable harmony with the rhythms of nature and makes full use of what is now called recycling.

On the basis of the Quran and *Ḥadīth,* the *Sharīʿah* has extensive teachings, both legal and moral, concerning the natural environment: the way that animals should be treated kindly, trees preserved and not cut unless absolutely necessary, vegetation guarded even in war, running water protected, and many other relevant issues. The Prophet himself was always very kind to animals. As for trees, he emphasized the significance of creating what is today called green space; He said, "It is a blessed act to plant a tree even if it be a day before the end of the world." The *Sharīʿah* promulgates certain general principles concerning the environment, such as that of balance *(mīzān)* between all parts of God's creation, the prohibition of waste, and respect for all life forms, and specific injunctions, such as the creation of protected areas for wildlife.

But in many areas where crises have been created during the past century as a result of the advent of modern technology, overpopulation, economic plunder, and so on, specific *Sharīʿite* laws are missing. For some time the Islamic world, like the rest of the non-Western world, neglected the environmental crisis and thought that it was a problem only for highly industrialized countries. As the dimensions of the crisis grew, however, the situation changed during the last two decades of the twentieth century. A whole new branch of the *Sharī'ah* is now being developed on the basis of the traditional sources of the Divine Law to address the crucial problems posed by the environmental crisis in the Islamic world as elsewhere. From Nigeria to Malaysia, legal scholars are applying themselves to these issues, and this branch of the *Sharī'ah* is one of the most challenging and dynamic aspects of it in the present day.

Economic Teachings: Before modern times there was no such thing as economics among the Islamic sciences, just as it was not part of European divisions of learning before the Renaissance. Both civilizations knew the Latin word *oeconomicus* (itself of Greek origin), from which the modern word is derived, but understood it in its original sense of managing the affairs of one's household. The modern Arabic word for economics, *al-iqtiṣād*, in fact, had the completely different meaning of "moderation" or the "just mean" in classical Arabic and is part of the title of one of the most famous works of Islamic theology by al-Ghazzālī. One could not say, of course, that there was no economics in Islam, but the area or activity known as economics as we understand it today was never isolated by itself in Islamic society. It was always combined with ethics and was seen as an organic part of the life of human beings, all of which should be dominated by ethical principles. That is why the very acceptance of economics as an independent domain, not to speak of as the dominating factor in life according to the prevailing paradigms in the modern world, is devastating to the Islamic view of human life.

If we were to accept the modern definition of economics, then we could say that the Quran has many verses that refer to economic life, including questions of inheritance, religious tax, opposition to excessive amassing of wealth, and so forth. It also contains, as does the *Ḥadīth,* numerous ethical teachings that bear directly upon economic life and are incorporated into the *Sharī'ah.* These include opposition to greed, the importance of honesty in all economic transactions, the inviolability of private property, and so on. As far as property is concerned, in principle "all property belongs to God," but God has given human beings the right to possess their own property, although a limit is set on the right to private property when it comes to what is meant for everyone and should remain public such as mountains, forests, and rivers.

The *Sharī'ah* promulgates a work ethic of central importance to economic life. The Quran states, "O ye who have faith! Be faithful to your covenants *('uqūd)*" (5:1). This verse connects work ethics explicitly to human religious life. Covenants can be between human beings and God, between the human being and his or her own soul, or between an individual or group and another person or group. The third covenantal relationship is at the foundation of Islamic work ethics, but at the same time is inseparable from the other two. On the basis of this and other verses, the *Sharī'ah* teaches that in all economic transactions the two sides must strictly observe the conditions on the basis of which a transaction is to take place. Both the employer and employee or the buyer and seller have a responsibility to keep their covenant, and the manner in which they carry out a transaction affects their soul as well as their relation to God.

As far as the relation between employer and employee is concerned, the *Sharī'ah* emphasizes the significance of personal relationship and recommends fairness and kindness on the part of the employer, who is in a position of power over the employee. According to a *ḥadīth,* a worker should be paid wages due before the sweat on his or her brow has dried. This personal relationship in economic transactions is so emphasized in Islamic civilization that to this day, even amid modern impersonal economic practices, most Muslims still rely on and trust personal contact above all else. This personal relationship was of course also very much emphasized in the production of goods, as we see in the guilds, to which we turn in the next chapter.

The *Sharīʿah,* moreover, opposes certain economic practices, some of which are forbidden and others discouraged. The practice of usury *(ribāʾ)* is forbidden in the Quran and according to Islamic Law, as it was forbidden in the Roman Empire, in Europe in the Middle Ages, and even in England before Henry VIII. The excessive amassing of wealth, to which the Quran refers in terms of gold and silver is also forbidden, as is dealing with substances that are themselves *ḥarām,* such as making or selling alcoholic beverages. Such acts are considered both illegal and sinful. Altogether the *Sharīʿah* envisages a society in which economic life is organic, based on the flow of goods and capital through various parts of society like the blood circulating through the human body.

In contrast to the Christian West, where mercantile activity was looked down upon up until the Renaissance, in the Islamic world from the beginning trade and economic transactions were seen in a positive light from the religious point of view. The Prophet himself had originally been a merchant, as had his wife Khadījah, and throughout Islamic history the merchant class associated with the bazaar has been among the most pious in Islamic urban areas, as have been farmers living in the countryside and villages. Traditional Islamic society succeeded in creating a notable integration of economic life and religion. It is also important to remember that in the economic domain, participation was not limited to men and integration concerned the whole of society. Women were active in the production of many goods from agricultural products to carpets and also as merchants and property owners. The *Sharīʿah* has given economic rights to women that did not exist in any large society, including the West, until very recently.

There has been a great deal of effort during the past few decades to study the economic principles and injunctions (in the Western sense) contained in the *Sharīʿah,* which many now call Islamic economics, and to put them into practice. Interest-free banks, called Islamic banks, have been created in several Islamic countries and in the West and interest-free loans made available. But the deeper issues have rarely been tackled in the face of problems created by the fact that the Islamic world is forced to be involved in a global economic system based on very different tenets and presumptions. But the field remains, nevertheless, among the most lively on the contemporary Islamic intellectual and religious scene.

Political Teachings: The Quran does not outline a particular political structure, but presents certain basic principles for rule, the most important of which is consultation, or *shawrā,* as stated in the verse, "and consult with them concerning conduct in affairs" (3:159). The rule of the Prophet in Medina and the document called the Constitution of Medina are also central to all later Islamic political thought and action, but, again, this constitution does not outline a particular form of government in the absence of the Prophet, who was both prophet and ruler of the community. What the Quran and *Ḥadīth* emphasize, however, is that the domain of politics cannot be separated from that of religion, which, however, must not be interpreted as "church" in the Western sense of the term. In

America one always speaks of the separation of church and state, although religion itself has never been totally separated from political life from the time of the writing of the American Constitution onward. In Europe, during the premodern period there were always two powers, the papacy and the empire or monarchy, and the latter received its religious legitimacy and investiture from the former. Later, states became secularized, especially after the French Revolution, but in many countries state religions have been maintained to this day, and in Great Britain the monarch is still the head of the Church of England.

None of these models apply, however, to the Islamic world, where there is no church or pope and where the classical caliphate was neither like the papacy nor like the emperorship of the Holy Roman Empire. Some have said that the Islamic model is a theocracy, but this is not exactly true as this term has been understood in the context of Western history or even that of ancient Egypt or classical Japan. A theocracy means the rule of the priesthood or the priestly class, of whom the ruler is the head or leader. In Islam, however, there is no priesthood comparable to that found in Christianity, Hinduism, or Buddhism; the closest class in Islamic society to priests is the *'ulamā'*, or religious scholars, who are knowledgeable in the Divine Law and serve as its guardians and interpreters. Moreover, except for Iran since the Revolution of 1979, the *'ulamā'* have never ruled directly over Islamic society, and even in Iran, the rule of the jurisprudent *(wilāyat-i faqīh)* is modified by the presence of an elected parliament. In any case, facile comparisons between the views of Christian fundamentalists concerning "theocracy" and Islamic views of government are simply false. Technically speaking, the Islamic ideal is that of a nomocracy, that is, the rule of Divine Law. It is true that all power, including political power, belongs ultimately to God, as the Quran states, "The command rests with none but God" (6:57; 12:40). But in the case of Islam, the rule of God was never associated with the rule of the priestly class; rather, it was associated with that of the *Sharīʿah.* The Islamic Republic of Iran is the first case in Islamic history in which the religious *ʿulamāʾ*, the closest one can come in Islam to a priestly class, has ruled directly over a major Islamic country.

During Islamic history, first the institution of the caliphate and then that of the sultanate were developed in Sunni Islam. Shīʿism rejected the caliphate as a political institution, but accepted the sultanate, or monarchy, as the least imperfect form of government in the absence of the Mahdī. This was even the view of Ayatollah Khomeini in his earlier writings, before he turned against the institution of the monarchy in favor of the new concept of the "rule of the jurisprudent" *(wilāyat-i faqīh)*. In any case, in all the different forms of government, the ruler sought legitimacy by protecting the *Sharīʿah,* or at least claiming to do so, and seeking the backing of those who were the custodians of the *Sharīʿah,* namely, the *ʿulamāʾ*. Even the legitimacy of the monarchy relied not so much on blood, as in Europe, but on the ability to preserve order and to protect the *Sharīʿah.* Of course, many rulers did not follow the teachings of the *Sharīʿah,* which in principle applied to them as to everyone else. But the ideal of protecting and preserving the *Sharīʿah* was always there, and, in fact, in practice the *Sharīʿah* often served as a shield for the protection of the people against the whims of powerful authoritarian rulers, although there were, again, exceptions.

In Islamic political theory, the role of the government is always limited, and in practice such major areas as justice, health, and education were left to the private sector before the rise of modern states in the Islamic world. Rule was also usually personal, and before modern times caliphs and kings would hold regular sessions with their ordinary subjects during which the petitions of the latter were received and answered. Today there is much talk of Islam and democracy. If democracy is understood as the rule of the will of the people, then there were mechanisms in traditional Islamic society where the will of the people was reflected to the ruling class, including the caliph or sultan, and it definitely played a role in those governments that were successful and that endured. If it means the particular institutions developed during the past few centuries in the West, then there is no parallel for them in premodern Islamic history, no more than there is for them in premodern Japan, China, or India. Although many Islamic countries have tried to introduce Western models of democracy during the past century, usually with little success, and although there is much turmoil in this domain today, the one principle that remains clear to all Muslims is that sovereignty belongs ultimately to God as expressed in the Divine Law and an Islamic society is one in which this sovereignty is accepted; but that still leaves a vast domain in which the people can exercise their views and act freely as long as they do not oppose the Divine Law.

With the fall of the Ottoman caliphate and the many twentieth-century revolutions based on the European model that followed, the whole question of political rule in its relation to Islamic teachings, the wishes of the people, and the form that an Islamic government should take has become central. There is today great confusion and turmoil in the Islamic world on this matter. Some have adopted Western republican models, others have continued the older form of sultanate or monarchy, and yet others want to revive the caliphate. It will take some time before Islamic civilization can again develop its own authentic political forms, a task that is being made much more difficult today by the fact that it is under constant external pressure and is not able to create institutions based on the inner dynamic of Islamic society. Paradoxically, many Western-oriented Islamic countries that are praised in the West for having "secularist" governments do not allow Western-style democratic practices; if they did in the sense of allowing people to really express their preferences, the result would be a much more Islamic government as far as the rule of the *Sharī'ah* is concerned. This is because the vast majority of all Muslims, even in the most Westernized and modernized countries, would like to live according to the *Sharī'ah* and to have their own freedom and democracy on the basis of their own understanding of these concepts and ideals rather than on how they are understood in the modern and postmodern West.

PUNISHMENTS AND RESTRICTIVE ORDINANCES

To speak of law is also to speak of restrictive ordinances and statutes *(ḥudūd)*, or punishment, under that law. Of course, to disobey the Divine Law is a sin, but it also has its legal consequences in this world, as we also see in Jewish law. In the modern world, religious statutes of this kind are often called "medieval" and "barbaric" on the basis of the idea that through progress people have now become much more "civilized" and "humane"—as if waiting on death row for a dozen years and then being executed is a lesser torture than being hanged shortly after being found guilty. And usually this criticism is immediately leveled at the Islamic restrictive ordinances. To make the situation clear it is necessary to point out, however, that these statutes and ordinances, called *ḥudūd* in Islamic Law, are fewer than in Jewish Law, where thirty-six crimes such as adultery, sodomy, idolatry, sorcery, and murder are punishable by death by hanging, beheading, burning, or strangling. I mention especially Jewish Law, because according to Islam, the Jewish laws brought by the Hebrew prophets remained valid as long as they were not abrogated by Islamic laws. A case in point is the stoning of an adulterer or adulteress, which is not mentioned in the Quran, but which was a Jewish practice that was continued in Islam with the addition of restrictions to the conditions needed to prove guilt in a *Sharīʿite* court.

The Quran says, "He [God] is the most swift of reckoners" (6:62), and many verses of the Quran, such as 2:187, 229, 230 and 4:13–14, are concerned with ordinances, or *ḥudūd,* which literally means "limits" set by God. For example, "Those who disobey God and His Messenger and transgress His limits *(ḥudūd)* will be admitted to a fire, to abide therein: and they shall have a humiliating punishment" (4:14). Quranic punishment, based on the concept that God is just and the reckoner of our deeds, involves acts forbidden in the Sacred Text; such acts are both illegal and a sin against God. These acts include illicit sexual intercourse and false accusation of it, drinking wine, theft, robbery, and murder. According to the *Sharīʿah,* the punishment for adultery is stoning, but there has to be either a confession by the party or parties involved or four just witnesses. That is why such a punishment has been extremely rare in traditional Islamic society. Punishment for theft and highway robbery, if it involves homicide, is death by sword or hanging, and if it does not, the amputation of a finger or in extreme cases a hand or foot. But many other conditions, according to some jurists twelve in number, have to be met before the punishment of amputation can be carried out. That is why this punishment has also been very rare. For lesser cases there is flogging. The punishment for murder is death unless the family of the victim accepts blood money. Although these are transgressions against God, repentance is accepted and the *Ḥadīth* strongly limits the application of *ḥudūd,* as we also see in the case of Jewish Law. In a *Sharīʿite* court, proof of offense is made very difficult, and the judge or *qāḍī,* is even permitted to accept the withdrawal of confessions. Many religious scholars, over the ages, have given the edict that the punishment for theft should only be carried out in a society that is Islamically just from the economic point of view and that it should not be applied to a petty thief who has stolen because of poverty and dire need.

Although a great deal is made today in the West of the extreme nature of such punishments in certain so-called fundamentalist countries, little is said about how rare, in fact, such punishments are in the Islamic world as a whole. More important, few want to face the fact that the number of people who die or are seriously injured in crimes involving theft and rape in America is far greater than the number of people punished for theft or adultery in a land such as Saudi Arabia, where they deal severely with these matters. In trying to understand the *Sharīʿite* restrictive ordinances, one must do so in the context of the historical reality of Islam and in light of all the mitigating circumstances that limit them in practice. Furthermore, it is important to see such matters not in the matrix of what is popular in the West today, but also in relation to the whole history of the West and the punishments meted out until only recently in both Europe and America for various crimes. The Islamic world is in the process of observing and studying the recent changes in the West in these matters and will not follow the same course as has the West, if the results of current social and legal experiments in Europe and America do not succeed in noticeably diminishing the crimes for which various societies, including the Islamic, had set punishments over the ages.

DIVINE AND HUMAN LAWS: CRISIS AND CONFRONTATION TODAY

Already in the middle of the nineteenth century in many Islamic countries, the rule of the *Sharīʿah* as a legal system was either limited to personal laws governing the family, inheritance, and so on or replaced by Napoleonic codes or English common law and European-style courts. By the time most Islamic countries gained their independence after World War II, the full *Sharīʿah* was applied only in a few lands such as Saudi Arabia, the Yemen, and Afghanistan. These countries may have had various political and economic problems, but at least they did not experience the tension between two different legal systems and philosophies that other Islamic countries did. Unfortunately, the application of the *Sharīʿah* did not prevent Yemen and Afghanistan from being invaded by foreign forces and having their traditional patterns of life, including their legal aspects, deeply disturbed and in some places shattered. Despite these tragedies, however, *Sharīʿite* Law played a central role in preserving the religious character of the life of the people of these countries even under great duress. Despite all the political turmoil in the Islamic world during the past half century, there has been an attempt in most

Islamic countries to return to the Divine Law as contained in the *Sharīʿah,* while incorporating and taking into consideration human laws associated with modern situations in which Muslims find themselves. Moreover, there continues to be extensive discussion on the *Sharīʿah* itself.

In the Sunni world, as already mentioned, many want to open the gate of *ijtihād* again, and there are those who speak of combining rulings from different classical schools of Law such as the Shāfiʿī and the Ḥanafī. Also, there are now a number of lay lawyers (not formal members of the class of *ʿulamāʾ,* the traditional custodians of the *Sharīʿah*) who believe that they have the right to make juridical decisions *(fatwās)* and formulate new *Sharīʿite* rulings. Even in Shīʿite Iran, where the *ijtihād* is practiced afresh in every generation, a number of modernized religious thinkers speak of the "dynamic *Sharīʿah,*" which they contrast with the old static one. In the field of law, just as in the field of politics, which is closely related to it, there is much debate and discussion going on throughout the Islamic world, but there is no doubt that the question of the revival of the *Sharīʿah* after its eclipse during the colonial period is at the center of the concerns of contemporary Islam.

THE DIVINE LAW, ETHICS, AND THE RELIGIOUS ETHOS

The *Sharīʿah* is not only concrete positive law, but also a set of values and framework for the religious life of Muslims. The books of jurisprudence *(fiqh)* contain the specific laws of the *Sharīʿah,* but the *Sharīʿah* itself also includes ethical and spiritual teachings that are, strictly speaking, not of a legal nature, although the legal is never separated from the moral in Islam. On the basis of the Quran and *Ḥadīth,* the

Sharīʿah teaches Muslims to respect their parents, to be kind to their neighbors, to be charitable, to be always truthful, to keep their word, to be honest in all affairs, and so forth. The whole ethics of Islam is related on the individual and social plane to the *Sharīʿah,* while the inner purification of the soul and the penetration into the inward meaning of the *Sharīʿah* are for the spiritual path, or the *Ṭarīqah,* which is of necessity always based on the formal practice of the Divine Law.

Today, in many parts of the Islamic world, Divine Law, or the *Sharīʿah,* is no longer fully practiced on the level of law, but the ethics that are contained in its teachings still permeate Islamic society. The *Sharīʿah,* in fact, determines the religious ethos of Islam on both the personal and the social level and is inseparable from the life of faith. For the vast majority of Muslims, the practice of the injunctions of the *Sharīʿah* is their manner of practicing their surrender to the Will of God and of living a virtuous and righteous life leading to felicity and salvation in the Hereafter. Even those who do not practice the *Sharīʿah* but still consider themselves Muslims draw their ethics, their understanding of right and wrong, and their frame of reference in the chaos of this world from the *Sharīʿah.* And those who aim to reach God in this life and to walk the path of the *Ṭarīqah* to that Truth, or *Ḥaqīqah,* which is the source of both the Law and the Way are more aware than anyone else how indispensable the Divine Law is, the law that alone can provide the sacred forms that are the sole gateways in this world of change and becoming to the immutable empyrean of the Formless.

Four

THE VISION OF COMMUNITY AND SOCIETY

People were one community and God sent unto them prophets as bearers of good tidings and as warners, and revealed therein the scripture with the truth that it might judge between people concerning that wherein they differed.

Quran 2:213

This community of yours is a single community.

Quran 21:92

THE CONCEPT OF COMMUNITY

One of the key concepts of the Quran and of Islam as a religion is that of community *(ummah)*. There is no doubt that Islam meant to create a community based on justice, one in which the pursuit of the Divine Law was made possible, not just injunctions for private behavior. In the debate between those who claim the primacy of society and those who emphasize the primal significance of the individual, Islam takes a middle course and believes that this polarization is in fact based on a false dichotomy. There is no society without the individual; nor can the individual survive without society. The social nature of the human being is part of the wisdom of God's creation, and the Quran asserts, "There is no secret conference of three but He is their fourth, nor of five but He is their sixth, nor of less that that or more but He is with them wheresoever they may be" (58: 7). This truth does not refer only to God's omniscience, but also to the profound reality of God's Presence in all human assembly. He is present in human community as He is within the heart or center of the individual.

Yet the role of religion is to save human souls, and on the Day of Judgment, according to Islam, human beings are judged individually and not collectively. The human community is judged in the Quran according to the degree to which it allows its members to live the good life, in the religious sense, based on moral principles. It judges a community to be good to the degree that it reflects the constant presence of the Transcendent Dimension in human life and is based on spiritual and religious ideals. A community as a whole can be judged and punished by God in this world, but a whole community does not enter paradise or hell as a collectivity. Only individual souls do so. Hence our personal responsibility before God remains, in whichever community we happen to live.

Islam recognizes communities according to their religious affiliation. Christians are referred to as the *ummah,* or community, of Christ and Jews as the *ummah* of Moses, as Muslims constitute the *ummah* of the Prophet. Abraham himself is called an *ummah* "obedient unto God" (16:120), and each community has a set of rites chosen for it by God, "And for every community have We appointed a ritual" (22:34). Originally there was only one *ummah:* "People were only one community" (10:19), but with the passage of history, different communities came into being and many faded away or were destroyed. The Quran depicts in elaborate terms the rise, decay, and falling away of various communities, which can also be understood as nations in the biblical sense. In fact, "every community has a term, and when its term comes, they cannot put it off an hour nor yet advance [it]" (7:34). And the decay and destruction of communities or nations has happened, according to the Quran, not because of loss of wealth or economic power or even military defeat, but because of moral corruption and straying from the religious norms willed by God for the community in question. The earth belongs to God, and He allows deserving communities or nations to rule over it as long as they deserve to do so. Once they lose their moral authority, they are replaced by God with other communities or nations.

For Islam, community implies above all a human collectivity held together by religious bonds that are themselves the foundation for social, juridical, political, economic, and ethical links between its members. In our period of human history, there is not one, but many communities or nations, which means many religions, as mentioned in Chapter 1, and this is set in the Quran as a condition willed by God, for, "Had God willed, He could have made them one community" (42:8). It is within the context of a world with many communities, all of which Islam sees in religious terms, that the Islamic understanding of itself as an *ummah* must be situated and understood.

First of all, Islam emphasizes the unity of its own *ummah*. Although after the first few years of Islamic history various theological and political rifts began to set in and although after the end of the Umayyad caliphate in the East in the eighth century the political unity of Islam was never again realized, the ideal of the unity of the *ummah* has remained strong throughout Islamic history. In modern times it has manifested itself in various pan-Islamic movements going back to Jamāl al-Dīn al-Afghānī in the nineteenth century. The unity of the Islamic community lies, however, primarily in ethical and spiritual realities within the hearts of the true believers, who emphasize the Quranic dictum that "Verily the believers are brothers" (49:9). Yet although this theme is repeated endlessly in sermons in mosques and elsewhere on various religious occasions, in practice some Muslims have made a mockery of it. This sense of unity and brotherhood, which also includes of course sisterhood, has become weakened by many ethnic, sectarian, and personal factors over the ages, especially in modern times.

Besides seeing themselves as an *ummah* ordered by God to "call to the good," Muslims also see themselves as the "middle community" in the world on the basis of the famous Quranic verse in which Muslims are addressed as follows: "Thus We have appointed you a middle community *(ummah wasaṭah)* that you may be witnesses unto the people and the messenger may be a witness unto you" (2:143). This verse can be and in fact has been understood in many ways. On the most external level, it means that Islam was destined to occupy the middle belt of the classical world from the Mediterranean to the China Sea, with many non-Muslim communities and peoples to the north and south. On a theological level and within the Abrahamic family, Muslims interpret this verse to mean that while Judaism emphasizes laws for this world and Christianity otherworldliness, Islam came to emphasize the middle ground, to strike a balance between this world and the next. Another interpretation, which is primarily ethical, is that "middle community" means that God chose for Muslims the golden mean, the avoidance of extremes in ethical and religious actions. Yet another meaning of this verse, with global implications, is that Muslims constitute "the middle community," because they have been chosen by God to create a balance between various communities and nations.

This last interpretation, however, does not at all mean that Muslims see themselves as the chosen people in the Jewish sense of the term. On the contrary, Muslims see all communities, Muslim and non-Muslim alike, to have been chosen by God, given their own sacred institutions and rites, and held responsible to Him. The role Muslims have always envisaged for themselves in the arena of human history as the "middle community" does not mean that other human collectivities do not have their own God-ordained roles to play. Nothing is further from Islam's traditional understanding of itself than being God's chosen people, unless one expands this claim to say that all *ummahs,* or communities, are God's chosen people, each brought into this world to perform a function in accordance with the Divine Wisdom and Will.

Today in the Islamic world, the *ummah* is politically more divided and even culturally more fragmented, as a result of the impact of modernism, than at any time in its history. And yet it would be a great mistake to underestimate the significance of the Quranic vision of community that most Muslims bear within their hearts and minds. This vision is still very much alive and manifests itself in unforeseen ways not only politically and economically, but also socially and culturally, not to mention within the domain of religion itself.

DĀR AL-ĪSLĀM AND *DĀR AL-ḤARB*

The Islamic idea of community, or *ummah,* is closely related to that of *dār al-islām,* or the "Abode of Islam," which corresponds in many ways to the Western notion of Christendom. *Dār al-islām* is the geographic area in which the Islamic *ummah* lives as a majority and where Islamic Law is promulgated and practiced, although there may be other *ummahs* such as Jews and Christians living within its borders. Classically, *dār al-islām* was juxtaposed with *dār al-ḥarb,* or the "Abode of War," in which Muslims could not live and practice their religion easily because the *Sharīʿah* was not the law of the land, although there were in practice always Muslim minorities living in various parts of it. Later Islamic jurists added a third category, *dār al-ṣulḥ,* the "Abode of Peace." By this category they came to mean a land that was not part of the Islamic world but one in which Muslims could practice their religion in peace. In the contemporary context Muslims living in America or Western Europe could be said to be living in *dār al-ṣulḥ*, in contrast to those living in the former Soviet Union or present-day Burma, who would be or are living in *dār al-ḥarb.*

The presence of the "Abode of War" did not necessarily mean, however, that the Islamic world should be at war with that region, as some have claimed. According to the Islamic law of international treaties, Muslims could make treaties of peace and live at peace with countries outside of *dār al-islām* if they themselves were not threatened by them. The best example of such a situation is the friendly relations the Prophet himself had with then Christian Abyssinians, who had in fact given refuge to some of the Muslims from Mecca shortly after the advent of the Quranic revelation. Many instances of such peaceful coexistence are also to be seen between Muslim and Christian kingdoms in Spain and Hindu and Muslim states in India. In this domain the Islamic principles must not be confused with matters of political expediency and particular actions of this or that ruler over the ages. What is important is to understand the Islamic principles involved.

As far as living in *dār al-ḥarb* is concerned, Islamic Law requires that Muslims in such a situation respect the laws of the land in which they live, but also insists that they be able to follow their own religious practices even if to do so is difficult. If such a way of living were to become impossible, then they are advised to migrate to the "Abode of Islam" itself. As for following local laws and practices, as long as they do not contradict Islamic laws and practices, the same injunctions hold for *dār al-ṣulḥ* as they do for *dār al-ḥarb.* The Shī'ites, who have been a minority during most of their history and often suffered persecution, have added the principle of dissimulation *(taqiyyah)*, according to which they should hide their religious beliefs and practices from the larger public if revealing them would endanger their lives or property.

MUSLIM MINORITIES

In the same way that throughout history many Christians have lived outside of Christendom, throughout Islamic history parts of the Islamic *ummah* have lived outside of *dār al-islām* in many different cultural and religious settings from West Africa to China. Today, the largest single minority in the world is the Islamic community in India, which has a population of around 150 million. There are also tens of millions of Muslims living in China, possibly 20 million in Russia, sizable minorities in many Black African countries, and small but old and firmly established communities in the Balkans, Finland, Bulgaria, Greece, Tibet, Nepal, Sri Lanka, Burma, Thailand, Vietnam, and Cambodia. There are also, of course, newer Islamic communities in most European countries as well as in North and South America. As already mentioned, in the United States alone there are some 6 million Muslims.

In practice, the situation of such minorities has varied and still varies greatly from country to country. In some places they have established a notable local culture of their own; in others they have remained as an enclave within the much larger society, clinging to their religious identity but not able to express much creativity on the larger cultural scene. These minorities have represented over the ages an Islamic presence in different parts of the world and have interacted with many diverse cultures, often acting as a bridge between those non-Islamic cultures and *dār al-islām*. Such Muslim minorities now have a major responsibility to fulfill this task as far as the relation of the Western world to *dār al-islām* is concerned.

MINORITIES WITHIN THE "ABODE OF ISLAM"

Except for the central part of the Arabian Peninsula, there is no area in the "Abode of Islam" where there are not minorities belonging, from the Islamic point of view, to other *ummahs*. In the heartland of the Islamic world these minorities have been usually Jews, Christians, and Zoroastrians, but there have also been and continue to be other minorities, such as the Druze, the Yazīdīs, and the 'Alawīs, who have survived over the ages in the very cradle of Islamic civilization. Traditionally Islam has categorized societal groups on the basis of religious affiliation, and therefore categories of minorities based on factors such as race or language have been of much lesser consequence. Kurds, who are linguistically a distinct minority, have become rulers of Arabs, as have Blacks, who in some cases were members of a racial minority in those lands where they gained political power.

Islamic Law requires the lives, property, and freedom of religion of religious minorities to be guaranteed if they are a "People of the Book," a category applied widely during Islamic history. On the basis of the verse of the Quran that speaks about fighting nonbelievers and those who do not acknowledge the Religion of the Truth even among the People of the Book "until they pay the *jizyah*" (9:29), religious minorities were required to pay a special religious tax *(jizyah)* and given in return protection from external attack and security for their lives and property. In the modern world, where the idea of the modern nation and citizenship in it has become prevalent, the classical Islamic theory has been often criticized, and in the contemporary Islamic world it is not even always practiced. That is because even in the Islamic world, on the outward level for certain groups loyalty to the state and the modern nation has lately come to replace to some extent loyalty to religion, something that did not occur even in Europe until fairly recently.

The Islamic system must be understood in terms of the premises of the Islamic conception of society, whose goal is to provide a just system and a beneficial environment for the spiritual and religious growth of human beings. From that point of view, minorities in the Islamic world certainly did not fare worse than those in the West, as one can see in a comparison of the history of Judaism in the "Abode of Islam" and its history in Europe. Also during five hundred years of Ottoman domination of Greece, Mt. Athos remained the most vibrant and living center of Orthodox spirituality. As for economic life, it might seem a paradox, but in most Islamic countries the religious minorities are in a better economic situation than the Muslim majority, as one can see in the case of the Christians of Lebanon and Egypt.

Of course, no human institution is without imperfections and abuses. Each theory of viewing the component communities that make up society is based on certain premises and provides certain advantages as well as disadvantages. The Islamic system, sometimes called the *millat* system (the word *millah,* "community," also means "nation" in the biblical sense), first of all eradicated distinctions based on race, ethnicity, or language. Second, by according protection to minorities on the basis of religion, it therefore created the means for these religions to survive in contrast to the situation in, let us say, Europe, where after

Christianization, other religions such as those of the Druids and the ancient Germans were totally eradicated, as were certain later movements within Christianity such as the Cathars.

In the Islamic world today, however, no nation lives any longer under the old Ottoman *millat* system, but people live according to the Western-style idea of citizenship in a nation. The modern nation-state system removes distinctions based on religion, at least in theory, but at the expense of subordinating minority *and* majority religious laws to secular laws. And yet within that system based on nationalism, people continue to insist upon the significance of religious laws and practices, and the very tension between the two has made the question of minorities more difficult than before. In days of old the Kurds did not have the same problems with the Turks and Iraqi Arabs that they do now, nor did the Copts in Egypt experience the same tensions they now face with the so-called fundamentalists, who are themselves reacting to the secularization of the laws of the land.

ISLAMIC SOCIETY: THE IDEAL AND THE PRACTICE OF THE GOOD LIFE

It is essential to distinguish between the ideal society described in the Quran and *Ḥadīth* and historical Islamic society. If the two were identical, there would be no evil or shortcomings in the world, and the world would not be the world with all its imperfections. In fact, throughout their own history, Muslims have looked upon the society of Medina at the time of the Prophet as the ideal society, as the golden age of Islam, religiously speaking, and have sought to emulate that society to the extent possible, but have always fallen short. Generations of young Muslims have been told stories of that period, when, one might say, Heaven and earth touched each other. I remember as a child hearing stories about the Prophet or other great early saints helping the poor, being honest in all affairs, administering justice, and the like from my parents and others. Almost always, numerous contemporary actions in society were contrasted with the ideals set forth by them. Yet tallying up and bemoaning shortcomings is far less profitable than seeking to understand the extent to which Islamic ideals *have* been implemented and realized in each Islamic society despite the imperfections inherent in the human state, imperfections that the original teachings of Islam itself have taken into consideration. Although every subsequent generation of Muslims has fallen below the standards established by the Prophet in Medina and despite human frailties, each generation until modern times has in fact realized many of the values established by Islam within the society in which it lived.

The ideal norms of society as envisaged by the Quran and *Ḥadīth* include the establishment of justice and equality before the Divine Law, economic fair play, and the just distribution of wealth, while legitimizing private property and encouraging economic activities, equitable treatment of all human beings (Muslims and non-Muslims living as members of their own respective religious communities within Islamic society), and the creation of a religious social environment in which the presence of the Transcendent is never forgotten. In such a society family bonds are honored over tribal ones, but the truth is considered to be above even family affiliations. It was Christ who said, "Leave all and follow me" and that one should hate one's parents if they oppose the truth. Likewise, the Quran states, "We have enjoined on human beings kindness to parents, but if they strive to make you join with that of which you have no knowledge, then obey them not" (29:8).

Since the goal of Islamic society is to make possible "Thy will be done on earth," in the ideal society it is the duty of each Muslim, as stated in several Quranic verses, to "enjoin the good and forbid the wrong" (3:110). This does not mean that individual Muslims should interfere in the affairs of others; rather, each person has the social responsibility to make certain that moral authority reigns in the community. In such a society keeping the peace and fostering social harmony are requirements, but if moral authority is destroyed for one reason or another and the religious norms flouted by those who wield political power, then there is a right to rebellion and the reestablishment of an order based on ethical norms and the Divine Law.

Also in the ideal Islamic society, virtue, goodness, and knowledge should be the only criteria for honoring and elevating individuals. The hierarchy of society should be based on the God-fearing quality called *taqwā* and on knowledge, both of which the Quran refers to explicitly. All other honors and distinctions should be evaluated in light of the truth of the transience of the world. This ideal has not been totally realized, but devout Muslims remain very much aware of it, as seen in the attitude of many powerful rulers toward the saintly and the knowledgeable. Even in my own life I have witnessed the great respect shown to virtuous and pious scholars not only by ordinary people, but also by the wealthy and the politically powerful.

Islamic social teachings also include support and help for those who have been oppressed or deprived in one way or another. In the reform that Islam carried out in Arabian society, it sided with the poor, and, like Christ, who said,

"Blessed are the poor," the Prophet said, "Poverty is my pride." Of course, in both instances poverty means, above all, spiritual poverty, but also on the material level the Prophet, like Christ, lived in simplicity and was closer to the poor and weak than the wealthy and the powerful. Although the Prophet said that wealth is like a ladder with which one can either ascend to Heaven or descend to hell, he always emphasized that the poor must be helped and respected regardless of their lack of worldly provisions. Likewise, Islamic social ideals emphasize being kind to slaves, treating women gently, and being generous to those who have suffered economic loss and are in debt or others in society whom modern sociologists would call the deprived classes.

Again, these and other ideals were not always fully realized by later Islamic societies, but as ideals set forth for one generation after another, they are crucial for the understanding of the dominant values in Islamic society. Of course, the sentiment that "my religion is the best" is to be found of necessity in every religious climate, and the Islamic is no exception. The Quran, in fact, refers to Muslims as the best community. But in practice individual Muslims often found that certain virtues that were supposed to be displayed among members of the Islamic community were in fact lacking in their own but found in members of other religious communities. For example, usually those who have performed the *ḥajj* and are called *ḥājjī* are deeply respected as pious and trustworthy, a reputation most have lived up to, but there have been exceptions, deceptive *ḥājjīs* who, in the guise of piety, have often dealt dishonestly with their customers in the bazaar. In my own family in Persia we always bought our carpets from an extremely honest Jewish rug dealer, and everyone in the family used to say that he was as honest as a real *ḥājjī*. In any case the dynamics between ideals and everyday practices for Muslims, as for Jews, Christians, or Hindus, is a complicated matter. They should not lead to either a self-righteous attitude or the deprecation of one's own religious community as being devoid of any virtues. As far as the Islamic world is concerned, both of these attitudes have been expressed by outsiders as well as by small groups within Islamic society itself in modern times. The phenomenon has led to unfortunate extremist positions and movements.

THE STRUCTURE OF ISLAMIC SOCIETY

Of course, not all Islamic societies are exactly alike and it would be wiser to speak of Islamic societies rather than society if one were to analyze every part of the *ummah* in detail. But for our present purpose and concentrating on the heartland of the Islamic world, where classical Islamic civilization was created, it is possible to speak about Islamic *society* when trying to bring out salient features of social structure shared by countries as far apart as Morocco and Persia. In contrast to the West and also Hindu India before modern times, Islamic society did not possess as rigid a stratification and there was, relatively speaking, more dynamism and fluidity within Islamic society than was the case with its two neighbors in medieval times. Social mobility in Islamic society was achievable, especially through the acquiring of religious knowledge, on the one hand, and personal, military, and administrative prowess, on the other. There was, strictly speaking, no feudal system in Islam, and there was nothing corresponding exactly to the landed aristocracy in the West with its lords and other feudal powers, although, in certain lands such as Persia and what is today

Pakistan, powerful landowners existed and in fact still exist. Nor did the peasantry play as important a role as it did in medieval European society.

One important factor present in Islamic society but absent from the Christian West was the nomadic element. In fact, as the great fourteenth-century Tunisian historian Ibn Khaldūn, whom many consider to be the father of sociology, wrote, the rhythm of Islamic history can be understood as the constant interplay between sedentary people and nomads. The Arabs were originally nomads, while Islam arose in Mecca, which was a sedentary environment. Yet something of what one might call "nomadic spirituality," with its emphasis upon the transience of the world, closeness to nature, love of language, and respect for the power of the word, is contained within the spiritual perspective of the Islamic revelation itself and is manifested clearly in Islamic art. On the social level also the constant dynamic between the nomad and the urban dweller continued throughout most of Islamic history.

The Prophet sought to replace tribal bonds with those of the Islamic community, or *ummah*, dominated by the truth of the Quranic revelation. Although he succeeded to a large extent, tribal allegiances did not by any means disappear and occasionally burst forth in political movements based on tribal affiliations. This tension between the unifying force of Islam and the dispersing and centripetal forces of tribalism has manifested itself in many ways in Islamic history and is still alive under new forms. Some have, in fact, interpreted the present opposition of local cultural, ethnic, and religious forces to globalization as "tribalism" and have considered both tribalism and globalization to be enemies of democracy. Such an analysis must not, however, be confused with the role and function of tribalism in Islamic history, which was witness to the tension between the nomads and sedentary people but also to the positive role of the tribal nomads in the constant renewal and revival of sedentary life and even in the unification of vast areas of the Islamic world under one "global" order as we see with the Seljuqs and Ottomans. The civilization of Islam, which was global in its own way, was created in urban environments, and, in fact, during the medieval period the Islamic world had many cities of much greater population than the largest European cities of the time. But the city is at once the locus of refinement in the arts and sciences, on the one hand, and moral decadence and excessive luxury, on the other. The city has produced great sages and saints, but it is also the only place that has produced skeptics and even atheists. History has not recorded any nomadic agnostics or skeptics, not to mention atheists. Even the Quran alludes to the fact that every city will be punished one day before the end of time.

In the Islamic world, nomads, who constantly threatened the cities, would invade and dominate them once decadence had set in. The nomads would inject new energy into the city, revive its moral character, and help keep the fire of tradition burning. Then they in turn would become sedentary, gradually losing their nomadic virtues and becoming immersed in decadent luxury until they were themselves swept over by a new wave of nomadic invasion. The Islamic world knew not only Arab nomads, but also Turkic ones, who began to migrate to the heartland of the Islamic world from the tenth century onward, and later the Mongols, who destroyed much of Islamic sedentary life, but also rejuvenated its art and architecture as well as its political power. To this day, despite the forced settlement of so many nomads, there are still Arab, Black, and Berber nomads in all of North and Saharan Africa, Turkish and Turkic nomads in Anatolia, Persia, and Central Asia, Arab nomads in Saudi Arabia, Yemen, Jordan, Syria, and Iraq, and even Iranian tribes such as the Pashtus, some of whom have now settled, in both Afghanistan and Pakistan. Even Egypt, which has been a sedentary society from time immemorial, has nomads in the south. Just recently, while visiting the tomb of a great Sufi saint in southern Egypt, I was surprised to discover that the Egyptian desert near the Sudanese border is still dominated by nomadic tribes. So one can hardly overemphasize the importance of the nomadic element, socially, psychologically, and spiritually in Islamic society. Moreover, one must not forget that something of the nomadic spirit survives even among those who have become settled in towns, for as the Arabic adage affirms, "You can take a nomadic boy out of the desert, but you cannot take the desert out of that boy."

As for classes within sedentary Islamic society, the most important before the advent of recent social changes included the learned and the scholarly *('ulamā')*, the ruling and military class, the merchants, the guilds, and in certain areas such as Egypt and Persia the peasantry. The *'ulamā'*, meaning literally "those who know," referred originally to savants in every field, including astronomy and medicine, not only Islamic Law, and it is still used to some degree in this general sense. But gradually it gained the more particular meaning of religious scholars, especially those who specialized in knowledge of the *Sharī'ah*. Although there is no priesthood in Islam, this class is the closest to that of rabbis in Judaism and to a lesser extent priests in Christianity or the Brahmins in Hinduism, although their religious function is not exactly the same. Throughout Islamic history the *'ulamā'*, who to this day usually wear the dress of the

Prophet and a turban to follow his example, have been the guardians and interpreters of the *Sharī'ah*. As a result, they have wielded great power and before modern times supervised both the educational and judicial activity of Islamic society. They were also traditionally protectors of the people against the power of political and military authorities. Generally Twelve-Imām Shī'ite *'ulamā'* have been more powerful than Sunni ones because, in contrast to the latter, they have been traditionally independent of political power and collected religious taxes directly, so that they have also been to a great extent economically independent. The Islamic Revolution of Iran in 1979 would not have been possible if such a power had not existed at the same time. The direct political rule of the *'ulamā'* in Iran today, for the first time in Islamic history, has, however, posed important challenges to it as a distinct religious class within Persian society and to its role and function within that society.

Many Sufis have been among the *'ulamā'*, and most Sufi masters are also well versed in Islamic Law, but they do not constitute a distinct class in Islamic society. They, in fact, constitute a "society" within society to which men and women from all walks of life can belong. According to a *ḥadīth*, "There is no monasticism in Islam," and the Quran states, "The monasticism which they invented for themselves, We did not prescribe for them" (57:27). Therefore there is no distinct class of monks in Islamic society, but the ideal of leading a spiritual life devoted wholly to God has been realized within the Sufi orders, which are integrated outwardly within society at large. It is also interesting to note that although Islam did not accept the monastic institution, the Prophet and, following him, generations of Muslims have looked very kindly upon Christian monks.

There is, moreover, a Sufism meant for the spiritual elite, who usually study advanced texts of Sufism combined with advanced spiritual practice, and there is a popular Sufism that brings the blessings, or *barakah,* of Sufism to a large number of people who usually participate in it passively and do not travel actively on the path to spiritual perfection of the first group. This distinction between the elite *(khawāṣṣ)* and commoners *(ʿawāmm),* so conspicuous in Sufism, can in fact be found throughout Islamic society and must not be confused with "elitism" in the modern sense. Today the word "elite" is disliked in public discourse especially in America, but in fact it exists in various domains of life and corresponds to what is widely practiced openly in its Islamic sense. For example, a small number of mathematicians know advanced mathematics. They are the elite of this field, while the rest of us are "commoners" in this domain. But one of the commoners can be an elite in knowledge of the medical properties of herbs, in which a mathematician who belongs to the elite in mathematics is a commoner. It is in this sense that the important category of *khawāṣṣ* and *ʿawāmm* used by the Sufis and elsewhere in Islamic society must be understood. When used in an absolute sense *khawāṣṣ* refers to those who possess advanced spiritual knowledge and exceptional virtue.

The practitioners of Sufism on all its different levels constitute an important group in Islamic society, even if not sociologically distinct as a class, and they have exercised great influence over the ages on fields as far apart as the inner life and public ethics, psychology and art, metaphysics and the guilds, poetry and politics. Sufism cannot be reduced to its social manifestations or analyzed simply in sociological terms. But one cannot understand the structure of Islamic society without considering fully the significance of the Sufis along with the *'ulamā'* and other distinct classes.

If in a sense the *'ulamā'* and the Sufis, at least their leaders, correspond to the sacerdotal class in medieval Christianity, the political and military classes in Islam can also be compared to their counterpart in the Christian West, although the differences between the types of monarchy and political aristocracy in the Islamic world and the West as well as differences in hereditary titles must be fully considered. Besides the supreme ruler of society, whether he is a caliph, sultan, or amir, whom we have already discussed, Islamic society has always had two groups involved in the political and military life of the country. The first is the class of administrators and the second that of the military.

The class of administrators developed early in Islam on the basis of older Persian Sassanid models. In earlier Islamic history this class was practically the only one in Islamic society outside of the cadre of *'ulamā'* to be well educated as a class in the arts of reading, writing, logic, and so forth; it even played a role in the development of a new style of Arabic associated with the activity of those who worked in the various *dīwāns,* which came to be known later in the West as ministries. The contribution of this class to Islamic learning, literature, ethics, and political thought as well as the running of the state has been of great importance in Islamic history. During the 'Abbāsid caliphate, from the eighth to the thirteenth century, while the Arabic element was primarily associated with religion and the Turkic element with military power, the Persian element was associated most of all with administration, and some of the most outstanding grand-viziers, or prime ministers, of the Arab caliphs or later Turkic sultans were Persian.

The military class has of course been important throughout Islamic history, as it has been in other societies, although Islam never emphasized the hereditary aspect as much as did many other traditional cultures. With the breakdown of the traditional political structures in modern times, however, many Islamic countries were witness to a military coup followed by a military rule very different from the traditional Islamic political order. Traditionally, a new military commander who was able to establish rule became a sultan or amir, but he was still bound by the *Sharīʿah* and traditions of rule. Such is not the case with the modern military dictators who took over the reins of power in so many Islamic countries during the second part of the twentieth century.

The merchant class has always played a major role in Islamic society and has been an important guardian of Islam. The Prophet began his adult life as a merchant and his wife Khadījah was also a major merchant in Mecca. From the beginning, the profession was considered a very honorable one, and the merchant class played a greater role in Islamic society than did the mercantile class in medieval Europe before the rise of the bourgeoisie in Italy during the Renaissance. To this day the bazaar is not only the heart of business activity in the still relatively traditional Islamic cities, but the religious heart of the urban environment as well, where major mosques and religious schools are usually located. In Persian as in other Islamic languages, the term *bāzārī,* that is, a merchant in the bazaar, is associated with piety and religious fervor, and this class has always been close to the *ʿulamāʾ*. I still remember my childhood days when during the mourning period of Muḥarram my mother would take me to the Tehran bazaar, where I was so moved by all the black flags and curtains covering everything. To this day the most intense religious activities, such as religious processions in streets and functions within mosques, in Persia are associated with the bazaar. Nor are matters different in the Arab world. The heart of Cairo is the mosque of Ra's al-Ḥusayn, and whenever I visit it, inevitably I also pay a visit to the Khān-Khalīlī bazaar adjacent to it, where one observes clearly the wedding between religious piety and trade.

In traditional Islamic society a major institution associated with the bazaar and the production of goods was the guilds *(aṣnāf)*. Considered to have been founded by 'Alī ibn Abī Ṭālib, the guilds combine apprenticeship in various arts and crafts with moral and spiritual discipline. In the guilds the masters are usually also moral and spiritual teachers, and apprentices receive initiation into a guild once they meet the moral and practical qualifications for acceptance. The Islamic guilds are like the medieval European guild of masons, which was a secret organization with knowledge of both theory and practical techniques that was transmitted orally. In fact, Freemasonry began when the guild of masons became "speculative" and cut off from the practice of masonry and turned into a secret organization with particular political and social goals. Although European Freemasonry came into the Islamic world through colonizing powers in the nineteenth century, the Islamic guilds themselves never underwent such a transformation. They remained closely wed to Sufism and the spiritual practices of the Islamic religion. With the advent of modern technology and the introduction of industrialism into many parts of the Islamic world, many of the guilds disappeared, but some survive to this day from Fez to Benares. It is interesting to note that the famous Benares silk has been made and is still made to a large extent by Muslim guilds of weavers and cloth printers. A few decades ago when I visited this holiest of Hindu cities, I was astonished to see the traditional Islamic guild still very much alive; the master of the guild that made the most beautiful saris was one of the dignitaries of the local branch of the Qādiriyyah order, which is one of the oldest Sufi orders.

Finally, in discussing the structure of Islamic society one must mention the peasantry, which of course exists throughout the Islamic world but which, except in certain areas, has not played the same central historical role it has in the West. In such lands as Egypt, parts of Persia, and the Punjab, there has always existed a large peasantry, which has usually been educated religiously from urban centers. In such lands the peasantry has also been a conservative social force and has provided many of the religious students for *madrasahs* in bigger cities, students some of whom later became major religious leaders. Popular Sufism has also been strong among the peasantry, as we see among the *fillāḥīn* of Egypt and in the spread of Maraboutism, which is a popular Sufi movement, in North and West Africa.

ISLAM AND SLAVERY

Islam came into a world in which slavery was almost universally practiced. The Quran and *Ḥadīth* advise kindness toward slaves and their humane treatment and encourage setting them free. The Prophet himself bought the Persian slave Salmān and immediately freed him, making him a member of his family. It is important to note that in Islamic society slavery was not equated with racism. Turkic slaves became military commanders and kings and leaders, as did some Black African slaves. Moreover, there was a great deal of intermarriage, and usually a slave's descendants would sooner or later melt into the general texture of society. There were of course Arab slave traders in Africa as well as European ones, but despite the fact that European colonial powers made the presence of Arab slave traders an excuse to colonize Africa, there has never been a Harlem or an Anacostia in any Islamic city. Even where there is a strong Black African presence, as in Arabia or Morocco, there is no feeling of racial distinction. Today in any grand mosque in Morocco at the time of prayers one sees worshipers ranging from Black Africans to blue-eyed Berbers, but one does not have a feeling of racial heterogeneity.

Many pious Muslims also refused to have slaves and wrote against it, but the practice in its Islamic form, which meant ultimate integration rather than segregation, continued sporadically but less frequently until the nineteenth century, when under internal forces and the impact of the ideas of Abraham Lincoln and others it was discontinued. If some write today that slavery is still practiced here and there, as in the Sudan or some other African lands, it is more like the slavery of sweatshops in China or the West today. In neither case is it a prevalent practice, nor are such practices condoned by religious authorities. Before modern times both Christians and Muslims had slaves, which does not mean that either religion created or encouraged slavery.

Various groups, not only Black Africans, were brought into the Islamic world as slaves, but all of them became soon integrated into the *ummah,* and Islamic society was never witness to the types of practices that went on in the American South before the Civil War. What is most important to understand is that even when it was practiced, slavery was not wed to racism in the Islamic world and therefore former slaves were soon integrated through intermarriage with the rest of the society in most parts and during most periods of Islamic history.

THE FAMILY WITHIN ISLAMIC SOCIETY

The basic unit of Islamic society is the family, which as a result of the Quranic revelation came to replace the Arab tribe as the immediate social reality for the individual. One of the most important social reforms carried out by Islam was the strengthening of the family and the bonds of marriage. In Islamic society, as in many other traditional societies, the family is not limited to the nuclear family of parents and children, but is made up of the extended family including grandparents, uncles, aunts, in-laws, and cousins. The extended family plays a major role in the upbringing of children, in protecting the younger generation from external social and economic pressure, and in transmitting religion, customs, traditions, and secrets of the family trade. One can hardly overemphasize the role of the extended family in Islamic society even today.

The impact of modernism has destroyed many Islamic institutions, but not, as yet, the family. In the West the extended family became reduced to the nuclear family and more recently, through a kind of splitting of the social atom, the nuclear family has been further distilled into the single-parent family, and the institution of the family as such has been placed under severe strain. Most Muslims look upon these developments in Western society, along with new sexual mores and new female and male roles, as incomplete social experiments the results of which are still uncertain, and not as definitely established and time-honored models to be emulated. This issue has therefore become a point of contention between certain ultramodernist circles in the West and the Islamic world, but then many modern practices are opposed with equal severity by conservative Jews and Christians within the West itself. The attitude of the ordinary Muslim to all these recent social experimentations with marriage and the family is not much different from those of traditional Jews and Christians in the West. I know of many Jewish, Protestant, and Catholic families in America who, in their understanding of the meaning and significance of the family, feel closer to their Muslim neighbors than to some of their own childhood friends.

As for the question of marriage itself, one cannot understand its status in Islam without first comprehending the significance of sexuality for Muslims. In classical Western Christian theology, sexuality itself is associated with original sin and accepted only as a means of procreation. To practice it in the context of the religion therefore requires that it be sanctified through the sacrament of marriage. In Islam, as in Judaism, sexuality itself is sacred and a blessing. Therefore, there is no need of a sacrament, in the Christian sense, to sanctify it. Rather, marriage in Islam is a contract drawn according to the *Sharīʿah* to legitimize the sexual act within marriage and to protect the rights of both partners. In both Christianity and Islam, however, as in Judaism, sexual activity outside of marriage is not allowed and is considered a sin in the eyes of God.

Islam does legally allow divorce, but makes it morally and socially difficult. According to a *ḥadīth,* of all the things that God has permitted, what He hates most is divorce. That is why, although legally it seems easy for a man to divorce his wife and a wife also has certain grounds for divorcing her husband, including being neglected and not supported, in practice divorce is relatively rare, especially in the more traditional segments of Islamic society, certainly much rarer than in present-day Europe or America. The current perception in the West about women's rights in Islamic society in matters of family and divorce is not accurate, because it fails to take into consideration the many social and ethical factors involved in most family situations, although there are, alas, also many tragic injustices. As far as actual practices in questions of family law and divorce are concerned, there is much debate going on in the Islamic world today about protecting the rights of women whose husbands abuse them but refuse to divorce them, and family courts have been established in many countries to try to administer justice according to the spirit and law of the Quran rather than current customs. There are, needless to say, abuses in Islamic society in this matter as there are elsewhere, but Islam emphasizes the importance of family and marriage and the responsibility that God has placed on the shoulders of both husband and wife, even if some of those who call themselves Muslims do not fulfill those responsibilities.

As for marriage itself, it must be recalled that the Christian and Islamic marriages are based upon two different spiritual prototypes. That is why Christians and even post-Christians in the West identify marriage solely with monogamy, while Islam includes the possibility of polygamy in certain cases and situations. No one has expressed this difference of prototypes better than Titus Burckhardt, one of the most profound Western scholars of the Islamic tradition. He writes:

> Europeans tend to look on Muslim polygamy as sexual licence. In so doing, they forget that the "licence" is largely compensated for by the monastic seclusion

of family life. The essential point, however, is that Islamic marriage presupposes a completely different spiritual prototype from that of Christian marriage: Christian monogamy reflects the marriage of the church—or the soul—to Christ, and this union is founded on a personal and non-transferable love. Islamic polygamy on the other hand finds its justification in the relationship of the one Truth *(al-Ḥaqq)*, to its several animic "vessels": Man, as spiritual officiant *(imām)* of his family, represents the Truth; his role corresponds to the "active" vessel, namely the Spirit; whereas his wife corresponds to the "passive" vessel, namely the soul. This is also why a Muslim man may marry a Christian or Jewish woman, whereas a Muslim woman may only take a husband of the same faith as herself. These spiritual prototypes—both cases—are not something imposed on marriage from the outside, but inhere in the nature of things. The symbolism in question is not necessarily in everyone's consciousness, far from it, but it is inherent in the respective tradition, and therefore part of the collective mentality.[1]

The spiritual principles and prototypes mentioned here do not in any way mean to reduce the relation of man and woman to simply that of the active and passive principles. As in the Far Eastern tradition, where males and females possess both *yin* and *yang*, but in different proportions, so in the Islamic perspective the male is not simply equated with the active principle and the female with the passive, for both the male and female contain both elements within their nature. What is elucidated by Burckhardt are the spiritual prototypes and principles involved.

If for Christians the multiple marriages of the Prophet diminish his spiritual status, for Muslims they ennoble sexual union and sanctify it. Moreover, if one relates marriage to the sexual act and accepts that there should be no sexual activity outside of marriage, then there has probably been a lot less promiscuity in the Islamic world, with polygamy, than there has been in the West, even before the 1960s sexual revolution, with its claim to monogamy. The Islamic world has for so long been accused in the West of being sexually licentious, while Christianity is pictured as favoring chastity and being severely opposed to extramarital sexual activity. The social reality is quite something else. There is no doubt that there is some polygamy in the Islamic world, and also temporary marriage in Shīʿism, but most men are monogamous and there is little extramarital sexual activity in traditional Islamic society. Moreover, there is also a great deal of extramarital sexual activity in the West, although polygamy is not officially practiced. In Islamic society, illicit sexual practice is rare, although it is not totally absent, and there are practically no illegitimate children because in all types of marriages, including the temporary, children are officially recognized by law and the father has the duty to support them.

The Prophet said, "Marriage is half of religion," and to marry is considered by Muslims a blessed way to follow the prophetic *Sunnah,* although it is not technically required by the *Sharīʿah.* Because of the religious significance of marriage, nearly everyone within the Islamic world, even in big cities, is married, and great pressure is put on the young to marry, especially to avoid sinful actions. There are hardly any unmarried men and women in Islamic society; only a few are to be found here and there. In the countryside even more than in cities, a woman whose husband has died often marries another man even if she is not young and has many children. Likewise, a widower is usually pressured to remarry. Even those who are not married, male and female, usually live with relatives and are part of the larger extended family.

THE MALE AND FEMALE IN THE ISLAMIC PERSPECTIVE

From the point of view of Islam, the distinction between the male and the female is not only biological or even psychological, but has its root in the Divine Nature Itself. The Quran asserts, "Glory to God, Who created in pairs all things" (36:36), and also, "We have created you in pairs" (78:8). The male and the female polarization is an essential part of the mystery of God's creation. Each gender is fully human with an immortal soul, and both sexes share equally in their religious responsibilities and are equal before God's laws. And yet each sex complements the other and together, like the *yin-yang* symbol of the Far East, they form a circle, which symbolizes perfection, totality, and completion. That is why the male and female both vie with each other and are attracted to each other. The alchemy of marriage and sexual union has the power to transmute and complete each side through the realization of both complementarity and wholeness through a love that transcends the two sides and yet encompasses them, a love that is rooted in God.

The bond between two hearts is made by God, as usual Islamic formulas of marriage state, and the love of one spouse for the other is an earthly reflection of the love of the soul for God, although the male and female forms of spirituality are not the same. This intimate bond between the male and female in marriage is indicated in the verse, "They [your wives] are raiment for you and ye are raiment for them" (2:187). Each spouse is a raiment for the other not only in the sense that he or she covers the intimate life and even faults of the other from public view as our clothing covers our bodies, but also in the sense that the raiment is the thing closest to our body. Husband and wife should be also the closest being to each other. Needless to say, not all marriages turn out to be perfect, neither in the Islamic world nor in the West. But the ideals set forth in the Quran have remained very much alive in every generation of Muslims and continue to be so today.

WOMEN IN THE FAMILY AND IN SOCIETY

Since the rise of feminism in the West, whole forests have been cut down to produce books by Western observers on the subject of women in Islam. In most cases current Western ideas have been chosen as absolute criteria to judge women in other societies and to preach to them about how they should behave. In the West today there is a tendency toward what one might call "the absolutization of the transient." Each decade absolutizes its own fashions of thought and action without the least pause and consideration of the fact that a decade later those very fashions and ideas will be buried in the dustbin of history as one turns to a new decade. Nowhere is this phenomenon more evident than in the question of women's rights and roles. If the West were carrying out this debate in 1900, there would be very different criteria for judgment, and most likely in 2100 there will be still others. Rather than using the question of women in Islam as a ram with which to batter the gate of Islamic society as a part of a new "crusade" coming from the West, it is best to first understand the situation from the point of view of Islam and Islamic society and then make whatever criticism one wants based on objective awareness of what criteria one is using.

It is, first of all, essential to realize that what is observed in the Islamic world is the result of not only explicit Islamic teachings, but also the customs and habits of the societies into which Islam entered. For example, in what is called the Middle East today, not only Muslim but also Jewish and Christian women have always covered their hair. The covering of the face is not mentioned in the Quran, nor was it practiced by the women around the Prophet; it was adopted from Persian and Byzantine models. In view of the fact that female education and the participation of women in politics were not common practice before modern times in non-Islamic societies as far away as Japan, China, and other Asian societies, it seems incorrect to highlight what is called the "patriarchal nature of Islamic society" as a unique phenomenon associated with Islam alone. Somehow, however, nearly all the criticism coming from secularist feminists is aimed these days at the Islamic world without bothering to ask practicing Muslim women themselves—women from the mainstream of Islamic society, not just those from the completely Westernized fringes—what their problems really are.

The teachings of Islam emphasize that, although men and women stand equally before God and the Law, they should complement each other in family and social life. Equality before God and the Law does not destroy the reality of complementarity. Some have asked me if men and women are equal in Islam. My answer has always been that before God, in the face of the ultimate eschatological realities, and before the Law, yes, but in this world, not always.

Women are not equal to men, but neither are men equal to women, a truth to which some American authors have been referring recently as distinctions between "persons from Mars" and "persons from Venus."

The traditional structure of Islamic society is based not on quantitative equality, but on the reality of complementarity, although there are exceptions. In this complementarity of functions, the man is seen as the protector and provider of his family and its *imām*, religiously speaking. The woman is the real mistress of the household, in which the husband is like a guest. Her primary duty has been seen as that of raising of children and attending to their earliest education, as well as being the basic buttress of the family. Like all traditional societies, Islam has honored the work of homemaker and mother as being of the highest value, to the extent that the Prophet said, "Heaven lies under the feet of mothers." Islamic society has never thought that working in an office is of a higher order of importance for society than bringing up one's children. Also an economic system was created in the cities, where, by and large, but not always, the wife was not forced for economic reasons to leave the home and her children during the day. From the Islamic point of view, the right of a child to a full-time mother rather than a nanny or day-care provider is more essential than many rights held dear today.

Within the home Muslim women usually wield great power and authority. In my own very large extended family on both the paternal and maternal side, I have known many mothers who were every bit as powerful and even autocratic as the most forceful "Jewish mother" or "Italian mother." Anyone who thinks that in Islamic society women have always been weak, downtrodden, and oppressed beings simply does not know the inner workings of a Muslim family.

The number of husbands oppressed by their wives is probably no smaller in Islamic society than anywhere else. That does not mean, however, that there has not been in the past or does not exist in the present terrible treatment of some wives by Muslim husbands, despite the explicit injunction of the Quran to honor the possessions of one's wife and to deal kindly with her, as when it says, "Consort with them in kindness" (4:19). Considering the practices that were going on in pre-Islamic Arabia, the regulations of Islam effected a remarkable transformation in bestowing economic and social rights upon women and protecting them from injustice. Nevertheless, human beings being what they are, there continue to be Muslim husbands who are cruel toward their wives and who abuse them physically—against the injunctions of Islam. But of course we know only too well that there are also many shelters for battered women in America and Europe, and this problem is not confined to any single part of the world. But to neglect for one moment the power that most Muslim women wield within the family and in the most important decisions affecting the lives of family members is simply to misunderstand the actual role and status of women in Islamic society.

As was stated before, in Islam the economic responsibility for supporting the family resides with the husband, even if the wife happens to be wealthy. The Quranic law of inheritance, according to which a male inherits twice as much as a female, must be understood in light of the husband's responsibility to support the whole family financially while the wife can do with her wealth as she wills. The famous Quranic verse "Men are the protectors and maintainers of women" (4:34) must be understood in this economic and social context, not taken to mean that the husband controls the wife's whole life. As for the testimony of two women equaling that of one man in legal matters, this concerns cases of crime and wrongdoing and not every form of testimony, as some jurists interpreted it later. When it comes to bearing witness to a crime, the Quranic injunction takes into consideration the more merciful, gentle, forgiving, and nurturing nature of women in comparison to that of men; the injunction does not at all belittle women—quite the contrary.

Islamic sources do not at all prevent Muslim women from working and receiving wages. In the agricultural sector of traditional Islamic society women always worked with men and were also very active in many of the arts and crafts. To this day most of the carpets and kilims of various Islamic countries are woven by women. Islam gave women complete economic independence even from their husbands, and over the ages many women have also engaged in trade and been merchants, as was the Prophet's wife Khadījah. Likewise, there is no objection in principle to Muslim women participating in politics. Before modern times there were even occasionally Muslim queens who ruled independently and many others who exerted great political power behind the scenes. If one objects that there were few such female political figures, one could answer that the same held true for Christian Byzantium or Confucian China and that this limitation was not imposed by the Quran. In fact, the granddaughter of the Prophet, Zaynab, played a major political role in early Islamic history, as did a number of other women. In modern times three Islamic countries have had women prime ministers and the Islamic Republic of Iran, which was established to implement Islamic teachings in the country, has a female vice-president and many other female officials, including members of the parliament.

As for education, there is a *ḥadīth* according to which seeking knowledge is a religious obligation for every Muslim, male and female. Throughout Islamic history girls usually completed only the elementary Quranic schools and only a few advanced further—not because of Islamic teachings, but because of social conditions—and from time to time women have become Islamic scholars. Sayyidah Nafīsah, whose sanctuary in Cairo is a major center of pilgrimage to this day, was so learned in the science of *Ḥadīth* that occasionally the greatest Islamic scholar of the day, Imām al-Shāfi'ī, would consult with her. Women, in fact, played an especially important role in the transmission and study of *Ḥadīth*. Also throughout Islamic history, there have been many women Sufis, some of whom were very learned, and fine women poets, from Rābi'ah al-'Adwiyyah, who lived in the eighth century, to Parwīn E'teṣāmī, who lived in the twentieth. Again, one must not equate educational practices in some parts of the Islamic world in modern times, such as Afghanistan under the Taliban, although they claimed to speak in the name of Islam, with the general Islamic view toward women's education. If one looks at such major Islamic countries as Egypt and Iran today, one sees a very large number of women in nearly every field of education, sometimes equaling or even surpassing men in number in the faculties of certain major universities.

The views of Islam concerning women bring us back to the question of the veil and covering. For a long time the West has had a distorted, exotic image of the mysterious Islamic world: women were covered head to toe in public, while harems of naked women were depicted reclining by indoor pools in so many nineteenth-century "orientalist" paintings in Europe. These depictions had much more to do with rebellion in the West against the restraints of the Victorian era going back to the sexual paradigm of Christianity, but they nevertheless introduced to Western society a completely false image of Muslim women. During the colonial period, head cover was taken by European colonizers as a sign of female oppression in Islamic society and Muslim modernists opted for this view themselves, as we see in the forced unveiling of women in Turkey and Iran by Ataturk and Reza Shah, respectively. As a result of these events, one sees today a whole spectrum of women, from those fully veiled to those in miniskirts, in many Muslim countries and especially in the Middle East, where more women have discarded their traditional dress than elsewhere in the Islamic world, such as South or Southeast Asia.

It is therefore especially important to be clear regarding the Islamic teachings on this matter. The Quran commands both men and women to dress modestly and not display their bodies, and the Prophet asserted that modesty is a central character trait of Islam. It also commands women to cover their "ornaments" *(zīnah)*, which is usually understood to mean their hair and, of course, their bodies. On the basis of this injunction, various forms of dress were developed in different parts of the Islamic world, but some forms of dress were carryovers from earlier pre-Islamic Near Eastern societies. In the earlier communities of Jews and Christians, women also covered their hair. The iconography of the Virgin in Christian art always shows her with her hair covered, and until quite recently Georgian and Armenian Christians as well as Oriental Jewish women covered their hair, as did Muslims. The covering of the hair was taken by women to be a natural part of life as a sign of modesty and especially a sign of respect before God. Even in the West until a generation ago Catholic women would not go to church without covering their heads.

Who has said that uncovering one's hair is more liberating than covering it? This is a very complex issue that, as far as the Islamic world is concerned, must be decided along with other women's issues by Muslim women themselves on the basis of Islamic teachings and prevalent social norms, not by others. Until thirty years ago, Muslim women who received Western education and became modernized would usually discard their head covers, but gradually matters began to change. Today in many countries, such as Egypt, many highly educated women freely choose to cover their hair again as a sign of self-identity and protection. Paradoxically, in the one Islamic country that is the most modernized and claims to be secularized in the European way, that is, Turkey, women do not have the right to cover their hair in public buildings, this ban showing total disregard for free choice and women's rights, so central to the concern of Western feminists.

The question of the veil and many other crucial issues having to do with education, legal rights, and so on have become the focus of attention of a number of Muslim women who want to modernize the rest of society after the model of the West, whatever that model, which is still in a state of flux, might be. They are abetted in this task by Western secularist feminists and certain other elements that would like to secularize Islamic society. It is unfortunate that most Western feminists do not bother to understand the underlying philosophy of the relation between men and women in Islam and, in fact, in other non-Western societies. Nor do they offer a clear alternative model that would have meaning for the vast majority of Muslim women.

During the last two decades a new movement has begun among believing Muslim women themselves to gain the rights they believe the Quran and *Ḥadīth* accord them, but that local social customs and regulations have prevented them from gaining. This so-called Islamic feminism is much more pertinent than Western-style feminism as far as the future of Islamic society is concerned, because those women who pursue it, most of whom are pious Muslim women, do so from within the Islamic worldview. Furthermore, they also know much better than their Western counterparts what their own real problems are. In any case, women's issues—their education, legal rights, participation in political affairs, and so forth—are one of the major challenges facing the Islamic world today, one that each part of the Islamic world has been trying to deal with on the basis of Islamic teachings and its own customs and traditions, in spite of the constant pressure from various forces in the West.

ISLAM AND THE INTEGRATION OF SOCIETY

Through the imposition of a Divine Law, the inculcation of moral values within its members, and the creation of bonds of relationship, Islam played a major role in the integration of human society. A series of concentric circles can represent the areas of relationship. At the center is the relationship between the individual and God. Surrounding that center is the circle of the family, then of the quarter of one's city or town, then of one's "nation" *(waṭan)* in the traditional sense of the term, then the Islamic community *(ummah)*, and finally all of humanity and in fact creation as a whole. In the same way that each circle in the series has the same center, each of these relationships was and remains based on the basic relationship between the human being and God.

Tawḥīd, or unity, which is the central doctrine of Islam and which also means "integration," therefore began with the integration of the individual soul into its Center, where God resides, and then extended to bonds between members of the family and other increasingly larger groupings until it encompassed the whole of creation. Despite the relentless downward march of time and numerous vicissitudes, Islam was able to integrate society to a large extent and create an *ummah* that stretched from the Atlantic to the Pacific. This *ummah* in turn created Islamic civilization, one of the major global civilizations, which, despite some weakening from the eighteenth century onward, is still very much alive. The Islamic *ummah* and civilization have seen periods of decline and rejuvenation, the appearance of those who have misled the people as well as authentic "renewers" *(mujaddid)* who, as promised by the Prophet, have periodically revitalized the religion and Islamic society from within.

Today the Islamic *ummah,* politically segmented and divided as never before, faces unprecedented challenges from the onslaught of modern secularism and consumerist globalization, challenges much greater than what it faced during the Mongol invasion. Of course, modern secularism and now globalization are also challenges to Judaism and Christianity in the West, but in their cases the challenges come from within their own society. For the Islamic *ummah,* it comes from the outside and is supported by exceptional military, economic, and political power. Reaction to this outside pressure has taken many forms, sometimes violent ones that go against the very tenets of Islam. These are, however, peripheral and transient phenomena. The profounder reality is the traditional religious truths of Islam embedded deep in the heart of Islamic society, which will have to survive these enormous challenges without betraying the principles of Islam itself.

More than ever before, it is important to remember that the empire of Islam resides in the hearts of men and women and not in worldly power alone. To perpetuate the life of the ***ummah*** and the rule of this "spiritual empire," it is essential to remember the truths for which Islam was revealed and the Prophet sent as the Messenger to the world. In one of his most famous *ḥadīths* the Prophet said, "I was sent in order to perfect [for you] the virtues of character." The role of Islamic society has always been to make possible the attainment of virtue and the perfection of character, and such Muslim authorities as al-Fārābī, like Plato, divided societies according to their ability to provide an environment that would foster this inner perfection of moral and spiritual qualities of the members of society. From the Islamic point of view, the value of a society before the eyes of God lies in its virtuous quality, its moral excellence, and not in power or wealth. It is this basic truth that Muslims must remember as they confront the powerful forces of secularism, globalization, and consumerism that threaten the very foundations of the Islamic order.

Five

COMPASSION AND LOVE, PEACE AND BEAUTY

My Mercy and Compassion embrace all things.

Quran 7:156

Those who believe and do good works,
the Infinitely Good will appoint for them love.

Quran 19:96

God is He than Whom there is no god,
the Sovereign Lord, the Holy One, Peace.

Quran 59:23

God is beautiful and loves beauty.

Ḥadīth

COMPASSION, LOVE, PEACE, AND BEAUTY AS DIVINE QUALITIES

According to a well-known *ḥadīth,* on the Throne of God is written, "Verily My Mercy and Compassion precede my Wrath." To be sure there is Divine Justice and need for justice in the world, as there is Divine Rigor and Wrath related to the Divine Majesty described so powerfully in both the Bible and the Quran. But the inner dimension of reality is inseparable from that Divine Mercy and Compassion but for which there would be no creation. Since this world is the creation of God, it must reflect His Qualities, and Islamic spiritual teachings emphasize that in fact the whole universe is nothing but the interplay of the reflections of God's Names and Qualities. Therefore His Names of Beauty and Mercy must be reflected in His creation as much as His Names of Majesty and Justice. Furthermore, the former Names, having to do with the inner dimension of the Divine Reality, take precedence when it comes to the inner life of the soul of the Muslim.

The idea propagated by certain Western scholars and Christian apologists that the God of Islam is only the God of Justice but not of Mercy, Compassion, and Love is totally false. God's Mercy, Compassion, Forgiveness, and Love are mentioned more times in the Quran than are His Justice and Retribution. All the four concepts mentioned in the title of this chapter, namely, Compassion (which is inseparable from Mercy in the Islamic view), Love, Peace, and Beauty, are Divine Names whose reflections must therefore be part of the very substance and root of the existence of human beings as well as that of other creatures.

COMPASSION AND MERCY

Of special significance for the understanding of the Islamic perspective on creation and revelation is the notion and reality of mercy and compassion. As the Quranic verse cited above bears witness, the Mercy and Compassion *(raḥmah)* of God embraces all things, and in fact the world would not exist if there were to be no *raḥmah*. The term *raḥmah*, which means both "mercy" and "compassion," is related to the two Divine Names *al-Raḥmān*, the Infinitely Good, and *al-Raḥīm*, the All-Merciful, with which every chapter of the Quran except one commences. They are also the Names with which daily human acts are consecrated. Because these Names are interwoven into every aspect of the life of Muslims, life is thereby wrapped in Divine Goodness, Mercy, and Compassion, which are inextricably associated with the Arabic word *al-raḥmah*. Moreover, this word is related to the Arabic term for "womb," *raḥim*. Therefore, it might be said that the world issues from the womb of Divine Mercy and Compassion. This truth is emphasized by Sufis who, as already mentioned, claim that the very substance of cosmic existence is the "Breath of the Compassionate." God breathed upon the archetypal realities of this world, and the consequence of this action was the realm of separative existence we call the world. It is most significant that this "Breath" *(nafas)* is associated with the goodness and compassion of God and not some other quality. Compassion is therefore at the root of our very existence, the gate through which both revelation and creation were brought forth and therefore a central reality in all aspects of human life. Every aspect of the traditional life of Muslims over the ages has been intertwined with *raḥmah* and inseparable from it, since compassion is woven into the very fiber of human existence.

A poem of Rūmī states, "Muṣṭafā [the chosen one—Muḥammad] came to bring about intimacy and compassion *(hamdamī)*." The term *hamdamī* in Persian means literally "having the same breath," therefore indicating close intimacy and what some ancient philosophers called *sympatheia*, which is closely related to compassion. Spiritually, the very message of the Prophet and the revelation of the Quran were to bring about a full flowering of the compassion that relates all beings to each other by the very fact that they exist. The Prophet is himself called *raḥmah* to all the worlds, and his inner reality plays a most important role in the spiritual economy of Islamic life as far as compassion and mercy are concerned.

If one asks how compassion and mercy function concretely in Islamic life, the answer begins with the distinctions between the relation of God to the individual, the individual to God, human beings to each other, and humanity to the rest of creation. As far as the relation of God to the individual and in fact to all of His creation is concerned, it always involves compassion and mercy. In addition to *al-Raḥmān*, the Infinitely Good, and *al-Raḥīm*, the All-Merciful, God is also known as *al-Karīm*, the All-Generous, *al-Ghafūr*, the All-Forgiver, and *al-Laṭīf*, the All-Kind. He possesses also other Names and Qualities that indicate His Compassion toward His creation and His Mercy, but for which there would be no religion, no human salvation, and in fact no existence. It is impossible for a Muslim to pray to God or even to think of God without awareness of this essential dimension of Compassion and Mercy, without, however, losing sight of the Divine Majesty, before which one must always remain in reverential awe.

I recall from the numerous Islamic holy sites I have visited, where one hears hundreds of audible supplications to God by women and men that besides the word Allah, or *Khudā* in Persian, no word is heard more often than *Raḥmān, Raḥīm,* and *raḥmah.* I remember especially this prayer uttered in Arabic with the utmost sincerity by a simple woman: "O Lord, have Mercy and Compassion, for if Thou dost not have Mercy, who will have mercy?" The heartfelt prayer of this simple pilgrim epitomizes the quintessential Islamic attitude toward God as the source of compassion and mercy. No matter what one has done in life, one should never lose hope in His Compassion and Mercy, for as the Quran states, "And who despaireth of the Mercy of his Lord save those who go astray" (15:56), and "Do not despair of God's Mercy" (39:53). A Muslim's prayer always contains an appeal to His dimension of Compassion and Mercy. This attitude can be summarized in the Quranic verse, "Have mercy upon us for Thou art the best of those who show mercy" (23:109). We may lose faith in the compassion and mercy of human beings and even close friends, although even this despair is spiritually incorrect, but we should never lose faith or hope in God's Compassion and Mercy. It might be said that in the Islamic universe the Face of God turned toward His creation is inseparable from His Compassion and Mercy, while the face of men and women turned toward their Lord must always be based on appeal to that Divine Compassion and Mercy that "embraceth all things."

As for the relationship between human beings, not only do the injunctions of the *Sharī'ah* recommend and require acts of compassion, charity, and mercy toward the poor, the sick, the weak, orphans, and the needy, but Islamic ethics, based on the model of the Prophet, emphasizes over and over again the importance of the virtues of compassion and charity, mercy and forgiveness. Muslims should be strict with themselves, but generous and compassionate toward those around them. This begins with the family, where the Quran and *Ḥadīth* emphasize in numerous verses the importance of exercising *iḥsān,* that is, spiritual virtue and goodness, which includes compassion and kindness toward one's parents, spouse, children, and other family members. Compassion and generosity must, moreover, be in deeds as well as in words, and here the whole tradition of *adab,* or traditional courtesy, manners, and comportment, plays a central role in making compassion, generosity, and the self-discipline and nobility that are inseparable from them a concrete reality.

Beyond the family there is the general category of neighbor, which usually includes one's physical neighbors and those living nearby. Again, there are numerous teachings in the Quran and *Ḥadīth* emphasizing the importance of having compassion toward the people who are one's neighbors and being aware of their needs. Then beyond one's neighborhood there is society at large, in which the same attitude of compassion and kindness must exist even beyond the boundary of one's religion.

When one looks at Islamic societies as a whole, one becomes aware how socially and economically significant the acts of compassion and mercy, in fact, are in the lives of so many people, especially the poor. Without these religiously motivated acts of compassion and charity, the social order would collapse, since in many places in the Islamic world governments are not strong or wealthy enough to provide a minimum income for all their citizens. Consequently the welfare of the poor is left to a large extent to the mercy of private individuals and institutions, all motivated, not by some kind of secularist altruism, but by the Islamic emphasis upon the importance of compassion, charity, kindness, and mercy to those less fortunate who turn to those better off for help. The hand of the needy beggar asking for help is in the deepest sense the Hand of Divine Mercy extended to us, for in extending our compassion and mercy to one of God's creatures we become ourselves recipients of Divine Mercy.

The last relation to consider is that of human beings to the nonhuman world. Despite the terrible abuse of both animals and vegetation in many big Islamic cities filled by recently uprooted people no longer in harmony with their natural environment, Islamic teachings themselves emphasize that compassion, mercy, and kindness must be extended to animals and plants as well as to human beings. Already in medieval Islamic cities there were animal hospitals and endowments established for the keeping of horses and donkeys that had become ill or incapacitated. The Prophet dealt with animals gently, and many *ḥadīths* refer to the importance of showing kindness to them as well as of respecting the life of the vegetal world, of not destroying trees and other vegetation unless absolutely necessary. Traditional Islamic societies have many examples of the exercise of compassion and mercy toward nonhuman realms of life as well as the human order.

Needless to say, not all Muslims heed the teachings of Islam as far as compassion, mercy, generosity, and kindness are concerned, any more than do all Jews, Christians, or even Buddhists, whose whole religion is based on the two foundations of compassion and enlightenment. Human imperfection is not the monopoly of any single people, race, or religious community; it exists everywhere. It is essential to bring out the significance of compassion and mercy in the Islamic religious universe, not in order to claim that all Muslims have abided by the teachings of their religion concerning this central matter, but to refute the false conception propagated by some in the West that Islam is a religion without compassion. If an impartial observer were to visit, let us say, ten major sacred sites in ten Islamic countries and record how many times in one hour words related to compassion and mercy, the Arabic *raḥmah,* are heard in the supplications and prayers arising from the hearts of those assembled at such sites, it would become clear how central compassion and mercy are to the Islamic understanding of God, the relation between human beings and God, and the rapport between human beings and all of His creation. The goal of Islam has always been to train individuals to be aware of God's Compassion and Mercy, to rely in their spiritual life upon these Divine Qualities, and to reflect these qualities in their human form in their relations with all other beings in God's creation. The aim of the Quranic revelation has also been to create a compassionate society, a society not based on ruthless competition and individualistic selfishness, but on the awareness that to gain inner felicity and be worthy of receiving God's Mercy and Compassion, we must exercise compassion and kindness toward others. In giving on the basis of compassion and mercy to others, we also give ourselves to God and gain freedom from the prison of our limited ego.

LOVE

One of God's Names is *al-Wadūd,* Love, and in the Quran there are numerous references to love, or *ḥubb,* as when it is said, "God will bring a people whom He loveth and who love Him" (5:54). There is a certitude for Muslims that God is all-loving, as He is all-compassionate and all-forgiving, as stated in the verses, "Surely my Lord is All-Merciful, All-Love" (11:90) and "He is the All-Forgiving, the All-Loving" (85:14). Even the Prophet's following of God's commands is related to his love for God, for as the Sacred Text states, "Say (O Muḥammad): If ye love God, follow me" (3:31). One of the titles of the Prophet is in fact Ḥabīb Allāh, usually translated as "Friend of God," but meaning also "Beloved of God."

In Christianity it is said that God is Love, and often from that perspective Islam is criticized for having a conception of God that lacks love. In this context it is of interest to turn to the observation of an outsider from the medieval period, the famous Jewish sage and poet Abraham ibn Ezra, who wrote:

> The Muslims sing of love and of passion
> The Christians of war and revenge
> The Greeks of wisdom and devices
> The Indians of parables and riddles
> And the Israelites—songs and praises to the Lord
> of Hosts.[1]

The assertion that Muslims do not know Divine Love is as absurd as claiming that Muslims know nothing of Divine Compassion. Neither Judaism nor Hinduism identifies God simply or purely with love, but that does not mean either of these religions, any more than Islam, is devoid of the notion of Divine Love, which flowered in them in the form of the Hasidic and *bhakti* movements, respectively. Islam states that God is Love, since this is one of His Divine Names, but it does not identify God solely with love, for

He is also Knowledge and Light, Justice and Majesty as well as Peace and Beauty, but He is never without love and His Love is essential to the creation of the universe and our relation with Him.

It is important to note that in the Islamic perspective God's Compassion for the world is not identified with suffering. Rather, it is translated into love. God's Essence transcends the created and temporal order, and He cannot suffer in His Essence for what happens in that order. This aspect of Islam is therefore in contrast to the theme of the suffering servant in messianic Judaism and the "suffering of God" in many strands of Christianity. As already mentioned, in the Islamic perspective God "loved" to be known and therefore created the world. Therefore love runs through the vein of the universe and, like compassion, is inseparable from existence. There is no realm of existence where love does not manifest itself in some way. One can even say that, metaphysically speaking, the gravitational attraction of physical bodies for each other is a particular instance of the universal principle of love operating on the level of physical reality.

On the more practical level, love in the life of Muslims has its exemplar in the love of God for the Prophet and the Prophet for Him. For human beings the love of God necessitates the love of the Prophet, and the love of the Prophet and the saints, who are his spiritual or biological progeny, necessitates the love of God. There are, furthermore, many levels of love natural to human beings: romantic love, love of children and parents, love of beauty in art and nature, love of knowledge, and even love of power, wealth, and fame, which, however, since they are turned toward the world, pose a danger for the soul. In the Islamic perspective, all earthly love should be in God and not separated from the love of God, and any love that excludes God and turns us away from Him is an illusion that can lead to the ruin of the soul. The Islamic sages have in fact asserted the doctrine that only the love of God is real love and all other love is metaphorical love. But metaphorical love is also real on its own level and is in fact a Divine gift, if it is understood properly and used as a ladder to reach real love, which is the love for the Source of all love, which is God.

The dimension of love gushed forth in Islam within Sufism and resulted in some of the greatest literary works about mystical love ever written. This perennial spring of inspiration began to inundate the soul and spirit of Muslims early in the history of Islam with the appearance of the woman saint of Basra, Rābiʿah al-ʿAdawiyyah. Her beautiful Arabic poems on the love of God are recited to this day in the Arab world even by popular singers. In one of her moving poems she writes:

Two ways I love Thee: selfishly,
And next, as worthy is of Thee.
'Tis selfish love that I do naught
Save think on Thee with every thought.
'Tis purest love when Thou dost raise
The veil to my adoring gaze.
Not mine the praise in that or this,
Thine is the praise in both, I wis.[2]

Although in Sufism love is never separated from knowledge, some schools have emphasized one and some the other. In early Islamic history the School of Khurasan in Persia was especially identified with love and its greatest masters, such as Bāyazīd Basṭāmī, Abū Saʿīd Abi'l-Khayr, and especially Aḥmad Ghazzālī, who developed a whole metaphysical language based on *ʿishq,* or intense love, wrote some of the most memorable hymns to Divine Love. This tradition finally led to what some have considered the greatest mystical poetry ever written, namely, that of the thirteenth-century poet Jalāl al-Dīn Rūmī, who was Persian but spent most of his life in Anatolia and is buried in Konya in present-day Turkey. Rūmī, who calls love "our Plato and Galen" and says that when the pen comes to the question of describing what love is, it breaks in half, is today the most widely read poet in America. This supreme troubadour of Divine Love, along with Ibn ʿArabī, who lived a generation before him, represents the highest peak of Islamic spirituality in that period that saw the inner renewal and revival of the spiritual dimensions of Islam and the creation of a sweet spring of spiritual knowledge and love whose tributaries have watered various Islamic lands from the Atlantic to the Pacific during the past seven centuries.

Such extensive manifestation of love within the Islamic religious universe was not in spite of Islam, but because of it. It cannot be traced to any foreign influences any more than Christian treatises on love can be reduced to the reading of Neoplatonic sources without consideration of the love for Christ. The very presence of this vast literature on Divine Love in nearly every Islamic language from Arabic and Persian to Turkish and Swahili, as well as most of the local languages of India and Southeast Asia, is the best external sign of the significance of the dimension of love in the inner life of Islam. This outpouring was so extensive and powerful in expression that it even influenced Jewish, Christian, and Hindu writers and spiritual practitioners. Raymond Lull, a Franciscan theologian who wrote against Islam, also composed a treatise entitled *The Lover and the Beloved,* in which he imitated Sufi terminology, and the greatest mystical writers of sixteenth-century Spain, St. Teresa of Avila and St. John of the Cross, adopted numerous Sufi symbols for the love of God. The inner signs of this dimension of love have always remained a secret between a human being and God, as they have in other religions, between "a people whom He loveth and who love Him" (5:54) to quote the Quran, and this intimate nexus between the soul and God is beyond external description. It is a fire that can only be known if it gives off sparks, as it has fortunately done in the luminous writings of those "lovers of God," those Islamic *fedeli d'amore,* who have expressed something of that love in human language. But then there are many fires that do not give off sparks.

Some might claim that all this Sufi emphasis upon love is only for the Sufis and has nothing to do with the rest of Islamic society. Nothing could be further from the truth, if one considers traditional Islamic society and not modernist or "fundamentalist" circles. Poetry celebrating the love and the yearning of the soul for God spread throughout traditional society and was often memorized by ordinary men and women who recited and still recite such verses with the deepest feeling and existential identification rather than simply as literature of historical significance.

Over forty years ago, when Lahore was still a beautiful garden city, I remember visiting the tomb of the famous Sufi saint Miān Mīr in the fields outside the city, a sanctuary now surrounded by the horrid sprawl of the once beautiful Lahore. It was nighttime, and I decided to take a horse-drawn carriage called a *tonga* back to town. The driver appeared to be very poor and was scantily dressed. At the beginning of our trip, he greeted me with the Islamic greeting and asked me in Urdu where I was from. I answered in Persian that I was from Persia. He became excited and smiled. Then he began to recite God knows how many sublime Persian poems of 'Aṭṭār, Rūmī, Ḥāfiẓ, and others on Divine Love and the nostalgia of the soul for God, rendering all those poems as if he had experienced what was described in them and had composed the poems himself. That example—riding in that carriage that night under the starry sky of the Punjabi countryside listening to an illiterate *tonga* driver reciting some of the most sublime mystical love poetry ever written, reciting both from memory and from the center of his heart—shows how universal the living reality of the love for God is in the Islamic spiritual universe. This love uses the sublime language of Sufi poets, but this poetry speaks for all those Muslims, technically Sufi and non-Sufi alike, who are aware of God's Love for His creation, those whose own love for God, hidden within the very primordial substance of their souls, has begun to stir and the steed of whose souls has turned in the direction of that spiritual homeland from which they have come and to which they yearn to return.

PEACE

If one walks along the Ganges River in Benares, one keeps hearing the phrase *"Shanti, shanti, shanti,"* meaning "Peace, peace, peace," and when one sees Jews greeting each other, one hears *"Shalom"* and from Muslims *"Salām,"* while for nearly two millennia the chant of *"Pacem, pacem, pacem"* has reverberated in the houses of worship dedicated to the figure known as the Prince of Peace. There is no major religion that does not emphasize peace, although only small groups such as the Quakers or Mennonites could afford to be pacifists. All the major religions preach peace, yet have to face occasions when war has become inevitable for one reason or another. Christ spoke of turning the other cheek, yet for centuries in Europe major and minor wars were fought in the name of Christianity or a particular brand of Christianity.

And yet in the West Islam is often singled out as being warlike and the "religion of the sword" in contrast primarily to Christianity as the religion of peace. Although such a major spiritual text of Hinduism as the Bhagavad Gita was revealed in the middle of a battlefield and the Old Testament has many more passages dealing with war than the Quran, among many Christians the opprobrium against religious war is generally saved for Islam. As this book is being written, some Filipinos are writing about how peaceful Christianity is in contrast to Islam by conveniently forgetting that, according to Spanish chronicles, when the Spaniards invaded the Philippines they defeated the Islamic sultanate, with its seat in Manila, and then slaughtered tens of thousands of Muslims, forcing the rest of those they were able to conquer to convert to Catholicism, as they had done to Jews and Muslims in Spain. Moreover, in the West the spread of Islam is associated with the "sword," while hardly anyone ever mentions the brutal manner in which northern Europeans were forcefully converted to Christianity and the older European religions destroyed. Even the Crusades, carried out in the name of Christianity, did not succeed in changing the Western image of Islam as the "religion of the sword" and Christianity as the religion of peace.

It is true that the sacred history of Islam begins as an epic with the rapid spread of the Arabs outside of Arabia in an event that changed world history forever. But this rapid expansion did not mean forced conversion of Jews, Christians, Zoroastrians, or others. In Persia three hundred years after Muslim rule much of the country was still Zoroastrian, and the province of Mazandaran by the Caspian Sea did not embrace Islam until the tenth century. In most areas Islamization was a gradual process. The history of Islam, like that of Judaism and Hinduism, is intertwined with a sacred epic, but that does not mean that Islam is any more or less the "religion of the sword" or the "religion of peace" than any other religion.

Since this accusation against Islam as the "religion of the sword" has continued in the modern West, which has fought more deadly wars than any other civilization, contemporary Muslims have usually developed a defensive attitude and simply respond that the very name Islam is related to the word *salām*, which means "peace." This response is, however, not sufficient. They need to point out that, since the goal of all authentic religions is to reach God Who *is* Peace and the Source of all peace, Islam also aims to lead its followers to the "Abode of Peace" and to create peace to the degree possible in a world full of disequilibrium, tension, and affliction. Furthermore, Islam has sought to limit war by legislating conditions pertaining to it, as will be discussed in the next chapter, and succeeded during the fourteen centuries of its history in reaching the goal of creating inner peace to a remarkable degree, while in the creation of outward peace it was certainly no less successful than any of the other major traditional civilizations such as the Japanese, Chinese, Hindu, or Christian. It is high time to put aside this curious historical characterization of Islam in a West that has carried out wars over the five continents often in the name of Christianity and even eradicated whole ethnic groups with impunity because they were not Christians.

It is easy for Muslims and Christians, or for that matter Hindus, Confucians, or Buddhists, to point to episodes of war in the history of other religions. The history of all societies, whether religious or secular, is replete with such examples, because human beings contain in their fallen state the seeds of strife and contention and take recourse in aggression and war, using for their cause whatever idea or ideology has the power to move people. When most Westerners were devout Christians, it was Christianity that was the banner under which wars were fought, and when religion became weak, nationalism, Fascism, Communism, and other ideologies as well as economic interests took its place. In the Islamic world, because religion remains a powerful force, its name is still used in support of whatever causes arise that lead to contention and conflict, although the Quran emphasizes that war must be only for defense of one's homeland and religion and not be offensive and aggressive. When we return to the teachings that are at the heart of all authentic religions, however, we see that the role of each religion is to seek to bring about peace and to accentuate those religious teachings that emphasize both heavenly and earthly accord, harmony, and peace. Seen in this light, it becomes clear how central in fact the emphasis on peace is in the teachings of Islam as traditionally understood.

Everyone today speaks of the need for peace, thanks partly to modern military technology, which has brought the horrors of war to a level inconceivable to even the most warlike people of old. But there is also an innate yearning for peace in the soul of human beings that is certainly not derived from experience. Even those who have never experienced peace yearn for it. One might therefore ask why people seek peace. Islamic teachings have a clear answer to this question, one that clarifies the concept and reality of peace in the Islamic context. In the Quran God refers to Himself as *al-Salām*, or Peace, so that one could, as a Muslim, say that God is Peace and our yearning for peace is nothing more than our yearning for God. Deep down in our primordial nature there is still the recollection of the peace we experienced when we bore witness to God's Lordship in pre-eternity before our fall into this world of forgetfulness. Through a process we might liken to Platonic recollection, we still recall now and then that peace that Christ said "passeth all understanding."

For Muslims, only religion is able to take us back to the "Abode of Peace," which is ultimately paradisal reality and Divine Presence. "God guideth him who seeketh His good pleasure unto paths of peace" (5:16). Over and over again the Quran identifies peace with the paradisal states: "And they call upon the dwellers of paradise: Peace be unto you" (7:46); the phrase "peace be unto you" is also the Muslim greeting taught by the Prophet as the greeting of the people of paradise. "In paradise there is not idle chatter but only the invocation of peace" (19:62). "'Peace'—such is the greeting from the Lord All-Compassionate" (36:58). In paradise there is "naught but the saying 'peace, peace'" (56:26).

Precisely because it is a celestial quality, peace is not easy to attain either outwardly or inwardly. To have outward peace, one must be at peace with oneself, and to be at peace with oneself, one must be at peace with God. Human beings have been created in the "form" of God, according to the *ḥadīth* already cited. Therefore every element of the soul is of some value. The problem is that the soul of the fallen human being has become chaotic, and various elements are no longer in their proper place. The great plays of Shakespeare can be understood as depicting this inner drama of the soul. In *Hamlet,* all is not well in the kingdom of Denmark, and the situation has become chaotic because no one is in his or her right place. The kingdom of Denmark is our soul, within which matters have to be put straight and elements put in their right place before harmony and peace can be established. But it is impossible for the soul to achieve this task by itself. It needs the help of Heaven. Like other spiritual traditions, Islam insists that without surrender to God *(taslīm,* which has the same root as peace, *salām),* we cannot attain peace, and without peace within ourselves there can be no external peace.

In the general discussion of peace today this hierarchy is often forgotten. Secularized men and women, for whom the spiritual world has become unreal, limit their vision of reality to the earth and life in this world; so they naturally want to live in peace and avoid the dangers of war and strife. But this talk of peace goes on while modern society is carrying out a brutal war against the natural environment and while, within human society, competition based on greed often eclipses compassion and the sense of social responsibility. Consequently, although there is no global war today, smaller wars, local strife, and acts of terror abound around the globe, not to mention the continuing economic and ecological warfare going on against nature in the name and under the banner of peace and prosperity. From the Islamic point of view, since Peace *(al-Salām)* is a Name of God and all peace is a reflection of that Divine Name, the question can be asked why God should allow humanity to live at peace in the forgetfulness of Him, negligent of the goal for which men and women were created.

For Muslims, the idea of living at peace while denying God is totally absurd, because only God can put the chaos and strife within the human soul in order, and when there is no peace within, there will be no peace without. Islamic teachings contain many injunctions for settling disputes between people and nations with the aim of establishing peace. But the highest goal of Islam is to lead the soul to the "Abode of Peace" by guiding us to live a virtuous life and to establish inner harmony with the help of Heaven. For Islam, as for all authentic traditions, the goal of religion is to save the human soul and consequently establish justice and peace in society so that people can live virtuously and live and die "in peace," which in the deepest sense means in the blessed state that leads to the experience of celestial peace. In Buddhism, the spiritual practices that lead to escape from *samsāra* and entry into *nirvāna* on the basis of the doctrine of no-self represent another perspective of the same reality. Buddhism is there to save its followers from *samsāra* and the wheel of rebirth, suffering, and death, as other religions are there to save their adherents from the world. Islam has been there to remind its followers over the ages that there is no possibility of peace on earth without peace with Heaven, and today it is called upon to also assert that peace with Heaven requires, as never before, peace between the messages that, through Divine Wisdom, have descended from Heaven over the ages. As Rūmī has said,

> If thou fleest with the hope of peace and comfort,
> From that side thou shalt be afflicted with
> misfortune.
> There is no treasure without wild beasts and traps,
> There is no peace except in the spiritual retreat of
> God.[3]

When speaking of peace, one should never forget the famous Quranic verse, "He it is who made the Divine Peace *(al-sakīnah)* to descend in the hearts of believers" (48:4). Whether one speaks of *sakīnah,* or the Hebrew equivalent *shekinah,* or for that matter *pacem* or *shanti,* the reality emphasized by Islam remains that the source of peace is God Who *is* Himself Peace and without Whom there can be no peace on earth.

BEAUTY

Like compassion, love, and peace, beauty is seen as a Divine Quality in Islam, one of God's Names being *al-Jamīl,* the Beautiful. Furthermore, according to the *ḥadīth* quoted at the beginning of this chapter, God loves beauty, meaning that the qualities of beauty and love are intertwined on the Divine plane. And this reality is reflected on the human plane as well by the fact that our soul loves what it perceives as beautiful and sees as beautiful what it loves. Beauty also has the power of radiation and emanation and shares therefore a basic characteristic with compassion and mercy. Furthermore, beauty brings about collectedness and helps the scattered elements of the soul gather together in a state of calm. Beauty is therefore also related to peace and has a remarkable pacifying power over the soul, a quality that is essential to Islamic spirituality, as reflected so clearly in Islamic art.

But what is beauty? In the Islamic universe, as in other traditional worlds, beauty is not simply a subjective state existing only "in the eye of the beholder," although each human being usually has the capacity to appreciate certain kinds of beauty and not others. Beauty is a dimension of reality itself, and throughout the ages Islamic philosophers and mystics have confirmed in their own terms the Platonic dictum "Beauty is the splendor of the truth." Now, the Arabic word *ḥaqīqah* means both "truth" and "reality" and the Divine Name *al-Ḥaqq* indicates the union of the two in God Who is both the Truth in its absolute sense, the Truth that makes us free, as Christ asserted, and absolute Reality.

Metaphysically speaking, since God is both Truth and Reality, He could not but be beautiful. As the Sufis would say, ultimately all beauty is the radiation on a particular level of reality of the Beauty of the Face of the Beloved.

One might say that Islam is the religion of beauty, which it never separates from goodness. In today's world, goodness and beauty have become separated from each other, and even religious people inclined toward the good often consider beauty a luxury. Some modern religious thinkers in the West have even developed a "cult of ugliness," the result of which is a large number of horrendously ugly churches to be seen especially in some Catholic countries, where one also finds the most beautiful manifestations of Christian architecture. Needless to say, this "cult of ugliness" has now also spread to the Islamic world, which knows many mosques that are in no way behind their Western counterparts in ugliness. They do not, however, represent Islamic art or thought but simply external influences. In any case, in the traditional Islamic perspective beauty and goodness are inseparable. In fact, in Arabic the word *ḥusn* means both "beauty" and "goodness," while *qubḥ* means both "ugliness" and "evil."

One might say that goodness corresponds to the outer dimension and beauty to the inner dimension of things, not that there is no outward beauty or inward goodness. There is a very telling saying in connection with this question that also clarifies the complementarity between the male and female, or *yin* and *yang*, which are seen cosmologically and spiritually as well as on the human level. It is said in Islam that a woman's beauty is outward and her goodness inward, while a man's goodness is outward and his beauty inward. Like the *yin* and *yang*, which complement each other and together make the perfect circle associated with the Tao, beauty and goodness complement and are inseparable from each other. In the Islamic perspective the role of religion is not only to teach the practice of goodness, but also to disseminate beauty on all its levels, spiritual, intellectual, and physical.

It is said in Buddhism that the Buddha image saves souls through its beauty. One might say, likewise, that the very beauty of Quranic recitation is salvific. In traditional Islamic society one never hears the Word of God except in beautiful chanting, which moves the very depth of the soul of even those Muslims who do not know Arabic and do not comprehend the message of what is recited. The same holds true for the writing of the Quran, which is the fountainhead of all Islamic calligraphy. From the earliest days, the Sacred Text was written in beautiful calligraphy, and certainly throughout the centuries the most beautiful books produced in any generation of Muslims have been the Quran. In the eyes and ears of Muslims the central theophany of their religion, namely the Quran, has always been associated with beauty, as have sites and structures associated with religious matters. Nor has this emphasis upon the link between beauty and the sacred been unique to Islam. Before modern times the most beautiful art of all civilizations was the sacred art associated directly with the rites and practices of religion, as seen in Gothic cathedrals, Torah scrolls, Hindu and Buddhist temples, and various types of icons, not to mention the sonoral arts of music and poetry.

It might be asked why, if Islam can be called the religion of beauty, religious thinkers, Islamic as well as Jewish and Christian, have also warned that the soul can be ensnared by beauty and distracted from God, and why some great mystics have avoided having or being surrounded by beautiful objects. The answer is that precisely because beauty is a powerfully attractive theophany, or visible manifestation, of the Divine Reality, it has the power to draw the soul to itself and can cause some to mistake that theophany for the Origin of all theophanies. It is precisely beauty's ability to attract the soul that makes it a double-edged sword. Beauty is at once a royal path to God and an impediment to reaching God if it is taken as a god in itself. One might say that if there were no beauty in this world, there would be no worldly distraction for the soul and every soul would be drawn only to God. In a sense the spiritual life would not be a challenge and the grandeur of the human state would itself be diminished. What makes the spiritual quest heroic is precisely that the soul must learn to distance itself from the worldly, which nevertheless appeals to it as attractive and beautiful, in order to reach the Source of all beauty.

It is here that the element of asceticism comes in, for Islam as for other religions. In order to see earthly beauty as a ladder to Divine Beauty, it is first of all necessary for the soul to pull its roots from this world and plant them in God. Hence the necessity of ascetic practice and spiritual discipline. There is no religious law and spiritual path that does not contain at least some ascetic practices. In Islam, although excessive asceticism as practiced by certain monks or yogis is not acceptable, asceticism and spiritual self-discipline certainly exist, as one sees in the prayers and the fast. Through the disciplines of the *Sharīʿah,* the soul is prepared to accept further spiritual discipline and embark upon the spiritual path that leads to God, where the source of attraction that makes this journey possible is beauty and love. There is also, of course, in addition, the spiritual and initiatic power *(wilāyah/walāyah)* transmitted through the Prophet to all later generations of Muslims who have sought and still seek to behold even in this life the incomparable beauty of the Face of the Origin of all beauty. For the realized sages, all beauty is the reflection of Divine Beauty. The soul of such persons has passed beyond the danger of being ensnared by the reflection of Beauty from beholding *the* Beautiful. For such persons no earthly beauty can become an obstacle to God. On the contrary, every form of beauty here below offers the occasion for the recollection of the Beauty of God and the remembrance of beholding the Beauty of His Countenance in our preeternal encounter with our Lord when we attested, according to the Quran, to His Lordship.

Islamic thought and artistic sensibility have always associated beauty with reality and ugliness with nonexistence. Today, it has become fashionable for many to seek the ugly and the evil and to parade them as the real, while the beautiful and the good are cast aside as being irrelevant, secondary, and ultimately unreal. For example, the media often search and search to find some evil in a person's life and then exaggerate it to such an extent that the good and the beautiful in that life are completely overshadowed. Even in the photography and film used in the media, the ugly is often more emphasized than the beautiful. The reign of the machine and the creation by modern human beings of an artificial urban ambience cut off from nature, which is overwhelmingly beautiful, have caused many to take the ugly to be the norm and the real while beauty is seen as a luxury for the rich. This is diametrically opposed to the Islamic perspective, which has always been opposed to the "cult of ugliness" and has always remembered that beauty, far from being a luxury, is as necessary for the soul as the air we breathe is for the body. It is no accident that only in those urban settings deprived of sacred and traditional art and the harmony and beauty of nature have agnostics and atheists arisen and thrived. Islamic civilization avoided this pitfall by creating an art and architecture both beautiful and still in touch with nature and its underlying rhythms and harmonies.

Wherever it went, throughout its history, Islam created an atmosphere of beauty. According to a *ḥadīth,* "God hath written beauty upon the face of all things." The mission of Islam has always been to guide the soul to God both through the Divine Law and the creation of art through which the beauty written by God on the face of things would be unveiled. There has never been an authentic expression of Islam without beauty, and one could even say that the criterion of beauty can be used along with that of the truth to judge the authenticity of the claims of any movement today that seeks to use the name of and identify itself with Islam. The Quranic verse "God is with the good" (29:69) can also be translated "God is with those enmeshed in beauty."

THE SPIRITUAL SIGNIFICANCE OF ISLAMIC ART

One cannot speak of beauty in the Islamic context without saying something about Islamic art and its spiritual and religious significance. Since Islam seeks to embrace all of life, it had to create its own art just as it brought forth the Divine Law. Now, human beings both act and make. The *Sharīʿah* concerns the plane of action, while Islamic art is concerned with the principles and methods of the making of things. Both Islamic art and Islamic Law derive from the Quranic revelation and the *Sunnah* of the Prophet, but they do so in different ways. The *Sharīʿah* is based on the legal aspects of the revelation and the literal and outward meaning of the Quran and *Sunnah,* while Islamic art is derived from the *ḥaqīqah,* or inner truth, of these sources. As in other major traditions such as Christianity, Hinduism, and Buddhism, the sacred art of Islam is related to its very essence and heart. If one wants to understand what Christianity is, all one needs to do is to go inside Chartres Cathedral and behold the sacred space and forms that surround the observer. Or what better explanation of Japanese Buddhism than the Golden Temple in Kyoto? Once a European asked Titus Burckhardt, who more than any other Westerner has succeeded in revealing the meaning and spiritual significance of Islamic art, what Islam was. He answered, "Go and see the Ibn Ṭūlūn Mosque in Cairo." He could have said the same of many other masterpieces of Islamic architecture, from the Mezquita in Cordova to the Qayrawān Mosque in Tunis to the Dome of the Rock in Jerusalem or the Shāh Mosque in Isfahan and the Sulṭān Aḥmad Mosque in Istanbul.

For Westerners sensitive to art, Islamic art is in fact one of the best means of understanding the heart of Islam. The metaphysical reason why something in the material world made of brick, stucco, or stone can play such a role is that, according to the famous Hermetic saying, "That which is lowest symbolizes that which is highest." By virtue of belonging to the physical level of reality, the plastic and sonoral arts are able to symbolize and reflect the highest level of reality, which is the Divine Realm. Far from being something peripheral, Islamic art is a central manifestation of the Islamic religion. It not only plays a decisive and essential role in the life of Muslims, but is also a key for the understanding of the deepest dimensions of Islam, if one is willing to seek beyond mere formal appearances.

In Arabic the words used for art are *fann* and *ṣināʿah*. The second word, like the original Greek term *techne* and the Latin *ars,* means simply to make something according to the correct principles. The first means the know-how in doing or making anything correctly and must be combined with wisdom, or *hikmah,* to become operative as art. In traditional Islamic society art was life itself and not a particular activity, and everything from sewing to cooking to playing music or composing poetry had its own *fann*. Once A. K. Coomaraswamy, the great twentieth-century Indian expert on traditional metaphysics and art, said that in modern society the artist is a special kind of person, while in traditional society every person is a special kind of artist. This observation holds completely true for traditional Islamic society as well, where no distinction was made between fine arts and industrial arts or major and minor arts or religious and secular art. Everything was marked by the seal of Islamic spirituality.

Of course, each civilization has its own hierarchy of arts based on the formal structure of the religion that created that civilization. For example, in the West the highest form of art has been painting because of the centrality of the icon in Christianity. In contrast, there is no iconic presentation in Islamic art, since Islam, like Judaism, prohibits the painting or sculpture of the image of the Divine and its sacred art is aniconic. For Islam the highest art is, as in Christianity, related to the Word of God, which for Islam, however, is not a person named Christ, but a book known as the Quran. The writing of the Word of God, that is, calligraphy, and chanting of it, that is, Quranic psalmody, stand at the top of the hierarchy of the arts. Next comes architecture, essentially of the mosque, but also extending to other forms, where the Word of God in the form of the chanting of the Quran reverberates. The art of dress, both male and female, follows, because after our body nothing is as close to our soul as the clothing we wear. Much of the artistic creativity of Muslims went into the art of the dress based on the modesty ordained by the Quran, the theomorphic nature of the human being and its sacerdotal function in the world, and the sharp distinction between the complementary functions of men and women, including the complementary nature of the beauty belonging to each gender. After dress come the articles of the house, the so-called minor arts, such as carpets, textiles, utensils, and the like, which affect the soul much more than paintings hanging on the walls of palaces or museums do. Then there is the art of the book, which includes paintings usually called miniatures. These were originally illustrations for various scientific, literary, and historical texts, but later developed as refined Persian miniatures, which reached their peak of perfection from the fourteenth to the sixteenth centuries. The Persian miniature also led later to the Ottoman and Moghul schools of miniature painting.

Although some Persian miniatures are among the great masterpieces of world art and Islamic paintings in general are deeply appreciated in the West, painting as a whole does not occupy the same position in Islamic art as it does in Western art. But that does not mean that all forms of painting were prohibited in Islam. What is forbidden is the painting or sculpture of the Divine and of the Prophet. Furthermore, Islam opposes a naturalistic art that would seek to imitate God's creation without being able to breathe life into it; hence the almost complete lack of the art of sculpture in Islam. The few lions or other animals that do appear in some gardens are highly stylized. As a whole, Islamic piety tries to avoid setting before believers any images that might become idols or negatively affect the imaginative faculty. Therefore, there are no images of any kind in any mosques or other places of worship, and the Quran and *Ḥadīth* are never illustrated. The prohibition of nonnaturalistic paintings has been strongest historically among Arabs, who as Semites are in greater danger of confusing image and idol than most other ethnic groups. Among Persians, Turks, Indian Muslims, Malays, and Black Africans the prohibition has not been as strict. In modern times, of course, there are painters everywhere, including in the Arab world, but most modern paintings, even if they are sometimes inspired by traditional Islamic themes and motifs, are not really Islamic art, but Western-inspired art executed by artists who are Muslims.

A word must also be said about music and poetry, both of which are sonoral arts and must be considered separately from the hierarchy listed above. Although the Quran is poetry of the highest quality and eloquence, it is not called poetry in the usual sense; in fact, in one of the Quranic chapters entitled "The Poets" it is said, "As for the poets, the erring follows them" (26:224). But this criticism was cast not against poetry in general, but rather against the influential poets of pre-Islamic Mecca, soothsayers who would compose poetry for any patron without being concerned with the truth (although their poetry was of a very high quality). In fact, as a result of the impact of the Quran, poetry became a highly appreciated art in Islam, and major works of poetry appeared in Arabic, Persian, Turkish, and other Islamic languages, some of which are among the greatest masterpieces of world literature. Wherever Islam has gone, poetry has flourished, and to this day poetry is very much alive as a major cultural force in nearly every Islamic society, where it plays a much more central role culturally, religiously, and socially than it does in America and in most European countries today.

Many Westerners have heard that music is forbidden in Islam and may have even heard Muslim individuals from certain religious backgrounds express the same opinion. Yet the Quran, whose psalmody is the supreme sonoral sacred art in Islam, and the call to prayer are chanted musically throughout the Islamic world, and if one turns on the radio in a country such as the Islamic Republic of Iran one will hear the most sublime pieces of classical Persian music played throughout the day. The question of the legality of music in Islam is a complex one and the Quran, it seems providentially, did not leave specific injunctions concerning it. However, on the basis of the *Sunnah* of the Prophet and the general tenor of the teachings of the Quran, music developed differently than it did in the West. First of all, for the chanting of the Quran and other liturgies the Arabic term *mūsīqā*, which is derived from the same Greek word that is the origin of the English word "music," has never been used. Moreover, the chanting of the Quran is always done only with the human voice, and musical instruments are not allowed in mosques. In the early history of Christianity also the use of instruments was forbidden in sacred music, as we see with Gregorian chant. Second, certain kinds of music, such as music played at weddings, for the march of caravans, and for military expeditions, were allowed explicitly by the Prophet and in fact the earliest Western military bands were based on Ottoman models. We even have Mozart's famous "Turkish March." As for other forms of music, what incited the passions toward evil acts was forbidden, and the door was left open for the development of the spiritual music that came to be cultivated by the Sufis over the centuries.

Several decades ago the world-famous violinist Yehudi Menuhin came to Tehran, and we arranged for him to hear classical Persian music for the first time. After listening to the concert he said, "This music is the ladder between the soul and God." Being the great musician and human being that he was, he detected immediately the spiritual quality of this classical musical tradition, a quality also shared by classical Arabic, Turkish, Muslim Indian, and other traditions as far away as the Sundanese music of Java. The famous theologian and Sufi al-Ghazzālī wrote that music intensifies the passions within the soul. If the passion is directed toward God, it makes this passion more powerful and increases the fire of love for God; and if there exists passion for worldliness, it increases the soul's worldliness and tendency toward concupiscence. Islam was fully aware of this reality and limited exteriorized forms of music in favor of interiorized music, which increases the love for God, is the means of recollection of paradisal realities, and intensifies the upward currents that help the wings of the soul to fly to its original celestial homeland.

The traditions of music in the Islamic world are among the richest in the world. Over the ages they have not only enriched the lives of numerous Muslims and played an important role in Sufi practice, they have also influenced Western music in many ways. Whenever I hear flamenco music I feel as if I were hearing classical Arabic or Persian music. The Western lute was adapted from the Arabic *ʿūd*, as the name itself reveals, and the guitar is the child of the Persian *tār*. Today there is much interest in the Islamic musical traditions in the West, in a musical language that speaks of the deepest realities of Islam without the use of alien theological categories.

In recent years many heard of the Taliban's banning of music in Afghanistan, a land that has always been a treasure-house for several musical traditions in the Islamic world.

But this ban was far from being a common norm in Islamic history. Rather, it was like certain bans imposed in the past by strict Protestant groups on certain forms of art, including music, in the West. In the traditional Islamic world, one always heard and still hears to a large extent the sound of spiritual songs *(nashīd)* in Egypt; the *ney* of the Mawlawīs in Turkey; the *tār* and *santūr* playing the *dastgāhs*, or systems of classical Persian music, in Persia; the Andalusian orchestra in Morocco; the *qawwālī* (made famous in the West by Nuṣrat Fātiḥ 'Alī Khān) in Pakistan and Muslim India; rhythmic drumbeats in Muslim Black Africa; and many other forms of spiritual music that permeated the air and accompanied throughout their lives those sensitive to the melodies and harmonies of music. Far from being un-Islamic, as some have claimed, the art of music in the Islamic world is one of the most powerful and universal means of expressing what lies at the heart of the Islamic message, which is the realization of the beauty of the Divine Face and surrender to that Reality which is at once Beauty and Peace, Compassion and Love.

Islamic art in its many forms is of the greatest import for the understanding of the essence of Islam and a central means of transmitting its message to the contemporary world. When one thinks of Islam, one should go beyond the repetitive scenes on television of wars and battles, which unfortunately abound in today's world, to behold the peace and harmony of Islamic art seen in the great mosques, traditional urban settings and gardens, and the rhythm and geometry of calligraphy and arabesque designs; read in the poems that sing of the love that permeates all of God's creation and binds creatures to God; and heard in the strains of melodies that echo what we had experienced in that primordial morn preceding creation and our descent into this lowly world. Today more than ever before, the understanding of Islamic art is an indispensable key for the comprehension of Islam itself. Those who are sensitive to the language of traditional art and the beauty of a paradisal order that emanates from it as well as the intellectual principles conveyed through it can learn much from this art.

IḤSĀN: VIRTUOUS BEAUTY, BEAUTIFUL VIRTUE

The highest form of beauty in this world is the beauty of the human soul, which is related to *iḥsān,* a term that means at once beauty, goodness, and virtue. To possess *iḥsān* is to have the virtues of generosity and love and to live at peace in one's Center, where God resides. The Quran states, "Surely We created man in the best of stature" (90:4). The word "best" in this verse is *aḥsan,* which comes from the same root as *iḥsān* and also means "beauty." The verse could therefore also be translated as "in the most beautiful stature." To embellish the soul with beauty, or *iḥsān,* through spiritual practice is therefore to realize the original beauty of the soul and to return it to its primordial state of "the most beautiful stature." To gain and practice *iḥsān* is also to respond with the beauty of one's soul to the Creator, Who is called the best or most beautiful of creators in the Quran (23:14) and to Whom belong the most beautiful Names (7:180). Even the famous Quranic verse "Is the reward of goodness ought save goodness *(iḥsān)*?" (55:60) can also be understood to mean "Is the reward of beauty but beauty?" Is the reward of the soul beautified through *iḥsān* but the Beauty of the One?

The goal of human life is to beautify the soul through goodness and virtue and to make it worthy of offering to God Who is *the* Beautiful. Those who possess *iḥsān* think through *iḥsān* and act and create with *iḥsān*. Their thoughts are based on the truth of which beauty is the aura and splendor, their actions are always based on *iḥsān* as goodness, and what they create reflects the beauty of the object "written by God upon its face" as well as the beauty of the soul of the artisan. To possess *iḥsān* is to be open to the Divine Compassion and Mercy and to be compassionate toward others. It is to love God and His creation in Him. It is to live at peace in the Center of one's being in a state of equilibrium and harmony with the worlds within and without. And it is to be immersed in beauty on all its levels of manifestation, beauty that liberates us from the confinements of earthly existence and ultimately immerses us in the ocean of Divine Infinitude. To realize *iḥsān* is, according to the already quoted *ḥadīth* of Gabriel, to worship God as if we were to see Him, and if we were not to see Him, He would see us. It is therefore to live in Divine Intimacy, where the perfume and vision of God's Compassion, Love, Peace, and Beauty are most evident. The person who has realized *iḥsān* is fully aware of the centrality of the qualities of compassion and love, peace and beauty in the Islamic spiritual universe and is able to see with the inner eye the verse written on the Divine Throne, "Verily My Mercy and Compassion precede My Wrath."

Six

DIVINE AND HUMAN JUSTICE

Peace and the Question of War

O believers, be ye steadfast before God,
witness for justice.

Quran 5:8

God loves the just.

Quran 5:42

Shall I inform you of a better act than fasting,
alms, and prayers? Making peace between
one another: enmity and malice tear up
heavenly rewards by the roots.

Prophetic ḥadīth

I bear witness that He is Justice
and that He acts justly.

'Alī ibn Abī Ṭālib, Nahj al-balāghah

THE INNATE HUMAN SENSE OF JUSTICE AND THE SEARCH FOR JUSTICE

Like the sense of peace and nostalgia for peace, the sense of justice and quest for its realization seem to have been kneaded into the very substance from which humanity was created. No matter how ambiguous and dim the philosophical, theological, and even juridical meaning of justice may be in our minds, our souls have in their depth a sense of justice that shines within our conscience, and a fire burns deep within us urging us to live justly, to administer justice, and to protect what we perceive to be just. Messengers, apostles, and sages—from the Hebrew prophets, Zoroaster, and Confucius to Solon, Plato, and Aristotle to Christ, the Prophet of Islam, and countless later religious thinkers, including Muslims—have uttered numerous statements and written many texts on the subject. Sacred scriptures from the Upanishads and the Bible to the Quran contain many illuminating passages on the centrality of justice to the moral and spiritual life. Every people and nation speaks of justice even when injustice abounds in this world, and the human spirit seems no more able to live without justice than it can without beauty, peace, love, and compassion.

And yet when it comes to the understanding of the exact meaning of justice, on the formal plane the concept differs in various religions and moral philosophies and even within a single religious universe. The case of Islam is no exception. The theme of justice permeates the whole of Islamic life and the Divine Law, the goal of whose implementation *is* the establishment of justice. The Quran is strewn with references to the subject of justice and identifies the good society with a just one. This virtue is so central to Islam that, according to a saying of the Prophet, "A kingdom might survive in infidelity, but it cannot survive in injustice and inequity." But for Muslims, as for Jews, who are addressed so often in the Torah on matters pertaining to justice, and Christians, so many of whose greatest religious thinkers have been primarily concerned with the issue, as well as for followers of other religions, some of the major questions are as follows: What does it mean to say that God is just and what does justice mean in this context? How does God judge and how can we judge in justice? What is the meaning of justice on the human plane and why, despite all the teachings of religion about justice, is there so much injustice in this world?

One truth, evident for and accepted by all Muslims, is that God is just and justice is related to Him and the truths revealed by Him through His prophets. But within this general framework, there have been many interpretations over the ages by various schools of Islamic thought on this central issue, as there have been for Christians and Jews. Needless to say, we cannot deal with these theological and philosophical differences here, but we can turn to certain basic tenets universally accepted by Muslims and seek to understand in the Islamic context some of the essential features of the central reality of justice and the means of living and acting justly, on the one hand, and opposing injustice, oppression, and inequity, on the other.

DIVINE JUSTICE

In the same way that Compassion and Love, Peace and Beauty are Names of God, Justice is also a Divine Name. God is *al-ʿĀdil,* as well as *al-ʿAdl, al-Muqsit,* and *al-*

Ḥakam, meaning the Just as well as Justice Itself, the Equitable, and the Bringer of Justice. As these Names show, one could say in the Islamic context that not only is God Just, but that He is Justice Itself in the highest sense of the term.

What, then, is the Islamic understanding of justice in itself and when applied to God? In one of his aphorisms 'Alī ibn Abī Ṭālib said, "Justice puts everything in its place." Justice is related to balance, to giving each thing its due *(ḥaqq),* to having everything be in its place according its nature, and, in keeping with what Plato said in the *Republic,* to having each person perform his or her duty in society in accordance with his or her nature. Now, God is *al-Ḥaqq,* the Truth and Reality, from which comes the word for what each thing is due and also the word for law and rights, to which we shall turn in the next chapter. Being absolute Truth and Reality, and ultimately the only Reality, without any division or delimitation in His Essence, God is Justice Itself, for He is all Himself and nothing but Himself. There is no possibility of disequilibrium or disorder, hence injustice, within Him, for there is no other reality within or outside of Him to even make possible bringing such a thing about. Metaphysically and theologically speaking, only God is in fact perfect and infinite justice as well as the perfect dispenser of justice.

Over the centuries, Muslim theologians debated whether whatever God did was just by virtue of its being His act, or whether God, being God, could not but act justly and His being just was comprehensible to us according to the discernment of our intelligence given by Him. The Ash'arites, who dominated Sunni theology for a millennium, took the first position and the Sunni Mu'tazilites as well as the Shī'ites took the second position. But the net result, as far as the general Islamic worldview is concerned, was the same, namely, that God is perfectly just and the perfect administrator of justice throughout His creation. The Quran asserts, "Perfect is the Word of thy Lord in truth and justice" (6:115); also, "Maintaining His creation in justice, there is no god save He" (3:18). God has created all things according to justice and wants men and women, to whom He has given free will, to be just. Three times in the Quran it is asserted that God loves the just.

It is on the basis of this cosmic and also human justice that God judges human beings. The Quran confirms the central importance of the role of God as judge as revealed earlier in the Torah. In fact, the Quran states explicitly, "We gave the Children of Israel the Book, the Judgment" (45:16), and "they [the Children of Israel] have the Torah where God has delivered judgments for them" (5:108). The pious among Muslims, when confronted with enmity and oppression, shared the sentiments so powerfully expressed in the Psalms: "Arise, O Lord, in Thine anger, lift up Thyself because of the rage of mine enemies: and awake for me to the judgment that Thou hast commanded" (7:6).

In the Quranic perspective God is also the supreme judge. "Thou shalt judge between Thy servants" (39:46), and "He is the best of judges" (12:80). Moreover, the Quran asks rhetorically, "Is not God the justest of judges?" (95:8). The judgment of God is final, for "God judges; none repeals His judgment" (13:41), although the gauge of the Mercy of God is known to Him alone. Ultimately God is in fact the only judge, for "the judgment is God's alone" (6:57), "His is the judgment" (28:88). Although, of course, human judgment exists in this world, for Muslims, as for devout Jews and Christians, who over the millennia relied upon the judgment of God and His justice above all human agencies, the ultimate refuge resides in Divine Justice and God's judgment of human actions. It is only He who knows all things and who can judge human actions not only outwardly, but according to the intention in the heart, the intention being what determines the value of an action according to the famous saying of the Prophet, "Actions are judged according to their intentions." Throughout their lives, Muslims, whenever called to human judgment, recall, "Shall I seek after any judge but God?" (6:114), although this spiritual attitude does not negate in any way their responsibility before the Divine Law or even human laws, or *'urf,* and the human agencies established to judge men and women in this world according to established laws. The ultimate judge is, however, God and the ultimate judgment, the events of the Day of Judgment, the only judgment that finally matters.

THE BALANCE

Before turning to the eschatological (end-time) realities and the Day of Judgment according to Islamic doctrines, a word must be said about a key Quranic symbol related to justice and God's ultimate judgment of us. That symbol is the balance *(al-mīzān),* mentioned several times in the Quran and repeated in many contexts in various classical texts dealing with ethics and other subjects. God created all things in the correct proportion and harmony, and the world is dominated by this remarkable harmony, which is the imprint of unity upon the domain of multiplicity. As the Quran says, "And the earth we have spread out: set thereon mountains firm and immovable and produced therein all kinds of things in due balance" (15:19).

The balance applies to every level of reality, from the physical to the alchemical, psychological, and spiritual. There is a balance of the elements within healthy bodies, and our psyche, if wholesome, is balanced. And for the spiritually accomplished Muslim there is a balance between the spirit, soul, and body and the satisfaction of their respective demands. To give each thing its due *(ḥaqq)* in accordance with its nature as created by God is to live in balance and realize the balance of things and hence to live in justice. Balance also involves human actions. The Quranic injunction "Give full measure and full weight in justice" (6:152) applies to selling things honestly in the bazaar as well as acting justly in every instance in life. Our actions in general are in fact "weighed" by God in a "balance," and we shall be judged accordingly on the Day of Reckoning, for "We [God] shall set up the just balances for the Resurrection Day" (21:47). The balance as the visible symbol of justice as well as harmony and equilibrium in the cosmos is so significant that the Quran asserts, "God it is who hath revealed the book with Truth and the Balance" (57:25). To observe the balance in all things is to live in justice. There is no sculpture in traditional Islamic art, but the Western statue of a blindfolded figure holding a balance found in so many courts and halls of justice is helpful here. The balance may be said to symbolize the Islamic idea of justice and the blindfolded figure to represent equality before God's Law. Muslims are ever reminded to "establish weight with justice and fall not short in the balance" (55:9), for one day they will face the supreme balance before the Judge whose justice is infinite and judgment perfect, although His Mercy and Compassion are also boundless.

ISLAMIC ESCHATOLOGICAL DOCTRINES

All Muslims, of whatever school, believe in the afterlife, Heaven and hell, the Day of Judgment, and other eschatological realities, which in many cases are similar to traditional Christian doctrines. Belief in *ma'ād*, literally "return" to God, or what is theologically known as eschatology, is part of the credo of Islam. It is discussed here rather than earlier, because the necessity of accepting the reality of the afterlife is so closely related to the realization of the reality of Divine Justice. People live in a world full of injustice, and if one accepts Divine Justice, it therefore becomes necessary to also accept the reality of other worlds and posthumous experiences for the human soul in which ultimate justice is to be found. Even Immanuel Kant, who was metaphysically "agnostic," turned to God in his moral and practical philosophy precisely over the question of justice. In any case, the reality of the afterlife is so intense for Muslims, even today, that the moral dilemma of a just God creating an unjust world so much discussed in the West does not seriously arise for them. They remain aware that our judgment of any life on earth is based on only a small segment of the total arc of a life whose fullness we cannot behold.

The scientistic philosophy that arose from modern science has deprived most of the well-educated classes in the West, and especially in Europe, of serious belief in the afterlife, and recently, on the basis of this skepticism, many have tried to make a mockery of the Islamic conception of the afterlife based on the Quran and *Ḥadīth.* Interestingly enough, the same skeptics say little about Hindu or Buddhist eschatology nor care to remember the text of the greatest work of Western Christian literature, the *Divine Comedy* of Dante. It therefore becomes necessary to say a few words about the complicated subject of Islamic eschatology, which is one of the main themes of the Quran and to which many *ḥadīths* of the Prophet are devoted.

Muslims understand eschatology in two senses: one concerning the individual and the other human history. As far as the second is concerned, Muslims, like Christians, believe that there is an end to human history and that this end will be marked by Divine intervention in the temporal order with the coming of the Mahdī and his rule, followed by the Second Coming of Christ—and not the Prophet—in Jerusalem, the destruction of the world, resurrection, and final judgment before God. Few in the West realize the central role that Christ plays in Islamic eschatology, just as he does in the Christian understanding of the last days. As for the individual, eschatological doctrines teach us that at the moment of death the angel of death appears to take a person's life, after which the person enters various paradisal, purgatorial, or infernal states depending upon that person's actions in this world. In the deepest sense we are weaving our posthumous bodies with our actions in this life. Muslims, like Christians, also believe in the resurrection of the body and not only in the immortality of the soul.

Now, the extreme complexities of eschatological realities cannot be expressed for most people in ordinary human language save through certain simplifications that we see in both Christianity and Islam. Islam, like Christianity, presents ordinary believers with the grand choice between Heaven and hell with purgatorial states in between. In esoteric Islamic teachings, such as the writings of Ibn 'Arabī and Mullā Ṣadrā, however, a more nuanced picture is developed that deals with the journey of the soul through various posthumous states and that also explains the hierarchies of the heavens, purgatories, and hells, in the manner of a Dante. There are, in fact, books in Arabic and Persian that are Islamic counterparts of the Tibetan *Book of the Dead*.

Furthermore, descriptions of posthumous realities must of necessity be symbolic, whether one speaks of the crystalline celestial Jerusalem of the Revelation of John or the gardens, houris, and rivers of paradise in the Quran. For centuries in the West certain critics of Islam sought to denigrate the Islamic paradise as nothing but a realm of sensual gratification in the same way that the paradise of the Native Americans was described pejoratively as "the happy hunting ground." This childish and shallow criticism has now returned when the question of suicide bombers who are considered martyrs by their supporters comes up in the Western media. It is true that the Quran uses very concrete language to describe paradise and hell, a language that should not be strange in its concreteness, if not the specific symbols used, for those who are familiar with the Book of Revelation or the *Divine Comedy.* This concrete Quranic language is, however, symbolic and must not be taken only literally, although the literal meaning also has its significance.

Now, the description of paradise seems at first sight to be simply the sublimation of earthly pleasures, including sexuality. In reality the reverse is true. Every legitimate experience of a pleasing nature here on earth is only a shadow and reflection of a paradisal reality. The most intense physical experience for the human being, which is sexual union, is a reflection of the union of the soul with God and reflects on its own level something of that supreme joy and expansion. The fruits we eat here on earth are blessings from God, reflecting fruits of paradise. Even the traditional gardens of the earth are reflections of heavenly archetypes. The very word "paradise" comes from the Middle Persian term *pardīs* (meaning "garden"), which is also the origin of the Arabic word *firdaws,* meaning "paradise." It is not true that *firdaws* is simply a sublimation of the experience of a cool garden in the desert heat, while the same word in its English form, namely "paradise," refers to spiritual realities. Rather, every traditional garden here below is the reflection of *firdaws,* and paradise is a spiritual reality for Muslims as well as Christians. The attitude of Muslims, including martyrs, toward paradise is basically no different from that of countless devout Christians, including, of course, martyrs and saints.

What is different in the present-day context is that many in Europe and to a lesser extent in America have lost all belief in the afterlife, and for them human life is limited to the years spent here on earth. For most Muslims, however, as for still devout Christians, earthly life is only a segment of our total life. Human life was created by God to transcend the few days spent here on earth. The ups and downs of this life are trials sent by God, as the Quran asserts. What is important is to live in justice and to do what is good, to which the Quran refers in numerous passages as *'amal ṣāliḥ,* or "good works," remembering that as the Quran says, "And whoso doeth good an atom's weight will see it then. And whose doeth ill an atom's weight will see it then" (99:7–8). Conscious of Divine Justice but also of God's infinite Mercy, Muslims live in open awareness of the realities of worlds beyond, and even today function in a world in which there is greater communication and rapport with realities that transcend the life of this world than there is for most modern Westerners. This awareness affects many aspects of life, including the understanding of God's Justice, the significance of our actions for the ultimate end of our soul beyond the grave, and the meaning of human life itself.

JUSTICE IN THIS WORLD: THE VIEWS OF 'ALĪ

Of all the companions of the Prophet no one said and wrote as much about justice as 'Alī, whose *Path of Eloquence (Nahj al-balāghah)* contains some of the most important metaphysical and practical discussions about justice.

It was ʿAlī who insisted that God is not only just, but Justice Itself and that the virtue of justice flows into the souls of human beings from God. Since God *is* justice, everything that He does is just. But according to ʿAlī human beings must also be just to God as well as to His creatures. To be just to God is to be godly and virtuous and to fulfill the goal for which He created us, namely to worship Him. To be just to His creatures is to pay each thing its due and act toward that creature according to its rights. ʿAlī insists throughout his sermons, aphorisms, and letters that justice is related to worship and sincere piety. By drawing closer to God, human beings also become more just, since the virtue of justice flows within their being to an ever greater degree as they draw nearer to the Divine Proximity. Justice is both the effect of worship, for through worship we are just toward God, and the cause of justice, for worship draws us even closer to the Source of all justice. In the same way that for Plato "gazing" upon the Supreme Good was the source of justice, so in Islam, as expounded explicitly by ʿAlī, worship of the One is the fount of justice.

ʿAlī also wrote much about justice in the practical realm of political and social life. Even when he held political power himself, he warned against the corrupting influence of power and pointed out how easily justice can be turned into its opposite, which is oppression or evildoing *(ẓulm)* in the hands of a heedless or corrupt ruler. He emphasized that God has made obligatory the rights of the ruler over the ruled, that the ruled will not be virtuous without their ruler being virtuous and just, and that, conversely, the ruler will not be virtuous if the ruled are not so. Each must pay the other its due *(ḥaqq)*, and only in this way can justice be established in society.

In the years when he was the political as well as spiritual head of the Islamic community, ʿAlī demonstrated his views of justice in many ways and established norms that became ideals, along with the *Sunnah* of the Prophet (especially his practices in governing the Medina community) and the practices of other "rightly guided" caliphs, for many during the centuries that followed. Among the most important texts of 'Alī on the question of justice on behalf of a ruler is his letter to the governor he had appointed for Egypt, Mālik al-Ashtar. This letter, which is still widely read in the Islamic world and whose message is set as an ideal by which existing rulers are judged by many pious people, Sunni and Shī'ite alike, demonstrates the centrality of justice and equity as well as forgiveness and compassion for a good government according to the traditional Islamic perspective. 'Alī writes to Mālik:

> In the Name of God, the Merciful, the Compassionate:
>
> This is that with which 'Alī, the servant of God and Commander of the Faithful, charged Mālik ibn al-Hārith al-Ashtar in his instructions to him when he appointed him governor of Egypt: to collect its land tax, to war against its enemies, to improve the condition of the people and to engender prosperity in its region. He charged him to fear God, to prefer obedience to Him (over all else) and to follow what He has directed in His Book—both the acts He has made obligatory and those He recommends—for none attains felicity but he who follows His directions, and none is overcome by wretchedness but he who denies them and lets them slip by. (He charged him) to help God—glory be to Him—with his heart, his hand and his tongue, for He—majestic is His Name—has promised to help him who exalts Him. And he charged him to break the passions of his soul and restrain it in its

recalcitrance, for the soul incites to evil, except inasmuch as God has mercy.

Know, O Mālik, that I am sending you to a land where governments, just and unjust, have existed before you. People will look upon your affairs in the same way that you were wont to look upon the affairs of the rulers before you. They will speak about you as you were wont to speak about those rulers. And the righteous are only known by that which God causes to pass concerning them on the tongues of His servants. So let the dearest of your treasuries be the treasury of righteous action. Control your desire and restrain your soul from what is not lawful to you, for restraint of the soul is for it to be equitous in what it likes and dislikes. Infuse your heart with mercy, love and kindness for your subjects. Be not in the face of them a voracious animal, counting them as easy prey, for they are of two kinds: either they are your brothers in religion or your equals in creation. Error catches them unaware, deficiencies overcome them, (evil deeds) are committed by them intentionally and by mistake. So grant them your pardon and your forgiveness to the same extent that you hope God will grant you His pardon and His forgiveness. For you are above them, and he who appointed you is above you, and God is above him who appointed you. God has sought from you the fulfillment of their requirements and He is trying you with them.

Set yourself not up to war against God, for you have no power against His vengeance, nor are you able to dispense with His pardon and His mercy. Never be regretful of pardon or rejoice at punishment, and never hasten (to act) upon an impulse if you can find a better course. Never say, "I am invested with authority, I give orders and I am obeyed," for surely that is corruption in the heart, enfeeblement of the religion and an approach to changes (in fortune). If the authority you possess engenders in you pride or arrogance, then reflect upon the tremendousness of the dominion of God above you and His power over you in that in which you yourself have no control. This will subdue your recalcitrance, restrain your violence and restore in you what has left you of the power of your reason. Beware of vying with God in His tremendousness and likening yourself to Him in His exclusive power, for God abases every tyrant and humiliates all who are proud.

See that justice is done toward God and justice is done toward the people by yourself, your own family and those whom you favor among your subjects. For if you do not do so, you have worked wrong. And as for him who wrongs the servants of God, God is his adversary, not to speak of His servants. God renders null and void the argument of whosoever contends with Him. Such a one will be God's enemy until he desists or repents. Nothing is more conducive to the removal of God's blessing and the hastening of His vengeance than to continue in wrongdoing, for God harkens to the call of the oppressed and He is ever on the watch against the wrongdoers.[1]

HUMAN JUSTICE AND ITS MODES

Of course, ordinary human beings are not like 'Alī, who had the guidance of the Quran and the Prophet in his heart and mind at all times. For ordinary men and women the question has always come up of how to be just in various concrete situations, how to recognize what is due all beings and treat them accordingly. The first guides given by God to Muslims about how to act justly are the Quran, the *Sunnah,* and the *Sharīʿah,* which, being God's Word, the teachings of His Prophet, and His Law, are of necessity the central means of understanding justice and acting justly. To live and act according to the *Sharīʿah* is to act in justice toward both God and His creation.

But what about those actions for which there are no clear Divine injunctions, Prophetic guidance, or *Sharīʿite* instructions? In such cases one must use the intelligence God has given us and rely upon the innate sense of justice written by God on the tablet of our souls. And what about situations in life when one experiences oppression rather than justice? God asks us to be just at all times, not only occasionally, and to refuse to accept oppression. "O believers! Be steadfast before God, witnesses in justice" (5:8). Muslims are constantly reminded that "My Lord hath commanded justice" (7:29), and that "You should be kind to them, and act justly toward them" (60:8). The Quran commands Muslims not only to act justly, but to speak in justice: "And if ye give your word, do justice thereunto" (6:152). And above all, Muslims must always seek to judge justly, for as the Quran commands, "If ye judge between them that ye judge justly" (4:58). Christ said, "Judge not, that ye be not judged" (Matt. 5:44). But in practical life it is not always possible to follow this exalted teaching. Although Muslims know that the supreme judge is God and ultimately only His judgment matters, there are always occasions in life when judgment is inevitable. In such cases they must act in truth and in justice.

In light of this essential necessity, courts were created on the basis of *Sharīʿite* teachings, and all cases were judged equally in such courts. In principle all Muslims are equal before Islamic Law and the judgments given on its basis. Strangely enough, while in the West an independent judiciary is the mark of the modern period, in the Islamic world *Sharīʿite* courts remained in the hands of religious scholars and were independent to a large extent of political authority until modern times. It is only since the nineteenth century that the state has come to dominate the judiciary in many Islamic countries, so that much of the earlier judiciary independence has been lost and the administration of justice has been compromised by political considerations. The question still remains about how to act justly in concrete situations when there are no clear *Sharīʿite* indications. General principles stated in the Quran and *Ḥadīth* provide an answer to this vexing question. Besides specific *Sharīʿite* injunctions, there are general teachings about doing good, being fair, seeing the view of the other side, placing truth over expediency, being objective and not self-centered, and similar moral and spiritual principles common to Islam and other authentic religions. These principles must be put into practice and the voice of one's conscience must be always heeded.

Fighting injustice, oppression, and evildoing is itself just and the means of establishing justice. The word for injustice, oppression, or evildoing in Arabic *(ẓulm)* is used as the opposite of justice and is in its various forms one of the most frequently used terms in the Quran, which states, "God wisheth not injustice for [His] creatures" (3:108). Those who are unjust and commit oppression break their covenant with God, for "My covenant shall not reach the oppressors" (2:124), and "Whosoever transgresses the bounds of God—those are the evildoers" (2:229). In more than one place in the Quran it is stated that, "God loveth not the evildoers" (e.g., 3:57) and in fact casts His wrath upon them: "The curse of God shall rest upon the evildoers" (11:18). Furthermore, the Quran and *Ḥadīth* make clear that those who are unjust and evildoing wrong themselves and that it is not God who wrongs human beings.

It might then be said that, in addition to following the *Sharīʿah* and acting according to the principles of the Quran and *Ḥadīth* mentioned above, to live and act justly means to combat oppression, evildoing, and injustice. The Quran itself unfolds the epic battle between justice and injustice in the individual as well as in the social domain. To live under unjust human laws or unjust applications of just laws or under tyranny and oppression with disregard for the law obliges Muslims to battle against the injustice being imposed upon them. It is even said that to accept oppression without reacting to establish justice is worse than the original oppression and injustice.

Of course, not all human beings are alike; nor have all Muslims always arisen against oppression and injustice, but the ideal is very central to the Islamic concept of justice and a just society. Furthermore, the presence of this ideal has from time to time led to exertion on both the individual and collective level to reestablish justice. This innate desire for justice is, of course, not unique to Islam; nor is the impetus to act to overcome injustice. The history of the West is also replete with episodes of individual or collective action to overcome oppression and injustice. When some people attack Islam for inciting struggle in the name of justice, they forget the Boston Tea Party and the American Revolution, not to speak of so many other major political and social movements based on the perceived notion of correcting the wrong of injustice and oppression. Where the case of Islam differs from modern Western phenomena of this nature is that the claim to the establishment of justice is still seen by Muslims in Islamic terms and not in secular, humanistic ones. That the establishment of justice entails struggle brings us to the major question of exertion and striving in the path of God, or *jihād*.

JIHĀD

Perhaps in modern times in the West no word in the vocabulary of the Islamic religion has been as distorted, maligned, misunderstood, and vilified as the word *jihād*, thanks not only to the Western media looking for demonizing epithets and stereotypes, but also to those extremist Muslims who readily provide them with examples to justify their propagation of the distorted image of this term. Now, matters are made worse by the fact that the word *jihād* has gained commercial appeal in Europe and America; a number of authors, seeking to attract a larger public and make their books commercially successful, have been trying hard to use the term in their titles in any way possible. Some have even changed the meaning of *jihād* to imply any local resistance and "tribalism" against the globalization process, whereas, in fact, in Islamic history itself, especially during the earlier centuries, *jihād* was often fought against "tribalism" and all the centrifugal forces that threatened the unity of the Islamic community. To explain the authentic meaning of *jihād* requires clearing the slate completely of all the prevalent misunderstandings that unfortunately continue to be perpetuated in the Western media and much of Western literature concerned with Islam.

In Arabic the term *jihād* is derived from the root *jhd*, meaning "to strive" or "to exert effort," and in the context of Islam this striving and exertion are understood to be in the path of God. The person who performs such a task is called a *mujāhid*, usually translated as "holy warrior" in the Western media, as *jihād* itself is conveniently translated as "holy war." One has only to recall that, in Sufi contemplation, the state of combating the distractions of the soul is also called *mujāhidah* to realize how limitative such a current translation is.

To understand the significance of *jihād* in Islam and its civilization, we must first of all distinguish between a general, popular meaning of the term and the theological and juridical sense of the word. In the first sense, it is used to mean any effort considered worthy, much like "crusade" in its general sense in English and not in particular reference to the religious wars carried out by Western Christianity against both Muslims and Jews in Palestine in the Middle Ages. In the same way that in English one says that such and such an organization is carrying out a crusade to eradicate poverty or disease, in Islamic languages one can say that this or that group or government agency is carrying out a *jihād* to, let us say, build houses for the poor. In Iran today there is in fact a movement and organization called *jihād-i sāzandigī* (that is, *jihād* for "construction"), whose function it is to exert effort to build housing for the poor and carry out similar projects. Also in the same way that throughout Western history certain wars have been fought in the name and spirit of a crusade, but without the blessing of the pope, who commissioned the medieval Crusades, in Islam some people have fought battles they have called *jihād*, although these battles were not, technically speaking, *jihād* according to Islamic Law or sanctioned by the *'ulamā'*, or religious scholars. To say the least, the West has no less of a crusading spirit than Islam has a *jihādic* one, if both terms are used in their popular sense. In fact, during the past millennium the West has carried out many more wars in foreign countries as crusades for all kinds of causes—such as spreading Christianity, "civilizing missions" (*la mission civilisatrice* of the French), and disseminating modern ideologies from Communism to capitalism—than Islam has carried out *jihād*.

In the same way, however, that we must distinguish between the medieval Crusades, condoned and in fact directed by the Church, and this general usage of "crusade" in European languages, we must not confuse the general social and cultural use of the term *jihād* with its strict theological and juridical sense in Islam. Beyond this dichotomy, it is important to consider what *jihād* means in the context of Islam and the practices of its followers. To understand this more exact and pertinent meaning, it is necessary to go back to the root meaning of the term as "exertion and striving in the path of God." On this basic level it might be said that all of life, according to Islam, is a *jihād,* because it is a striving to live according to the Will of God, to exert oneself to do good and to oppose evil. We are cast into a world in which there is disequilibrium and disorder both externally and within our souls. To create a life of equilibrium based on surrender to God and following His injunctions involves constant *jihād,* in the same way that a sailor on a windy sea needs to exert constant effort just to keep the boat on an even keel and continue to sail toward the chosen destination.

To wake up in the morning with the Name of God on one's lips, to perform the prayers, to live righteously and justly throughout the day, to be kind and generous to people and even animals and plants one encounters during the day, to do one's job well, and to take care of one's family and of one's own health and well-being all require *jihād* on this elemental level. Since Islam does not distinguish between the secular and religious domains, the whole life cycle of a Muslim involves a *jihād,* so that every component and aspect of it is made to conform to Divine norms. *Jihād* is not one of the "pillars" *(arkān)* of Islam, as are the canonical prayers or fasting. But the performance of all the acts of worship *(ʿibādāt)* certainly involves *jihād.* To pray five times a day regularly throughout one's life is certainly not possible without great effort, or *jihād,* on our part, save for the saints, who are always in prayer and in a sense have to carry out a *jihād* to tear themselves away from prayer to perform the chores of daily life. Likewise, for ordinary believers fasting from dawn to dusk is certainly a *jihād* and requires great effort on the part of the human will for the sake of God. The same holds true for the other acts of worship, or *ʿibādāt.*

Jihād is, however, also required in the domain of transactions, or *muʿāmalāt,* if one is going to live an honest and upright life. Not only acts of worship, which directly concern our relation with God, but also other human acts affect the soul and must be carried out ethically and justly. But the soul is not always given to the good and the just. Therefore, to be upright and to perform acts of everyday life in accordance with the Divine Law and Islamic ethical norms is to carry out a constant *jihād.* There are many simple people in the Islamic world trying to make an honest living in difficult circumstances who consider their everyday work to be a *jihād.* I have heard many a taxi driver in Persia and the Arab countries say he had to support a large extended family and worked fourteen hours a day to do so, adding that every day for him was a *jihād.* To live in equilibrium in a chaotic world and a morally upright life in a society in which there are so many temptations to accept and participate in corruption is to carry out *jihād.* Also to try to overcome ignorance and to attain knowledge, the highest kind of which is the knowledge of God, is a major form of *jihād* and in fact its highest form. In its widest sense, therefore, it might be said that for a Muslim life itself is a *jihād* and that the peace one seeks is the result of the equilibrium created through *jihād* in its basic sense of exertion on the path of God and striving to act according to His Will. The saying of the Prophet "*Jihād* remains valid until the Day of Judgment" must be understood in this universal sense of the *jihād* inherent in the general human condition in this imperfect world.

Beyond this general understanding of *jihād*, which embraces life itself, Islamic authorities over the ages have distinguished between the lesser and the greater *jihād* on the basis of a famous saying of the Prophet after the great battle of Badr, which was crucial to the survival of the newly born Islamic community. Despite the momentous significance of this battle, in which the still idolatrous Meccans sought to defeat and destroy the nascent Islamic community in Medina, the Prophet, after having achieved victory, said, "You have returned from the lesser *jihād* to the greater *(akbar) jihād*." When asked what the greater *jihād* was, he said, "It is the *jihād* against your passionate souls."

The greater, and one might also say greatest (in Arabic the word *akbar* means both "greater" and "greatest"), *jihād* is therefore the inner battle to purify the soul of its imperfections, to empty the vessel of the soul of the pungent water of forgetfulness, negligence, and the tendency to evil and to prepare it for the reception of the Divine Elixir of Remembrance, Light, and Knowledge. The greater *jihād* is undertaken only by those spiritual warriors who are willing to sacrifice their ego before the Throne of the One.

In the same way that external *jihād* as battle or war is not required of every Muslim, but only of those physically and mentally qualified, the spiritual *jihād* is also not required of every Muslim, only of those who have the spiritual and mental capability—along with the spiritual will—to follow the path to God in this life and the virtues to be worthy of remaining on it. In light of the meaning of *al-jihād al-akbar*, or greater *jihād*, it can be said that the greatest "spiritual combatants" in Islam are the saints, whose instrument of battle is, however, not the sword, but prayer and the rosary. Sufism in general is concerned with this greater *jihād*, which is similar to the "spiritual warfare" known so widely in Orthodox Christianity and also mentioned by certain Western Christian mystics and to the spiritual exertions of Hindu and Buddhist sages, in whose words and deeds numerous parallels can be found.

As for the lesser *jihād*, in the sense of outward struggle and battle, the meaning of *jihād* as the Western media use it, a distinction must first of all be made between the struggles and battles carried out within Arabia against idolatry at the dawn of Islam and events in later Islamic history. In Arabia the idolaters were given the choice of embracing Islam or fighting against Muslims, because according to Islamic belief God did not want such a crass form of idolatry to survive. This was similar to arguments given by Christianity when it rooted out by force what remained of the decadent Greco-Roman and northern European religions, once it gained sufficient power. But even in Arabia *jihād* was not carried out against Jews and Christians in order to force them to convert to Islam, nor was this policy carried out generally later outside Arabia against Jews and Christians, or for that matter against Zoroastrians or Hindus, as was mentioned earlier. During Islamic history some rulers invaded non-Muslim lands and even spoke of *jihād*, but rarely was a juridical edict given by the *'ulamā'* that such battles were a *jihād* to convert people to Islam. The view of Western orientalists and centuries of Christian polemicists on this issue is simply not correct. The principle of "There is no compulsion in religion" (2:256) did not allow *jihād* outside of Arabia during the lifetime of the Prophet to include forced religious conversion of the "People of the Book." Likewise, it is forbidden to carry out *jihād* against other Muslims to bring them to one's own persuasion.

In fact, all Shī'ite and most Sunni jurists, especially in modern times, believe that *jihād* is legitimate only as defense *(difā'ī)* and cannot be originated as aggression *(ibtidā'ī)*. As far as Twelve-Imām Shī'ism is concerned, throughout the centuries and including today, all the eminent authorities have asserted that *jihād*, except for defense, is *ḥarām*, or forbidden, by Islamic Law in the absence of the *ma'ṣūm*, that is, "the inerrant one" (or one who is impeccable in the etymological sense of this term), which in the context of Shī'ite Islam means the Prophet and the Imāms. In Sunni Islam, historically some jurists have ordered a *jihād* in an offensive mode based on a argument one might call "the best defense is an offense," but since the 1950s with the pronouncements of the Shaykh al-Azhar of the time, Maḥmūd Shaltūt, who occupied what is the most influential and significant religious position in the Sunni world, the mainstream Sunni position has been like the Shī'ite one. The reputable religious scholars of the Sunni world agree that the only *jihād* permissible is a defensive one, which is incumbent on the Islamic community as a whole once its existence is threatened. This does not mean, however, that any extremist group can carry out violence by appealing to the need to defend Islam, for in every case authorization of the *jihād* by the head of the Islamic state and the authoritative *'ulamā'* is required.

The Quranic verse "Fight in the way of God against those who fight against you, but begin not hostilities. Verily God loveth not aggressors" (2:190) has provided the scriptural basis and the principle for judging the legitimacy of *jihād*. It must be recalled that, during the past century and a half, all those who have fought against foreign invaders or occupiers, whether they were in West Africa, Algeria, Bosnia, Kosovo, Palestine, Kashmir, or the Philippines, and have spoken of *jihād*, have done so in a defensive sense. There have been no Muslim *jihāds* in non-Islamic lands. Those who carry out terror in the West or elsewhere in the name of *jihād* are vilifying an originally sacred term, and their efforts have not been accepted by established and mainstream religious authorities as *jihād* in the juridical and theological sense of the term. The declarations of Shaykh al-Azhar, the most authoritative religious voice in Sunni Islam, condemning in no uncertain terms the terrorist acts of September 11, 2001, in America is a clear example.

This naturally brings up the important question of who can declare *jihād*. In classical Sunni theory based on the existence of an Islamic state, it was the sovereign in consultation with the *'ulamā'* who could declare *jihād* in the juridical and theological sense. And without the existence of an authentic Islamic state, it was the leading religious authorities, the *'ulamā'*, and more precisely *muftīs*, who had such a prerogative. Although each Muslim stands directly before God and there is no priesthood in Islam, no one can simply declare *jihād* by virtue of being nominally Muslim and wielding some political or military power. The difference between the declaration of *jihād* in the Islamic sense and its everyday declaration by various extremist groups here and there is as great as the difference between the declaration of a crusade against this or that evil by a Western political or social leader and the declaration of the Crusades by Pope Urban II in 1095.

When a legitimate *jihād* is to be carried out, it must not be based on anger and hatred that would blind one to justice. The Quran warns Muslims in no uncertain terms when it states, "Let not hatred of a people cause you to be unjust" (5:8). Grievance can turn to anger and hatred, but that cannot be the basis of blind revenge. *Jihād* cannot be carried out against the innocent, and even the enemy must be treated in justice and even kindness. One should "repel the evil deed with one which is better, then verily he, between whom and thee there was enmity (will become) as though he were a bosom friend" (41:34). And above all *jihād* must be carried out for the truth and the truth alone, not on the basis of anger, hatred, or revenge. Traditionally even external *jihād* has been associated in the Muslim mind with magnanimity, generosity, and detachment, with all the virtues associated with chivalry.

A story in Book I of the *Mathnawī* of Rūmī about 'Alī ibn Abī Ṭālib, the prince of those who carry out *jihād* for God alone, is very revealing as far as the Islamic understanding of *jihād* is concerned. In a one-to-one battle with a great enemy of Islam who was a powerful warrior, 'Alī was able to subdue his opponent and throw him to the ground. As a last act of hatred the enemy warrior spat in 'Alī's face, upon which 'Alī immediately got up from his position of sitting on the enemy's chest and sheathed his sword. The warrior became surprised and asked 'Alī why he had done such a thing. 'Alī answered that until then he was fighting for the Truth *(al-Ḥaqq),* but as soon as he was spat upon he became angry; recognizing this, he ceased to battle because he did not want to fight on the basis of personal rage and anger. As Rūmī puts it:

He spat on the face of 'Alī
The pride of every prophet and saint. . . .
And 'Alī responded,
He said, "I wield the sword for the sake of the Truth,
I am the servant of the Truth, not commanded by
the body.
I am the Lion of the Truth, not the lion of passions,
My action is witness to my religion."[2]

The action of this prototype of all authentic Islamic *mujāhids,* which led to a change of heart in his enemy, should serve as a salutary correction for, first, those who in the name of Islam carry out actions based on rage but call them *jihād* and, second, those in the West who continue to speak of holy or sacred rage among Muslims who are trying on the basis of justice to protect their home and religion. When one looks beyond current aberrations of so-called *jihād* by certain extremists to the long history of Islam, one sees numerous examples of the kind of chivalry exemplified in its supreme form by 'Alī in such warrior-heroes as Saladin, whose chivalry was proverbial even among his Western enemies, and in more recent figures such as Amīr 'Abd al-Qādir, 'Abd al-Karīm, and 'Umar al-Mukhtār in North Africa; Imām Shamil in Caucasia; the Brelvis in the northwest provinces of India; and more recently Aḥmad Shāh Mas'ūd, who participated in the Afghan war against the Soviet Union and was assassinated shortly before the September 11, 2001, tragedy in America. All such figures were not only pious and chivalrous, but were attached to the inner dimension of Islam and some were saints. None was the product of a narrow, literalist, and exclusivist interpretation of his faith.

CONDITIONS UNDER WHICH WAR CAN BE FOUGHT

Not all wars are *jihāds,* and Islam has also promulgated certain regulations for conflict in general. First of all, war should be in self-defense and Muslims should not instigate wars, as the already cited verse, "Fight in the way of God against those who fight against you, but begin not hostilities. Verily God loveth not transgressors" (2:190), demonstrates. If, like the Bible, the Quran does speak of fighting against one's enemies, it must be remembered that Islam was born in a climate in which there were constant wars among various tribes. Still, after ordering Muslims to battle against their enemies, the Quran adds, "Except those who seek refuge with people between whom and you there is a covenant, or (those who) come unto you because their hearts forbid them to make war on you. . . . So, if they hold aloof from you and wage not war against you and offer you peace, God alloweth you no way against them" (4:90). War can be fought to avoid persecution and oppression or to preserve religious values and protect the weak from oppression. The Quran does mention the biblical "an eye for an eye," but recommends forgoing revenge and practicing charity, as in the verse, "But whoso forgoeth it [that is, an eye for an eye] it shall be expiation for him" (5:45). Also war should not go on indefinitely; as soon as the enemy sues for peace, hostilities must terminate, "But if they desist, then let there be no hostility" (2:192).

Of the utmost importance is the injunction that innocent human life must not be destroyed in any warfare, for the Quran says, "Whosoever killeth a human being for other than manslaughter or corruption in the earth, it shall be as if he had killed all humanity" (5:32). The Prophet forbade explicitly attacking women and children and even killing animals or destroying trees during war. His own magnanimous treatment of his most bitter enemies upon his conquest of Mecca has remained the supreme concrete example to be followed. Likewise, Muslims recall to this day how, upon conquering Jerusalem, 'Umar dealt with Christians and their respected sites of worship with remarkable magnanimity and justice. Needless to say, not all Muslims have followed these precepts during Islamic history any more than have all Jews, Christians, Hindus, or Buddhists followed the injunctions of their religions. But it is essential here not only for Western observers but also for many Muslims who, having lost hope, have fallen into despair and commit desperate acts to remember what the teachings of Islam as a religion are on these matters. Human nature being what it is, it is not difficult to find reasons why not all Muslims have followed the teachings of their religion in matters of war. What is remarkable is the degree to which over the ages many of the values of this spiritualized chivalry *were* followed, as witnessed over the centuries even by Western invaders from medieval knights to French officers in Algeria.

Today a new challenge has been created by the invention of modern means and methods of warfare, of the invention of weapons of mass destruction causing so-called collateral damage over which one has no control, of bombs that cannot distinguish between combatants and women and children. Now, Islamic civilization did not invent these monstrous technologies, or even the idea of total war involving whole civilian populations, but it is faced with their reality on the ground and, one might add, in the air and at sea. This situation creates an additional challenge of monumental proportions for Muslims, as it does for those Christians in the West who seek to live according to the teachings of Christ and even for many secular humanists. It is precisely at such a juncture of human history that Muslims are called upon to be most vigilant in the defense of what their religion has taught them about *jihād* and the regulations it has promulgated for any form of warfare. Moreover, any Muslim who has a sense of responsibility before God must be especially careful when he or she carries out an act explicitly in the name of Islam in a world in which inhuman and even infrahuman tools of military combat are in the hands of the powerful who dominate the global scene. Although defense of oneself, one's homeland, and one's religion and the overcoming of oppression remain religious duties, the regulations of warfare, especially the protection of the innocent, that is, nonaggression against noncombatants, and dealing with the enemy in justice, also remain part and parcel of the religion and essential to it; they cannot be cast aside with the excuse that one is responding to a grievance or injustice. If one does so, one is no longer speaking or acting in the name of Islam and is in fact in danger of defiling the religion more than its enemies ever could.

MARTYRDOM

As a result of suicide bombings and the extensive use of the term "martyr" in recent years in various Islamic countries, many people in the West have turned to the question of martyrdom in Islam, and some have even described it in the most pejorative manner as an object of ridicule. First of all, martyrdom exists in every religion. Second, Christianity relies particularly on martyrdom and celebrates its martyrs as saints more than Islam does, especially Islam in its Sunni form. It is therefore particularly strange to see some observers in the West speak of martyrdom as if it were a peculiar, solely Islamic concept. The Quran states, "Think not of those who are slain in the way of God that they are dead. Nay, they are living being nourished by their Lord" (3:169), and "They rejoice because of favor from God and kindness and that God wasteth not the wage of believers" (3:171). Therefore, just as Christian martyrs enter paradise, Muslim martyrs are also blessed and allowed entry into the paradisal states. For both, martyrdom is victory over death, and Muslim martyrs share with Christians in asking at the moment of their ultimate victory, "O Death, where is thy sting? O grave, where is thy victory?" (1 Cor. 15:55).

Who is a martyr? In Christianity, at least Catholic Christianity, this question has been decided over the centuries by the Church, but in Islam there is no official magisterium to decide ecclesiastically who is a martyr. In Twelve-Imām Shīʿite Islam martyrdom plays a more central role than in Sunnism. All the Imāms, except the Twelfth (who according to Shīʿism is still alive although in occultation), were martyred, and the martyrdom of the Third Imām, Ḥusayn ibn ʿAlī, who is called *Sayyid al-shuhadā'*, or the Master of Martyrs, is particularly important in Shīʿite piety. The Shīʿite community has also recognized a number of other martyrs who were clearly killed for religious reasons. In Sunni Islam, likewise, a number of figures have been given the title of martyr over the ages by the Islamic community *(al-ummah)*, which is the final arbiter on this matter in Sunni Islam. Sometimes the term "martyr" has also been used more politically for those killed in a religio-political struggle even within the Islamic world and by other Muslims.

The term "martyr" in Arabic is *shahīd,* which is related to the term for the supreme testification *(shahādah)* of Islam regarding Divine Unity. Furthermore, it is truly remarkable that the word *shahīd* is also related to the word *shāhid,* which means "witness," exactly as does the Greek word *martos,* from which "martyr" derives. Even the word "martyr" has therefore the same root meaning in Christianity and Islam. Furthermore, in both traditions often the same symbols were used to describe a martyr. In Shī'ism a martyr is often referred to as the lamp that burns itself but illuminates the world about it; the most famous English Catholic martyr, Thomas Becket, was also called the "bright candle on God's candlestick." In the truly spiritual sense, the *shahīd* is the person who has born witness with his or her whole being to Divine Oneness. He or she has made the supreme sacrifice of his or her own life for the sake of God, a sacrifice that has been truly for God and not for any worldly cause. Such people go to paradise because they have given their life in all sincerity to God. In this context it is also important to recall the *ḥadīth* of the Prophet, "The ink of the scholar is more precious than the blood of the martyr," which means that although martyrdom is such an exalted state, the inner *jihād* leading to the knowledge of God and His revelation (hence the ink of the scholar) is of even higher value.

But can a person become a martyr by committing suicide? Suicide itself is forbidden by Islamic Law, and those who commit it are condemned to the infernal states because they have taken upon themselves a decision that belongs to God alone. Life can be terminated legitimately only by the

Giver of life. But suicide as a desperate act to overcome oppression or to defend oneself has manifested itself on the margin of human existence everywhere. Many brave American soldiers in various wars have thrown themselves on bombs, which is an act of suicide, to save others, and we all know of the Japanese kamikazes during World War II. An especially telling case is mentioned in the Bible: Samson committed suicide by bringing the Temple of Dagon down not only on himself, but on thousands of Philistines, including women and children, because his people had been oppressed by the Philistines. Some Jews consider him a hero and some a prophet, whereas, interestingly enough, Muslims do not consider him one of the Hebrew prophets.

For Muslims, the difficult question on both moral and religious grounds concerns those who live under appalling oppression and in a state of despair and have no other means of defense except their bodies. Even in such cases the Islamic injunction that one cannot kill innocent people even in war must of necessity hold. As for using one's body as a weapon against combatants, this is an issue that is being hotly debated among experts on Islamic Law in the Islamic world today. Most believe that an act that is certain suicide must be avoided, while some believe that it is permissible as self-defense or for the protection of one's people if it does not involve innocent victims. The great tragedy is the existence of a situation in which young people fall into such a state of desperation that the question of suicide even arises. Here again, as with total warfare, the phenomenon itself, which exists among Hindu Tigers in Sri Lanka, in the case of the person who killed Rajiv Gandhi, and among Palestinians and others, is one of the fruits of modern technology that make what is now called terrorism possible, but about which few are willing to speak.

TO ESTABLISH JUSTICE AND PEACE

In conclusion, we must remember that there is no peace without justice, and justice implies a constant struggle to establish equilibrium in a world, both within and without, in which forces and tensions threaten chaos and disorder at all times. A Muslim's duty is to seek to establish peace and justice within, and on the basis of the Divine injunctions to establish justice in the world about him or her through an effort, or *jihād*, that must avoid outward war and confrontation except when absolutely necessary and in defense. But even in war, regulations set down by the religion must be observed. Today we live in a world full of strife with powerful economic, political, and cultural wars that occasionally also result in military confrontation. In such a situation Muslims must be vigilant, but also seekers of peace. Some have said that Islam displays a greater combative spirit than other religions. Now, all religions are guardians of the sacred, and Islam, coming at the end of the present human cycle, has a particularly important role in carrying out this duty. Therefore, whenever the sacred is attacked and challenged by the forces of desacralization and nihilism, Islam is destined to display a particularly combative spirit to respond to this challenge. But this response must not be at the expense of destroying the sacred message of Islam itself, based on peace and surrender to the Divine Will. Therefore, Muslims must strive to preserve the sacred and to defend justice, but not by succumbing to means that contradict and in fact destroy the very reality of not only Islam, but religion as such. Muslims must seek justice, but with humility and charity, not in self-righteousness, ever aware that absolute justice belongs to God alone and that one of the cardinal meanings of the *shahādah* is "There is no justice but the Divine Justice."

Seven

HUMAN RESPONSIBILITIES AND HUMAN RIGHTS

He it is who produceth gardens. . . . Eat ye of the fruit thereof when it fruiteth, and pay the due thereof upon the harvest day.

Quran 6:141

Let me free so that like the Sun I shall wear a robe of fire,
And within that fire like a Sun to adorn the world.

Rūmī

But is it always man who "chooses"? And who then is this "man who chooses"? Where is his limit and his center? If it is man who defines himself, what objective value can be attached to this definition? And if there is no objective value, no transcendent criterion, why think? If it is enough to be a man in order to be in the right, why seek to refer to human error?

Frithjof Schuon

TO BE HUMAN

Before speaking of human responsibilities or rights, one must answer the basic religious and philosophical question, "What does it mean to be human?" In today's world everyone speaks of human rights and the sacred character of human life, and many secularists even claim that they are the true champions of human rights as against those who accept various religious worldviews. But strangely enough, often those same champions of humanity believe that human beings are nothing more than evolved apes, who in turn evolved from lower life forms and ultimately from various compounds of molecules. If the human being is nothing but the result of "blind forces" acting upon the original cosmic soup of molecules, then is not the very statement of the sacredness of human life intellectually meaningless and nothing but a hollow sentimental expression? Is not human dignity nothing more than a conveniently contrived notion without basis in reality? And if we are nothing but highly organized inanimate particles, what is the basis for claims to "human rights"? These basic questions know no geographic boundaries and are asked by thinking people everywhere. Christianity in the West has sought to answer them on the firm theological basis that "human beings were created in the image of God" and it is the immortal soul and the spark of the Spirit within men and women that constitutes the basis for human dignity, the sacredness of human life, and ultimately human rights. In fact, many Christian thinkers, both Catholic and Protestant, as well as Jewish thinkers insist that human dignity is based on the Divine Imprint upon the human soul and that historically in the West the idea of human rights, even in its secularized version, is derived from the religious conception of the human state.

For Islam, likewise, human beings are defined in their relation to God, and both their responsibilities and rights derive from that relationship. As mentioned earlier, Islam believes that God breathed His Spirit into Adam and according to the famous *ḥadīth,* "God created Adam in His form," "form" meaning the reflection of God's Names and Qualities. Human beings therefore reflect the Divine Attributes like a mirror, which reflects the light of the Sun. By virtue of being created as this central being in the terrestrial realm, the human being was chosen by God as His vicegerent *(khalīfat Allāh)* as well as His servant *('abd Allāh)*. As servants human beings must remain in total obedience to God and in perfect receptivity before what their Creator wills for them. As vicegerents they must be active in the world to do God's Will here on earth. The Islamic conception of *insān,* or man, as the *anthropos* encompassing both the male and female states, can be summed up as the wedding of these two qualities in him. But God has also given human beings free will; this means that they can rebel against their own primordial nature and become active against Heaven and passive to their own lower nature and the world of the senses, so that not all human beings remain God's servants and vicegerents. In fact, the perfection of these passive and active modes belongs to the prophets and saints alone. Nevertheless, all human beings possess dignity, and their lives are sacred because of that primordial nature, which all the progeny of Adam and Eve carry deep within themselves.

Throughout Islamic history many philosophical, theological, and mystical discussions have taken place about this issue, but one basic element with which all schools of Islamic thought and in fact ordinary believers agree is the truth that God is our creator, or, philosophically speaking, the ontological cause of our existence. It is therefore we who owe everything to Him and our rights derive from our fulfilling our responsibilities toward Him and obeying His Will.

To understand our relation to God, we must first ask what God wants of us. The Quran makes this demand clear when it states, "I have not created the *jinn* and humanity except to worship Me" (51:56); also "Verily I, I am God. There is no God save Me. So worship Me and establish prayers for My remembrance" (20:14). The word "worship" *(ʿibādah)* in Arabic also means "service." To worship God is also to serve Him. Many interpretations have been given of the term *ʿibādah* by commentators; its meaning ranges from ordinary acts of worship to loving and knowing God. The purpose of human existence is considered by Islam to be the worship and service of God, and only in carrying out the aim and purpose of our existence are we fully human. Otherwise, although we carry the human reality within ourselves, we fall short of it and live beneath the fully human state.

HUMAN RESPONSIBILITIES

Responsibility comes from the word "response," and one might say, in the Islamic context, that all of our responsibilities issue from that original response to God, when, according to the Quran, before the creation of the world God addressed all the children of Adam asking them, "Am

I not your Lord?" and they said, "Yes" (7:172). In this affirmation lie all our responsibilities as human beings, for in saying "yes" we accepted the Divine Trust *(amānah)*, which we must bear in this world. At the heart of this trust resides the affirmation of Divine Oneness and acts of worship and service. The very word for servant *('abd)* of God is related to the word for worship and service *('ibādah)*. To accept to be God's servant and to represent Him in this world means, above all, worshiping and serving Him. All the rights we have issue from the fulfilling of our responsibilities, and in the Islamic perspective responsibilities always precede rights. Although everyone these days speaks all the time of human rights and little of human responsibilities, in practice, even in the modern West, in many cases responsibilities precede rights. For example, we have to be responsible drivers before we are given the right to drive on public roads, and we have to accept the responsibility of mastering the laws of the land before being given the right to practice law. In Islam this relationship is not a matter of expediency, but of principle, and its acceptance dominates the cultural and intellectual landscape.

Now, we have responsibilities not only toward God, but also toward His creation. Traditional religious texts, in fact, delineate a hierarchy of responsibilities for human beings. At the apex are our responsibilities and duties toward God through acts of worship and service and obedience to His Law. Then there is the responsibility one has toward oneself. Since human life is sacred and is not created by us, we are responsible for trying to keep our souls as well as bodies healthy and not causing ourselves spiritual or physical harm (unless it is in battle or some other cause for the welfare of others or in self-defense). Therefore, as already stated, suicide is considered a grave sin in Islam. The modern idea that "This is my body and I can do whatever I want with it" is totally absent from the Islamic perspective; Islam states, "My body is not mine, for I did not create it—it belongs to God." Responsibility to ourselves also, of course, involves our soul and mind. Our greatest responsibility to ourselves is, in fact, to try to save our soul and to be good. This is not at all a selfish act, because one cannot do good unless one *is* good, and to save one's soul is also to introduce virtue and goodness into the ambience in which we live. We also have the responsibility to our minds to seek knowledge and the truth to the extent possible.

Next in the hierarchy we have responsibility toward society, starting with our family. This set of responsibilities ranges all the way from working honestly to support ourselves and our families, to performing acts of charity, to respecting others and strengthening community bonds, to supporting and sustaining all that is positively creative in human society. The vast spectrum of these social responsibilities is delineated in traditional works on the *Sharīʿah* and ethics and cannot be enumerated here. Furthermore, the world around us is not limited to the human sphere—we also have responsibilities toward animals and plants and even inanimate parts of nature such as water, air, and soil. This latter set of responsibilities involves what modern Western writers now refer to as environmental ethics. Our rights on all different levels derive from the acceptance of our responsibilities, which precede our rights in a principial manner. To flout responsibilities in the name of inalienable rights is not at all within the Islamic perspective and is considered putting the cart before the horse.

The question arises, however, about those who do not fulfill their responsibilities. Do they then have no rights? In everyday life in society it is not difficult to provide an answer. If we do not fulfill our responsibilities at work, we will be fired and have no right to receive a salary, or if we have too many traffic violations, which means that we are irresponsible drivers, our license and right to drive will be taken away. The question becomes more difficult in the modern context when we refer to that first category of responsibilities, that is, our duties and responsibilities toward God. In modern society, the rights of citizens do not change whether those citizens fulfill their responsibilities toward God or even believe in God or not.

Some in the West have contrasted this state of affairs with the situation in the Islamic world and claim that, from the Islamic point of view, such persons would have no rights. This assertion is, however, not at all true. If certain Muslims fall into religious and intellectual doubt even about God's existence, their right to the protection of their life and property by society still remains as long as they do not try to impose their views on others or act against social norms and laws. Even if they hold philosophical discussions on such matters, their basic rights cannot be removed. Needless to say, throughout Islamic history some have been imprisoned or occasionally even put to death for theological and religious reasons, but usually their situation has involved a political dimension, and in any case such occurrences have been much rarer in Islamic history than in Western history. The usual Islamic theological and juridical reasoning followed for the protection of such people is that as long as a person is alive, he or she may always come back to God, and that therefore the life of such a person must be protected like any other. As for performing acts of worship, that is between each individual and God, and Islamic society cannot force anyone to carry out acts of worship. What is expected of everyone is to observe the

Sharīʿah as law in public and as it concerns others and not to break religious injunctions publicly; this is analogous to prohibitions in the Christian or even post-Christian West against performing acts against public morality.

HUMAN RIGHTS

It is only in light of this understanding of human responsibilities that the question of human rights must be considered. To comprehend the meaning of human rights in the Islamic context, it is essential to ask how Muslims refer to the concept of "rights" and what they understand by it. In Arabic the basic term for "right" is *ḥaqq,* which is first of all a Name of God, who is *al-Ḥaqq,* that is, Truth and Reality. The term *ḥaqq* also possesses the meaning of "duty" as well as "right," obligation as well as claim, law as well as justice. It means also what is due to each thing, what gives reality to a thing, what makes a thing be true. Its derivative form, *iḥqāq,* means to win one's rights in a court of law, while another derivative, *taḥqīq,* means not only to ascertain the truth of something, but on the highest level to embody the truth. The term *ḥaqq,* which is one of the richest in the Arabic language, involves God, the Quran (which is also called *al-ḥaqq*), law, our responsibilities before God and His Law, as well as our rights and just claims.

Everything by virtue of the fact that it exists has its *ḥaqq,* which means both responsibilities to God and rights. Each thing has its due by virtue of the nature with which it has been created. Rights do not belong to human beings alone, but to all creatures. Today, as a result of an emphasis of human rights over the rights of other creatures, we are rapidly destroying the natural environment, and as a result people now speak of animal or plant rights. This latter perspective is perfectly in accord with the Islamic view, according to which rights are not the prerogative of the human state alone, but belong to all creatures. In the deepest sense "rights" means to give each being, including ourselves as human beings, its due *(ḥaqq)*.

Turning to the more specific question of human rights as currently understood in the West, according to Islam human beings have rights that are directly related to the responsibilities they have accepted as God's servants and vicegerents on earth. These rights range from the religious and personal to the legal, social, and political. The first rights of human beings concern their immortal souls. Men and women have the right to seek the salvation of their souls, which Islam, like other religions, considers our first duty toward ourselves and toward God, to Whom we must offer our souls. This right means the freedom of conscience in religious matters. God does not wish to compel His creatures to believe in Him, but wants them to do so on the basis of their own free will and conscience. To obey the laws of society is one thing, but to be coerced to have faith is quite another. The great drama of every human soul to accept or reject the call of Heaven is inseparable from the human state itself, and Islam, while emphasizing our duties to God, also emphasizes our right and even duty to engage in this drama. No external authority can take this right—and duty—away. Furthermore, the right to practice one's religion or not to, as long as the latter does not destroy social norms and laws, is at the heart of the Islamic understanding of human rights. The rights of non-Muslims to practice their religion is also guaranteed by Islamic Law, as mentioned above, unless it is a pseudo-religion or cult, which Islam has opposed as much as have Christianity and other traditional religions. Needless to say, the understanding of what constitutes an authentic religion and what constitutes a cult is not the same in the traditional Islamic world and in modern Europe and America, where many cults, some quite dangerous, dot the landscape, but the principle of the right to the practice of one's religion, whether it is Islam itself or any of the other heavenly inspired religions, is ingrained in the Islamic understanding of human rights. Furthermore, in this crucial matter there is no difference between men and women, who stand equal before God.

Next are personal rights pertaining to one's life, property, personal choices, and so forth. According to the principles of Islam, which have not always been followed any more than have those of Christianity, every human being has the right to life and the possession of property unless he or she commits crimes, as a result of which society takes away certain or all of these rights. Human beings also have the right of choosing their personal way of living in such matters as what form of livelihood to engage in, whom to marry, how to raise their family, where to live, and so on. Of course, in every society there are external constraints, including economic ones, that do not always allow these rights to be fulfilled according to one's wishes, but the principles are there. For example, in contrast to many premodern societies, Islamic society allowed each individual according to the law to learn and practice whatever profession he or she wanted and in practice could follow.

Likewise, according to Islamic Law both women and men have the right to choose their spouse. Now, in practice there have often been family pressures and economic and other considerations that have limited this right, especially for many women, but the social pressure exerted by many families has had nothing to do with the rights accorded by Islam to both men and women to choose their mates freely. In this matter, again, the situation in the Islamic world has not been very different from that in various Western societies until quite recently and in many cases even today.

In speaking about personal rights, one must remember that the thrust of the message of Islam is not only to give rights to human beings to perform this or that act, but especially to encourage them to lead a good life in every way possible. If certain personal rights such as sexual promiscuity have been taken away in Islam, it has been done in light of what religion considers to be the attainment of the good, which is the goal of human existence and the purpose of human rights. From the religious point of view, not only must rights follow obligations, but they must themselves be conditioned by various "thou shalt nots" in order to guarantee the rights of others and also the right of our immortal soul to be protected against the tendencies toward evil that each of us bears within himself or herself.

As for legal rights, which include the right to equality before the law and the right to a trial and self-defense, they are defined and in principle defended by Islamic Law itself. They include the right to be treated equally before the law, right to a fair trial and self-defense. In traditional Islamic society, where the Divine Law was widely applied, these matters were handled according to extensive procedures developed by Islamic jurists. Since the nineteenth century in numerous Islamic countries many of the laws as well as court procedures have come to be based on European models, while the judiciary has at the same time lost much of its independence. Needless to say, in many instances tyrannical governments have prevented the legal rights of many from being upheld, and consequently today there is a great deal of pressure by Muslims within various Islamic societies to allow everyone to live according to the rule of law and to have the legal rights of all members of society respected. When we speak of legal rights in Islam, we do not therefore mean simply what is going on in the Islamic world today, but the teachings of Islam itself.

Even more problematic than legal rights in the Islamic world today are political rights, which, in their current Western understanding, are, of course, a modern idea neither understood nor applied in other parts of the world in the same way as they are in countries that are culturally European. The whole array of historical processes—democracy rebelling against dictatorship, freedom of the individual versus tyranny, transformation from the England of George III to the America of Washington and Jefferson, the Third Reich and present-day Germany, the Gulag and Yeltsin's Russia—belong to Western history and do not have their equivalents in the Islamic world, which has had its own distinct struggles in the colonial and postcolonial periods. It is not possible to delve into all these issues here, but we must always remember the differences in the historical experiences of Islam and the modern West. What we need to focus on, however, is the classical Islamic ideal of political rights, which serves as a background for all that goes on in this domain today in various Islamic countries.

Traditionally, Muslims were to be consulted in matters of rule, and each person had the right to live in justice and the right to fight against injustice and oppression. With the rise of secularism, many people in the West saw the rule of God through religion as tyranny and identified the tyranny of their rulers with the tyranny of religion, as is seen so clearly in the French Revolution. In contrast, in the Islamic world the tyranny of worldly rulers was never identified with what agnostic philosophers in the West called the tyranny of religion, and in this matter there are certain resemblances between the views of Islam and those of America's founding fathers. Nor must the situation in the present-day Islamic world be confused with what occurred historically in the West, despite the presence of a small but vocal secularized minority in various Islamic countries for whom political rights mean freedom from tyrannical rule as well as secularization in the Western sense.

In much of the Islamic world today, Muslims are governed by dictatorial regimes, usually supported by the West if they happen to have a pro-Western stance and preserve Western interests. Muslims see Islam as a means of protecting themselves against this worldly tyranny as they had done in ages past. One of the appeals of so-called fundamentalism is this deeply rooted Islamic view of the role of religion in protecting the people from tyranny. In any case, under no condition should the lack of political rights in many Islamic countries today be seen as being simply the Islamic understanding of this matter. In the political realm there is much turmoil in the Islamic world today resulting from the consequences of the colonial period, the destruction of many traditional institutions, and the establishment of governments that are not based on the culture and religion of the people themselves. These governments are supported and sustained by powers from another civilization that still dominate much of the Islamic world and make it impossible for authentic structures and norms to be born from within Islamic society itself. If there were really free elections in the Islamic world today, in nearly every country there would come to power a less Western-oriented regime; it would not be necessarily anti-Western, but it would place the interests of Islamic society itself above everything else. Many who criticize Islamic countries for their lack of political rights are shedding crocodile tears, for in their hearts they are happy that such is the case and that in not many places in the Islamic world are members of society allowed to exercise their political rights according to classical Islamic teachings.

In discussing the whole question of human rights, it is essential to realize how the cultural values of each society determine to a large extent its understanding of this term. At the present moment many in the West consider human rights to be universal. Yet the Western understanding of this term has itself changed over time. Moreover, over the years Western powers have often used this issue for political gain and sometimes with astounding hypocrisy, which has amazed not only non-Westerners, including Muslims, but also those in the West who believe sincerely in human rights as they understand them. In addition, the issue of human rights has become central in the struggle between forces of globalization and forces seeking to preserve local cultures, economies, and ways of life. One cannot in all honesty discuss human rights on a global scale without turning to these issues and also to the different understandings that various cultures and civilizations, including the Islamic, have of human rights on the basis of their understanding of what it means to be human.

Let us for a moment compare priorities in human rights according to the secular and the Islamic understandings of what it means to be human. From the secular point of view, the human being is a purely earthly creature and what matters most is the rights of the individual as a purely earthly being. If one curses God or Christ on the street today in some American city, nothing will happen legally, but if one insults an individual, one can be arrested or sued. Clearly in this perspective, the rights of the individual stand above not only those of God, but also those of faith as a social and public reality. The priorities in the Islamic world are reversed. The rights of God stand above the rights of human beings, and for a person to insult the religion of others is not considered a right at all, even if the prevention of such an act decreases one's individual rights. The same holds true for questions of morality, including sexual morality, over which there has been so much debate during the past few decades even in America and Europe, and the issue of "freedom of speech" as individual right versus the rights of the public.

This difference in priorities came out clearly a few years ago in the infamous Salman Rushdie affair, where a writer of Islamic Indian background living in England wrote a blasphemous work seeking to denigrate and destroy a central part of Islamic sacred history. The publication of his work led to riots, which resulted in several deaths, and finally to his condemnation to death by Ayatollah Khomeini, followed by severe reaction from Western writers, especially secularist ones. One side argued that what was most important was the right of the individual to free speech; the other championed the right of a society to preserve its sacred history. Lest one think that this is only a dichotomy between Islam and the West, one should recall that blasphemy laws are still on the books in Great Britain, although they do not include blasphemy against Islam. In any case, it was difficult in the Rushdie affair for either side to understand the intensity of the indignation of the other, for each was operating from within a different worldview and with a different set of priorities.

If a debate were to be carried out today on the question of the understanding of human rights and the hierarchy presumed within it, one of the Westerners on the panel might say that Muslim women have few rights. A Muslim mother might answer that Western children have few rights; their most basic right, that of having a full-time mother, has been taken away by a new economic system in which many mothers are forced to spend, at best, a couple of hours each day of so-called quality time with their children after a full day's work and in a state of fatigue. The Muslim might add that, after the need for a mother, the most basic right of a child is to have two parents, and that this right is taken away from nearly half of the children in many sectors of Western society by complex socioeconomic factors and the prevalent "morality," which places the desires of the individual above responsibility in marriage to one's spouse and children. A Westerner might say that most Muslims do not have the right to a vote that counts for anything. A Muslim might respond that he agreed, but, as important as the right to vote was, along with it came the "right" to gain a livelihood in a just and reasonable manner and not by struggling from morning to night as a result of difficult economic conditions, many of them due to what is called the international economic and political order. Other Muslim debaters might further add that in their village, they always voted for their village elder on the basis of his experience and character, whereas in so many places, especially America, the choices offered in an election are strongly conditioned by the pressure of financial factors that have nothing to do with authentic democracy.

The debate could continue for a long time, but at the end the Muslim interlocutors would thank their Western counterparts and state that they were grateful for their concern, but that if they really wanted to be friends and fellow human beings, they should not impose their views but ask the Muslim team what *they* considered to be the rights that were most missing in their lives and that their Western friends could help to realize. If human rights are related to love of humanity, they must be combined with humility, not hubris. One of the Muslims might ask a Westerner if she would like to experience humiliation instead of humility. What would happen if a group of human rights activists in Cairo with access to all the international media kept holding press conferences, at which a few token Americans were present, on the rights of battered women and alcohol abuse or the tragedy of adolescent pregnancy in America? Would this moralistic hectoring be real concern for human rights in America, or an attempt to humiliate those who are unlike the activists and hold a value system the activists do not accept, even if the activists' own value system is in constant flux and transition?

Anything less than mutual respect in understanding the other side makes a sham of the question of human rights. And when the issue of human rights is used as a tool for policy by Western powers, it tends to nullify the efforts of those in the West who, with sincerity and good intention, are seeking to help others all over the globe to preserve the dignity of human life, a belief that not only Muslims, Christians, and those from other religions, but also many secularists share.

FREEDOM *FROM* RELIGION VERSUS FREEDOM *OF* RELIGION

The very thought of freedom creates joy in one's mind and heart, and there is no man or woman in the East or West who does not cherish freedom. But what is freedom? We need to answer this question in a fundamental way, especially since "freedom" has now become a shibboleth of the West, especially America, that is then presented to the world as the highest ideal. To answer the question in the Islamic context, it is first necessary to remind ourselves how religions in general view this matter.

The very word "religion" in English comes from the Latin *religare,* meaning "to bind," which seems to be the opposite of "to free." The Ten Commandments, which form the foundation of Jewish and Christian morality, consist of a number of "thou shalt nots," that is, limitations rather than freedoms. The Gospel of John (8:32) speaks of the Truth, which will set us free, but only if one accepts the conditions set by Christ, "If any man will come after me, let him deny himself, and take up his cross, and follow me" (Matt. 8:34). In the Indian religions freedom is also identified with deliverance from the bondage of all limitation, or what Hindus call *mokśa,* and from the recurring cycles of *samsāric* existence, or the chain of births and deaths in the world of becoming, which Buddhism emphasizes. In most sacred scriptures freedom is identified with release from the limitations of our own existence, rather than the freedom of the individual qua ego. As many Muslim sages have said, religion is to enable us to gain freedom *from* the self and not to abet the freedom *of* the self.

Metaphysically speaking, God alone is infinite; so God alone is absolute freedom. Every mode of separative existence is limitation and to some degree bondage. Only in God are we truly free, and He has given us free will in order that we may freely submit this free will to His Will in order to gain genuine freedom, freedom from the prison of our limited egos and our never-ending passions generating unending waves of unreal wants and desires, which are then turned into needs. Once it was asked of the prince of the Sufis of Khurasan, Bāyazīd, "What do you want?" He answered, "I want not to want." That is ultimate freedom, which Islam, like other heavenly inspired religions, places at the center of its teachings. That is why the Quran, like the Bible or the Vedas, for that matter, never speaks of freedom in quantitative and earthly terms, but seeks to help one unbind the tethers that confine one's immortal soul to the dictates of the lower passions. And that is also why Sufism, the inner dimension of Islam concerned with spiritual training of the soul, speaks so often of freedom, but always as freedom *from* the self, not *of* the self. In the deepest sense even our outward love for freedom is nostalgia for the freedom of the infinite expanses of the Divine Empyrean.

The attitude of Islam toward freedom is based on this metaphysical reality. Like other traditional religions, Islam sees its role as that of helping human beings to overcome the clutches of the power of their lower souls and thereby to be able to gain real freedom, rather than to foster an individualism that, in the guise of freedom, only strengthens the bonds of slavery of our immortal soul to that powerful slave master within it that is the agent of rebellion, passion, concupiscence, and ultimately bondage. This highest sense of freedom has, however, never prevented Islam from believing that human beings should possess the freedom to live in dignity in this world and to practice their duty toward God as His servants and toward His creatures as His vicegerents. Indignation and rebellion against tyranny have always been encouraged in Islam.

There is, however, an important distinction that needs to be clarified. For a person of faith, whether Jew, Christian, or Muslim, to love God and obey His commandments is not considered a loss of freedom. In contrast, those who have lost their faith regard that submission itself as a loss of freedom. In the American Revolution, the founding fathers made clear that the freedom of religion was a cardinal human right, but for many during the more than two centuries that have followed, this right has come to mean freedom *from* religion, not *of* religion. Current cultural wars in America over school prayer and other issues pertaining to the separation of church and state bring out this distinction clearly. Now, obviously the secularizing experience of the West during the past centuries has not been shared by the Islamic world, and most Muslims still live in the world of faith, in which submission to God is not seen as a curtailing of one's freedom any more than going to church and obeying the teachings of Christ would be seen as a restriction of freedom for a devout Christian. In both cases the acceptance of the authority of God would be seen as the gateway to the gaining of real freedom. It is simply meaningless for secularized Western intellectuals seeking to flee religion in order to gain "freedom" to try to apply their existential plight to Muslims who still live in the world of faith.

The love of God and surrender to His Will do not mean, however, for one moment that Muslims therefore have no interest in political and social freedom. The human desire for freedom according to who one is and what one's cultural values are is a universal trait, and throughout history Muslims have shown as much desire for freedom for themselves and their society as anyone else, as the courageous wars of independence fought against the British, the French, the Russians (which is still going on in Chechnya), and others bear witness. Paradoxically, after all these struggles, most Muslim societies came to be saddled with governments that have provided less freedom to them than before. Not only because of modern technology, which makes the state so much more powerful than in earlier times, but also because of the loss of many traditional institutions, the modernized parts of the Islamic world enjoy less freedom today than they did before the modern period. The contrast between talk about freedom by the West and pursuit of self-interest, usually of an economic nature, which causes support of oppressive regimes in much of the Islamic world, is certainly not lost on the general Islamic public.

If one asks if Muslims want freedom, the answer is definitely yes. But the vast majority of Muslims would add that, first of all, for them freedom does not mean freedom from God and religion; they would embrace other freedoms, provided they do not destroy their faith and what gives meaning to their lives. Second, they would point out that to be free means also to be free to understand what one means by freedom. They certainly do not want "freedom" to be imposed on them as an ideology by a more powerful West that knows better than they do what is good for them. Coercion under the guise of freedom is still coercion. What Muslims would like most of all is to be allowed the freedom to confront their own problems and find their own solutions. During all those centuries when the West was experimenting with all kinds of ideas and institutions, from the French Revolution to Napoleon, from the Bolshevik Revolution to Fascism and Nazism, from laissez-faire capitalism to socialism and back, the dynamic came from within Western civilization itself and the West had the freedom to develop as it did, for better or worse, without outward constraint. There was no external force, no powerful civilization breathing down its neck and preventing it from acting freely from within itself to create new institutions and norms as it deemed necessary. The Islamic world does not have such a privilege. The very Western civilization that talks of freedom has placed numerous constraints on the Islamic world in the name of protecting its own "interests," constraints that are greater obstacles to freedom of action than any that could come from within Islamic society itself.

Under such pressure some Muslims during the last century turned to Western liberalism, others to Marxism while the Soviet world was still alive, and yet others to politicized forms of Islam. But none of these movements has been free of the external constraints the West did not have to face in its own recent historical development. In any case, the Islamic world certainly seeks its freedom, but wishes to do so according to its own understanding of the nature of the human state, its ultimate goal of freedom in God, and, in light of that reality, freedom in the human order. Muslims are no less intelligent than other communities, and if given the freedom, they could discern for themselves between venom and the elixir of life offered to them in their societies. What the Islamic world would like most from the more powerful West, which keeps preaching freedom, is to be given this freedom by the West itself, so that the Islamic world can respond to the challenges of the present-day world on the basis of its own inner dynamic. But most in the Islamic world realize that this wish is not going to be realized and that the West's geopolitical and economic interests in the Islamic world take precedence over the question of real freedom. And so Muslims must find a way themselves to struggle for freedom, rule of law, and human rights, all Islamically understood, while under unprecedented external and internal constraint and without sacrificing the possibility of that spiritual freedom that is the ultimate goal of human life on earth.

Muslims agree that Islam is pertinent to all conditions and circumstances, including therefore the present one. Hence serious Muslims must seek to act correctly and to seek freedom despite outward constraints and not to blame their own lack of initiative and drive and their inability to overcome inertia on outside forces. It is possible to live Islamically even in the most difficult historical circumstances and to seek at least certain kinds of freedom on the basis of Islamic understanding, even in situations where both external and internal constraints are ever present.

CONTEMPORARY MUSLIM RESPONSES TO THE ISSUE OF FREEDOM AND HUMAN RIGHTS

Far from being passive to the challenges posed by the West on the issues of freedom and human rights, during the past few decades many Islamic responses have been issued by those who have tried to analyze what freedom is for an Islamic society today beyond going to the ballot box, and what both theoretical and practical engagement on the question of human rights involves. In most Islamic countries there are now human rights groups, opposed by some governments and even considered agents of the West in others. There have also been extensive discussions among theologians, philosophers, and jurists, including some of the most eminent traditional authorities, on the question of Islam and human rights. Many deliberations, conferences, and debates at the beginning of the fifteenth century of the Islamic calendar, corresponding to the early 1980s, led to the publication of an Islamic declaration of human rights that gained the support of many traditional Muslim authorities and many notable organizations and has become widely disseminated throughout the Islamic world.

Based totally on the Quran and *Ḥadīth,* the rights enumerated in this document include the right to life, freedom, equality, and prohibition against impermissible discrimination; the right to justice, fair trial, protection against abuse of power, protection against torture, protection of honor and reputation, and asylum; the rights of minorities; the right of participation in the conduct and management of public affairs; the rights of belief, thought, and speech; freedom of religion, free association, freedom to pursue what concerns the economic order, protection of property, social security, and founding a family and related matters; the rights of married women; and the right to education, privacy, and freedom of movement and residence.

A skeptical Westerner might say that these are simply modern Western concepts of human rights couched in Islamic terms. The reality of the matter is that every one of these rights is supported by Quranic and *Ḥadīth* references. Surely what constitutes the *content* of human rights, and not its *form,* is not specifically modern, but is to be found in one way or another in moral and spiritual teachings of various religions and the writings of moral philosophers from many lands stretching from China to France, including, of course, those of the Islamic world. What this and similar documents present are responses of the Islamic world to the challenge posed by the West on this matter, but the substance of the response comes from Islam itself.

Some may say that even if these are Islamic ideals, they are not realized in the Islamic world today. Such an observation is true to some extent, but not absolutely. But the Islamic world is not unique in this matter. No society from China to Mexico lives up to such ideals. Nor does the West itself live up to these ideals completely, as one sees in the continuous presence of racism in America. To be fair, one would have to say that some of these ideals are more fully realized in the West and some in the Islamic world, if the full gamut of human rights in relation to our duties to God and His creation are taken into consideration. In any case, the mainstream of Islamic thought does not have a dispute with the West, even its secularist component, on the question of the substance of human rights or even the necessity of their implementation. Where there is a basic difference is on the relation between human rights and human responsibilities and also on our rights vis-à-vis God's rights over us and the rest of His creation. On this issue many Western Jewish and Christian thinkers are in fact closer to their Muslim counterparts than to their secularist compatriots.

On the practical level, despite numerous political and social obstacles, in recent years in several Islamic countries there have been developments toward greater respect for the law and the rights and freedom guaranteed therein. In countries as different as Malaysia, Indonesia, and Iran, there is an attempt afoot to develop what is called an Islamic civil society governed by law, a society that would not be secularized yet be a civil society in which the rights of citizens would be guaranteed. The dichotomies established by so many so-called experts in the West between a "theocracy" and a secular society and government in the Islamic world are simply false and do not apply to the Islamic world. Saudi Arabia or Iran are not theocracies in the Western understanding of this term, and Egypt is not secular. The Islamic world today is in the process of responding to the challenges posed by modernism in this as in other domains. Many experiments are under way in countries as different as Turkey and Iran. And because this process is carried out under conditions in which there is not complete freedom either within or without, sometimes extreme forms of action manifest themselves with tragic consequences. But these tragic eruptions must not make one forget that on the deeper level something much more basic is happening. And what is happening is the response to the difficult challenges of the modern world by a major world civilization, which, despite its current political and military weakness, has the spiritual resources to emphasize the significance of human dignity and the rights that God has bestowed upon human beings and at the same time to never tire of emphasizing that all our rights issue from the fulfillment of our responsibilities to God and His creation and that without accepting our responsibilities emphasis upon our rights alone can turn us into a species that is at once endangered and endangering.

THE HUMAN CONDITION AND THE ROLE OF ISLAM

Since the beginning of the decade of the 1990s, a number of leading figures in the West have sought to create a universal declaration of human responsibilities to complement the one on human rights declared by the United Nations. Many have become aware that the sole emphasis on human rights without emphasizing our responsibilities to the rest of society and also the natural environment can only accelerate the suicidal course that the modern and now postmodern world seems to be taking. One does not need to be a prophet to realize that the rapid destruction of both the natural environment and the social fabric of the most highly industrialized societies cannot but end in total disaster for the whole of humanity. Islam has a crucial role to play in bringing out the primacy of responsibilities over rights in accordance with its vision of the human being as a theomorphic being and its emphasis on the ontological reliance of human beings upon God. It can also be a major force, perhaps the most powerful on earth, to oppose the process of the desacralization of both human beings and nature, a process the result of which is the monumental crisis we now face.

Beyond the din of political and military confrontations going on today, Muslim thinkers must address themselves to the questions of human responsibilities and human rights, joining hands with both Western and other thinkers engaged in such matters globally, bringing to the table without apology the Islamic contribution to these vital subjects and especially the emphasis upon the theocentric worldview and sacred conception of creation, which are not only Islamic but are shared in one form or another by all the historical religions. The participation on a global scale by Muslims in the creation of awareness of human responsibilities to complement and precede human rights is itself a responsibility of primary order placed by God upon the shoulders of those Muslims endowed with sufficient knowledge combined with virtue to carry out such a task.

Within the Islamic world itself, Muslim thinkers must address themselves to the ever greater understanding of human rights on the basis of the Islamic conception of the nature of the human being. All the elements of human rights as delineated in the Islamic declaration above are found within traditional Islamic sources, from the Quran and *Ḥadīth* to poetry, aphorisms of sages, and works of moral philosophers and Sufis. But they need to be reformulated in a contemporary context in such a way as to be able to respond to modern Western challenges and also the current situation within various Islamic societies. Why must there be respect for human life and in fact all of life? If all Muslims are equal before the law, why is this not actually the case in so many Muslim societies, and what about non-Muslims? What is the foundation of the freedom of religion and worship? To what extent is personal life sacrosanct and what is the limit of state intrusion upon personal life? Such questions must be answered in a clear and convincing manner for the present generation of Muslims, not by quoting Jean-Jacques Rousseau and John Locke as an earlier generation of Muslim modernists did with blatant lack of success, but by drawing from the most authentic sources of the Islamic tradition.

The Islamic understanding of human rights will not necessarily be identical with the most current Western interpretations of it, but that is not a negative matter at all. What is important is that the Islamic response be authentic and deeply rooted in the Islamic tradition. The attempt to harmonize the Islamic understanding of these matters with the current Western appraisal of these issues is not only metaphysically and religiously not always feasible, but also impossible in practice, because the Western understanding of these issues is constantly changing from decade to decade. What is important for Islam is to accept the challenge of the reality of the issues involved and then provide Islamic responses, which may in fact be also of interest to certain Western thinkers grappling with the pertinence of these issues on a global scale.

A particularly difficult task, which is also a new one requiring intellectual effort *(ijtihād)* on the highest level by Muslims, is determining the rights of those who do not believe in God and therefore in any responsibilities that people of faith believe they have toward God. The classical Islamic works on ethics and rights, whether written from a juridical, philosophical, or theological point of view, envisaged a universe in which there was a multiplicity of religions, as we have already discussed in the first chapter of this book. Today there is a new situation in the modern and post-modern world that is indeed an anomaly in world history. Since extensive secularism developed within the West itself, through a gradual process, the attitude of Western Christian thinkers could accommodate itself to secularism over time.

For Islamic theological thought, the presence of a powerful secularist force in the world appears as a great shock, despite the advent of modernism starting two centuries ago in many Islamic lands and after seventy years of domination of a good part of the Islamic world by the officially atheistic Soviet regime. Today, the mainstream of Islamic thought, both Sunni and Shīʿite, must address itself to this question of secularism and agnosticism as it did in earlier days concerning the rights of followers of other religions within the Islamic community. Whatever understanding of human rights from the Islamic perspective comes to dominate the center of consciousness of the Islamic community in the future, it must take account not only of followers of other religions, a matter that is relatively easy in light of the Quranic doctrine of the universality of revelation, but also of those who do not believe in any transcendent or immanent Principle beyond the human. And that is more difficult to achieve in light of the Islamic conception of the human state. Yet it is a task to which the *ʿulamāʾ*, or religious scholars, who wield influence over the people and who are the guardans of the *Sharīʿah,* as well as other Islamic thinkers must address themselves. This task will of course become easier if those within the Islamic world who have decided to leave the world of faith do not act as a fifth column for modern Western secularism. But even if this is the case, a way has to be found to protect their rights under the law along with those of non-Muslims of no religious persuasion who happen to be living within the Islamic world.

Islamic thought must also challenge on the highest intellectual level the current Western notion that the present-day Western understanding of human rights is universal, which in this context means global. Now, all values are related to the worldview, or *Weltanschauung*, within which they are understood, and not all worldviews are the same. The religious worldviews have basic principles in common that they do not share with views that deny the Transcendent and the Sacred. When it comes to the question of the human state, Christians speak of people being the children of God, Muslims of their being His vicegerents on earth, and both of humans being made in the "image" or "form" of God, although with different meanings of the term "image" or "form." Hindus speak of the sacrifice of the Primordial Man to create the world and Neo-Confucianism of the human being as an anthropocosmic being and bridge between Heaven and earth. These views can be easily correlated, but they cannot be harmonized with a view of the human being as an aggregate of molecules brought together by chance out of the original cosmic soup.

Nor can human rights, which must of necessity be based on the concept of who the human being is, be considered global and universal because of such crass differences about what constitutes the human state. Islamic thinkers must come forward to point out that, yes, there are human values that are global, such as respect for human life or opposition to torture, but other human rights are dependent upon the worldview of various civilizations that together compose humanity. Are the rights of human beings more important than the rights of God? Can we have human rights without human responsibilities? Are political rights superior to economic rights? Do the rights of the individual have priority over those of the community? If human rights are not to be a form of cultural and political coercion in the name of the love of humanity, the answer of various religions, cultures, and civilizations to such questions must be respected whatever the current strength in this world of these religions or cultures might be. One of the roles of Muslims as members of a major world civilization is to answer such questions in all honesty from the Islamic point of view. It is also to insist upon mutual respect between civilizations and the values they bear instead of accepting one-sided imposition. It is, moreover, to seek actively to cooperate with not only Westerners, but also with members of other cultures and civilizations to point to those values that we do all hold dear and that must be respected by everyone if we are going to live and function as human beings on a globe on which there seems now to be no other choice but to live in mutual respect with compassion and love for others or to perish together.

Not only the Islamic world, not only the West, but the whole world is passing through one of the darkest pages of its history, which no amount of triumphalism and chest-beating can hide. In these dark times Muslims must remain vigilant as never before about all that goes on about them and concerning all those who use the name of Islam for various purposes, including deviant ones. On the basis of the traditional teachings of Islam, some of which have been outlined above, they must be as critical of what goes on among themselves in the form of bigotry and fanaticism as they are of the shortcomings of modern Western societies, from sexual promiscuity and the breakdown of the family to the desecration and destruction of the natural environment. Muslims must fulfill their responsibilities before God and His creation as taught in Islam, responsibilities for which they were created as human beings, and on the basis of these responsibilities they must seek to exercise the rights God has given them while also respecting the rights of others.

In a world in which the hierarchies of the states of being are denied, and in the minds of many, human beings are elevated to the level of God, and the "kingdom of man" has come to replace the "Kingdom of God," it is the duty of Muslims to proclaim the primacy of the Sacred, the absolute necessity of sacred laws as foundations for social morality, the ultimate goal of human life beyond the earthly, the centrality of justice in human society, and the need to seek peace within before searching for outward peace. Muslims must remind themselves again of their responsibilities to God, to human beings, and to the natural world and also of their basic rights, the most important of which is the right to be God's servant and vicegerent here on earth. They must extend their hand in friendship to followers of other religions as ordered by the Quran and to live and let live with regard to those who have moved away from the world of faith altogether. They must even extend their hand to those Christian and primarily Protestant evangelists who express ignorant, hurtful, and even malicious and egregious views about Islam. Muslims must in this case turn the other cheek and prove in their actions that for them also Christ is sent by God and his words revered.

Men and women in the West who are still devoted to the life of faith should also know that those closest to them in this world are Muslims, if only the veils of mutual misunderstanding and distrust, which have grown so thick of late, were to be rent asunder. Every practicing Muslim, which includes the vast majority of the population of the Islamic world, could not but agree that his or her highest wish is none other than the prayer uttered by Christ, "Thy Will be done on earth as it is in Heaven." No matter what the aberrations that cloud the horizons today, the Islamic tradition remains and must remain witness to God's Oneness and dedicated to the effort to carry out His Will here on earth. Only in remaining true to itself, clinging to the "firm cable" mentioned in the Quran and the message it has been destined to bear in this world, will the Islamic community fulfill its duties before God and the rest of humanity and contribute as the "middle people" to the creation of harmony between religions, peoples, and civilizations the world over. Only in turning to the heart of its teachings will Islam be able to bear witness in this age of forgetfulness to the basic truth about the nature of human beings as creatures destined for the spiritual world with the possibility even in this world of "seeing God everywhere," creatures who are agents of His Will here on earth, bearers of peace, and channels of the waters of compassion that issue from the spring of Life Divine.

Epilogue

THE ETHICAL AND SPIRITUAL NATURE OF HUMAN LIFE, EAST AND WEST

The Quran asserts that God is the Lord of both the East and the West and also that the Blessed Olive Tree, which symbolizes the spiritual axis of the world, is of neither the East nor the West. It is more necessary today than at any other time in history to realize the universal nature of the truth, which belongs to both the East and the West and yet is confined to neither. And yet there are those in the West who see Islam as the "totally other" and then vilify and identify it with all that they disdain, while there are also those in the Islamic world who look upon the West as the innate enemy of Islam. Those who realize that God is the Lord of both the East and the West must raise their voices against such ignorant and sometimes malefic attitudes.

There is not, however, a simple symmetry between East and West today. Before modern times the "Abode of Islam" was the only "other" the West knew, and the self-consciousness of Western civilization during its period of maturation and its crystallization was to a large extent defined by that "other." For Islam, however, there were several other civilizations, such as those in India and China, with which it had contact and which it saw as the "other." This factor itself contributed, through Islam's image of itself as the central world civilization, to the neglect for several centuries by Muslims of the rise of European power during the Renaissance and the major intellectual and religious transformations that were taking place at that time in the West, including the rise of modern science followed by the new technology.

Some have tried to fault Islamic civilization for not following the same trajectory of development that took place in Europe and have asked, "What went wrong?" in reference to the Islamic world. If we look at world history, however, the question should not be "What went wrong in the Islamic world?" but "What went wrong in Europe?" The very question "What went wrong?" implies a norm or a right against which something is judged to *be* wrong. Now, the global norm was once traditional civilizations based on religious and spiritual principles and rooted in a theocentric or anthropocosmic worldview, as we see in Japanese, Chinese, Hindu, Islamic, Byzantine, and medieval European civilizations. It was postmedieval Europe that deviated from this norm by substituting an anthropocentric worldview for a theocentric one, making human beings the measure of all things or, to use a religious language, replacing the "Kingdom of God" with the "kingdom of man." This "freedom" of reason from revelation and intellectual intuition, combined with emphasis upon humanism, rationalism, empiricism, and naturalism, led to many new developments, including a new science based on power rather than wisdom, and made it possible for Europe to expand over the globe and become dominant over other civilizations. It led to the Industrial Revolution, modern technology, and modern medicine. Now, modern medicine has eradicated many diseases but has also caused the population explosion, while modern technology has created many comforts along with the catastrophic destruction of the natural environment.

The death of tens of millions of Europeans in the twentieth century, thanks to modern means of warfare, combined with the loss of the meaning of life, the secularization of the world, the dehumanization of humanity, the breakup of the social fabric, the unprecedented destruction of nature and many other consequences of modern civilization, led a number of leading Western thinkers and poets during the last century to profoundly criticize the course taken by modern Western civilization. If not everyone has read René Guénon's masterful *Crisis of the Modern World*, most people in America are familiar with T. S. Eliot's *The Waste Land* and some remember Theodor Roszak's *Where the Wasteland Ends,* along with many other works written by European and American authors during the past decades either depicting the spiritually tragic condition of human life in modern society or criticizing the tendencies driving modern Western civilization to its destruction.

Are all these criticisms to be forgotten and modern civilization made the norm that is right and in comparison to which everything else is considered wrong? No thinking person who is aware of what we are doing to our natural environment and what forces are tearing away the fabric of our society and, more important, our souls can claim that the path followed by the West should be the norm by which one should judge other civilizations, Islamic or otherwise. Moreover, if Islamic or Chinese civilizations *had* followed the same course as the postmedieval West and we had had the Industrial Revolution not only in England, but also in China, India, Persia, Turkey, and Egypt, the environmental impact would have been so great that we might not even be around today to pose the question of what went wrong.

In reality, each civilization, whether in East or West, has decayed and deviated in its own way and must pose the question to itself about what went wrong, rather than exclaiming with hubris and self-righteousness about what went wrong somewhere else because the people in that "somewhere else" have not followed its way of thinking and acting. We must desist from identifying ourselves with pure goodness and the other with pure evil. Even Christ said only God is good in the absolute sense. Each civilization must become ever more aware of its own shortcomings and evil elements as well as its virtues and what is good in it. Muslims must ask themselves what went wrong within their own societies, but the West must also pose the same question about itself. And this task of self-examination is even more urgent for the West, for at this particular juncture of human history it possesses much greater power than other civilizations and has greater global influence.

Moreover, today one can no longer speak strictly of the West and the Islamic world as two civilizations facing each other across a line like two armies ready to do battle in medieval times. In days of old Islam occupied the southern shores of the Mediterranean and the West the northern shores, and later the Ottomans occupied eastern Europe and Western civilization ruled from Vienna west. Today the relation between the Islamic world and the West is more like the *yin-yang* symbol of the Far East. Let us recall that there is an element of *yin* in *yang* and of *yang* in *yin* and together they comprise a circle, which is the symbol of totality. Likewise, there are many Westerners living in the Islamic world along with many Westernized Muslims and there are also sizable Islamic communities in both Europe and America. Whereas the contribution of Westerners in the Islamic world to the West is essentially economic and to some extent political, the contribution of Muslims living in the West to the Islamic world itself is primarily intellectual and only secondarily economic. In fact, at no time in Islamic history have so many influential intellectual leaders of Islam lived outside the "Abode of Islam" in another civilization, which, interestingly enough, provides the favorable climate for free intellectual discourse not found under present-day conditions in many Islamic countries themselves. The destinies of the West and the Islamic world are intertwined in such a way that one cannot reduce the situation simply to "us" and "them" in total mutual exclusion.

It is in the destiny of not only Islam and the West but all other civilizations to be forced to confront at this particular moment of history the powerful forces of globalization. If secularism sought earlier to demolish and destroy the older worldviews based on the Sacred, the process of globalization as usually understood seeks in an ever more accelerated manner to articulate a single worldview and "value system." But this "value system" is what one might call "trans-human," because it is based on the ephemera of the marketplace and its corporate denizens and not on enduring truths and spiritual values. The political and economic objects of globalization are therefore as inimical to the perennial values of religion as the forces of secularism were in earlier days and still are today. In this unprecedented historical situation, fraught with the greatest danger for the whole spiritual legacy of humanity, it is essential that the particular aspects of each tradition be preserved and sharpened, that the universal aspects be recalled, and that both be used to inform other traditions. It is only on the basis of a positive and mutually enriching dialogue between religious traditions that respects their particularities as well as recognizes the universal truths lying in their heart or center that the answers must be sought for the most acute problems facing humanity today.

In this critical moment of human history both Muslims and Westerners, and in fact all human beings, must seek to live an ethical life based on mutual respect and greater knowledge of each other. Turning more particularly to Islam and the West, it must be emphasized that whether we are Muslims, Jews, Christians, or even secularists, whether we live in the Islamic world or the West, we are in need of meaning in our lives, of ethical norms to guide our actions, of a vision that would allow us to live at peace with each other and with the rest of God's creation. It is in the achievement of this task that both the formal aspect and the inner message of Islam as well as those of other religions can come to our aid as can nothing else in this world. Of special importance is the inner message, for this message is none other than the universal truth that was placed by God in the hearts of all human beings and that stands at the center of all heavenly revelations.

The heart of Islam is also the Islam of the heart, which is that spiritual virtue, or *iḥsān,* that enables us "to see God everywhere" and to be His "eyes, ears, and hands" in this world. The heart of religion is the religion of the heart, wherein all external forms are transcended, the heart that according to the Prophet is "the Throne of the Infinitely Good and Compassionate." It is within this religion of the heart that is to be found that eternal wisdom, or *sophia,* which shines like a jewel at the center of every Divine message. This wisdom alone can provide for us, in this period of darkness and confusion, the light of harmony based on principial knowledge and the warmth of compassion and love of the other. As the last major historical religion in this cycle of human existence, Islam has been able to preserve to this day, and despite all the external turmoil and even subversion of our times, that message of the eternal *sophia* in its heart. To understand Islam fully is to understand this universal message from the heart and the manner in which the external elements of the tradition are related to this hidden center.

Muslims themselves must draw ever more from these inner springs of wisdom and all men and women of good will in the West must seek to understand Islam in light of these central truths, which are also to be found in Judaism, Christianity, and other religions. We must all seek to rediscover the heart of religion, which is also the religion of the heart, to drink deeply of the spring of wisdom gushing forth from the heart, to live in peace and harmony on the basis of the universal truths contained in the perennial wisdom shared by all traditions, and to love all of God's creation as the consequence of being ourselves touched by the love and compassion of the One who resides in our hearts. Nothing less than the wisdom and love of the religion of the heart can save us in a world torn apart by so much evil and selfishness, a world that has the chimerical dream of living in peace in the forgetfulness of God. The heart of Islam is none other than the witnessing to the oneness of the Divine Reality, the universality of the truth, the necessity of submission to His Will, the fulfilling of human responsibilities, and respect for the rights of all beings. The heart of Islam beckons us to awaken from the dream of forgetfulness, to remember who we are and why we are here, to know and respect the religions of others. It is for Muslims to heed the call from the heart of Islam and live an ethical and spiritual life accordingly, but it is also for those in the West who seek meaning in their lives to turn to their own center and to realize that in coming to know better the heart of Islam they may gain more than greater insight into another religion and civilization; they may gain greater insight into their own heart and soul. The heart of any religion is none other than that single, universal Truth that resides at the heart of all authentic religions and that is itself the foundation of the religion of the heart.

> In love no difference there is between monastery and Sufi tavern of ruins,
> Wheresoever it be, there is the glow of the light of the Beloved's Face.
>
> Ḥāfiẓ

Wa'Llāhu aʿlam—And God knows best.

Notes

CHAPTER ONE

1. Trans. Martin Lings, in *Muhammad: His Life Based on the Earliest Sources* (Cambridge, UK: Islamic Texts Society, 1991), p. 69.
2. Trans. Muhammad Marmaduke Pickthall, *The Meaning of the Glorious Koran* (many editions), modified.
3. Trans. Lings, in *Muhammad,* p. 102.
4. Trans. Martin Lings, *A Sufi Saint of the Twentieth Century* (Berkeley: University of California Press, 1973), p. i.

CHAPTER TWO

1. Trans. Martin Lings, in *Muhammad: His Life Based on the Earliest Sources* (Cambridge, UK: Islamic Texts Society, 1991), pp. 333–34.

CHAPTER THREE

1. Trans. Martin Lings, in *Muhammad: His Life Based on the Earliest Sources* (Cambridge, UK: Islamic Texts Society, 1991), p. 69.

CHAPTER FOUR

1. Titus Burckhardt, *Fez: City of Islam,* trans. W. Stoddart (Cambridge: Islamic Texts Society, 1992), pp. 102–3.

CHAPTER FIVE

1. Trans. B. Lewis, *Music of a Distant Drum* (Princeton, NJ: Princeton University Press, 2001), p. 193.
2. Trans. A. M. Schimmel, *As Through a Veil* (New York: Columbia University Press, 1982), p. 18.
3. Rūmī, *Mathnawī* II, v. 593.

CHAPTER SIX

1. Trans. W. Chittick, *A Shiʿite Anthology* (Albany: State University of New York Press, 1981), pp. 68–69.
2. Rūmī, *Mathnawī,* Book I, v. 3735f.

Bibliography

Ahmed, Nazeer. *Islam in Global History*, 2 vols. Chicago: Kazi Publications, 2000.

A clear and detailed history of the Islamic world from the advent of Islam to the modern period.

Armstrong, Karen. *Muhammad: A Biography of the Prophet.* San Francisco: HarperSanFrancisco, 1992.

A detailed and fairly sympathetic account of the life of the Prophet by a major Western writer on religion.

Asad, Muhammad. *The Road to Mecca.* Louisville, KY: Fons Vitae, 2001.

A moving account of the experience of an Austrian journalist who went to the Islamic world in 1927, embraced Islam, and became a major Muslim intellectual figure.

Bill, James, and John A. Williams. *Roman Catholics and Shīʿi Muslims: Prayer, Passion and Politics.* Chapel Hill and London: University of North Carolina Press, 2002.

The first comparative study of Catholicism and Shīʿism showing some of the remarkable resemblances between the two traditions.

Burckhardt, Titus. *Fez: City of Islam.* Cambridge: Islamic Texts Society, 1992.

A unique in-depth study of the spiritual, religious, artistic, intellectual, and social life of one of Islam's greatest traditional cities, with numerous insights that apply to the Islamic world as a whole.

Cleary, Thomas. *The Essential Koran*. Edison, NJ: Castle Books, 1998.

A lucid and highly readable translation of selections from the Quran.

Eaton, Charles le Gai. *Islam and the Destiny of Man*. Albany: State University of New York, 1985; Cambridge: Islamic Texts Society, 1985.

A profound study of some of the basic tenets of Islam by a leading British Muslim writer.

———. *Remembering God: Reflections on Islam*. Chicago: Kazi Publications, 2000; Cambridge: Islamic Texts Society, 2000.

An eloquent treatment of Islamic spirituality and the existential problems created by living as a Muslim in the modern world.

Esposito, John. *Islam: The Straight Path*. Oxford: Oxford University Press, 1998.

An account of Islam and the development of contemporary Islamic trends by a very perceptive scholar of modern developments in various parts of the Islamic world.

Hallaq, W. *A History of Islamic Legal Theories*. Cambridge: Cambridge University Press, 1999.

A scholarly treatment of the historical development of the theories of Islamic Law.

Herlihy, John. *In Search of the Truth*. Kuala Lumpur: Dewan Pustaka Islam, 1990.

An American's journey to Islam and his reflections on traditional Islamic themes.

Kamali, Mohammad Hashim. *Principles of Islamic Jurisprudence*. Cambridge: Islamic Texts Society, 1991.

The best available work in English on the Islamic understanding of the principles underlying Islamic jurisprudence.

Khadduri, Majid. *The Islamic Conception of Justice*. Baltimore, MD: Johns Hopkins University Press, 1984.

A detailed study, on the basis of the most authentic Islamic sources, of justice in Islam from a political, theological, philosophical, and ethical perspective, including the question of justice among nations, social justice, and changing conceptions of justice among some Muslims under modern conditions.

Lings, Martin. *Muhammad: His Life Based on the Earliest Sources.* Cambridge: Islamic Texts Society, 1991; New York: Inner Traditions, 1983.

The best biography of the Prophet in English based on traditional Islamic sources, written with great elegance and narrative power.

Murata, Sachiko. *The Tao of Islam.* Albany: State University of New York, 1992.

A unique work using the Far Eastern *yin* and *yang* to explain gender relationships in Islam on both the spiritual and the social level.

Murata, Sachiko, and William Chittick. *The Vision of Islam.* New York: Paragon House, 1994.

An exposition of all the major facets of Islam and Islamic thought on the basis of the *ḥadīth* of Gabriel, in which the meaning of *islām, īmān,* and *iḥsān* are explained.

Nasr, Seyyed Hossein. *Ideals and Realities of Islam.* Chicago: ABC International Group, 2001; Cambridge: Islamic Texts Society, 2001.

Deals from the traditional point of view with the major aspects of Islam including the Quran, the Prophet, the Law, the spiritual path, and Sunnism and Shīʿism.

———. *Islam and the Plight of Modern Man.* Chicago: ABC International Group, 2001; Cambridge: Islamic Texts Society, 2002.

Deals with both metaphysical and existential questions arising from the encounter between Islam and modernism.

———. *Traditional Islam in the Modern World.* London: Kegan Paul International, 1990.

A clarification of the differences between traditional, modernist, and so-called fundamentalist Islam and an elucidation of various aspects of traditional Islam.

———. *A Young Muslim's Guide to the Modern World.* Chicago: Kazi Publications, 1996; Cambridge: Islamic Texts Society, 1994.

A summary of the teachings of Islam and various aspects of Western civilization and the manner in which young Muslims must face the challenges of the modern world.

———, ed. *Islamic Spirituality: Foundations.* New York: Crossroad, 1989.

Contains numerous seminal essays on basic aspects of Islamic spirituality by some of the leading scholars from both the Islamic world and the West.

Pickthall, Muhammad Marmaduke. *The Meaning of the Glorious Koran.* Many editions.

One of the most widely read renditions of the Quran in English, one that also received the approval of leading Islamic religious authorities at the time of its appearance before World War II.

Renard, John. *Seven Doors to Islam: Spirituality and the Religious Life of Muslims.* Berkeley: University of California Press, 1996.

A perceptive introduction to the inner meaning of Islam through seven different doors leading to the inner courtyard of the religion.

Schimmel, Annemarie. *And Muhammad Is His Messenger.* London and Chapel Hill: The University of North Carolina Press, 1985.

The only work in English that explains through various Islamic literary texts the veneration of the Prophet and his role in Islamic piety.

———. *Islam: An Introduction.* Albany: State University of New York, 1992.

A succinct account of the different basic teachings of Islam, written with much love and empathy.

Schuon, Frithjof. *Understanding Islam.* Bloomington, IN: World Wisdom Books, 1994.

The most profound work on the inner meaning of Islam and its relation to other religions ever written by a Western author.

Sells, Michael. *Approaching the Qur'ān: The Early Revelations.* Ashland, OR: White Cloud Press, 1999.

Highly poetical renditions into English of selections from the Quran that bring out some of the literary quality of the original text.

Ṭabāṭabā'ī, 'Allāmah. *The Quran in Islam.* London: Routledge & Kegan Paul, 1987.

A short but masterly work on the significance of the Quran and the manner in which to study it by the author of the most monumental commentary written on the Quran in the twentieth century.

Index

Page numbers of illustrations appear in italics.

'Abbāsid caliphate, 73, 89, 178
'abd (servant), 8, 278
'Abd al-Karīm, 265
'Abd al-Qādir, Amīr, 104, 110, 139, 265
'Abd Allāh (the servant of God), 13, 35
Abode of Islam. *See dār al-islām*
Abraham, 8, 18, 30, 141; tomb in al-Khalīl, 41; *ummah,* 160
Abū Bakr, 30, 65–66
Abū Ḥanīfah, Imām, 68
Abū Sa'īd Abi'l-Khayr, 212
Abu'l-Qāsim, 35
adab (spiritual etiquette), 59
'ādah (custom), 121–122
Adam, 12, 13–14, 17, 30; expulsion from paradise, Eve's role, 14; humanity as progeny of, and Eve, 276
Afghānī, al-, Jamāl al-Dīn, 103
Afghānistan: Ḥanafism in, 68; history of, 91; Islamization of, 106; Kafirestan, 78; *Sharī'ah* in, 154; Shī'ism in, 65; Taliban in, 78, 233–34
Aga Khān, 74–75
aḥādīth, 37
Ahl al-bayt, 67
Aḥmad al-'Alawī, Shaykh, 105
Aḥmad Bamba, 139
Aḥmad ibn Ḥanbal, Imām, 69
Aḥmad Shāh Mas'ūd, 265
Aḥmadiyyah movement, 79–80, 87
Aḥmad, 35, 36
aḥsan al-taqwīm, 7
akbar (greater, greatest), 260
"*al-salāmu 'alaykum,*" 23
Alamut, 74
'Alawīs of Syria (Nuṣayrīs), 78
'Alawīs of Turkey, 77
Albania, 96
alcohol, abstention from, 128
Algeria: 'Ibādīs in, 77; independence movement, 104, 105; secularism in, 109
Alḥamduli'Llāh, 22
'Alī al-Riḍā, 91
'Alī ibn Abī Ṭālib, 26, 30, 65–66, 70–71, 77, 139, 180, 237, 241, 248–52, 264
'Alīallāhī, 77
Allah (God): as absolute freedom, 291–92; "beautiful Names," 4–5, 13; compassion and mercy, relationship of God to humanity, 205–6; Creator and Sustainer, 4, 9–15; Divine Beauty, 225–26; Divine Compassion and Mercy, 204; Divine Justice and, 240–43, 245; Divine Love, 209–11; Divinity, 4; Essence, 4, 13; Face, 4; feminine form, 4; God as Lord of both East and West, 309; as "hidden treasure," 11; humans defined in their relationship to God, 276–77; Inward (*al-Bāṭin*), 26; masculine form, 4; nearness of, 5; as One and Absolute, 3–9, 16, 21; Outward (*al-Ẓāhir*), 26; primacy of the Sacred, 305–6; revelation of, 3; as *al-Shāri',* 119; transcendence, 5; what God wants of humans, 277. *See also* Quran
Allāhu akbar, 5
'amal ṣāliḥ (good works), 248
America: African-Americans, Nation of Islam, and Malcolm X, 97; crime and punishment in, 153–54; freedom and, 290; Muslim community in, 97, 165; persecution, oppression, and bias against Muslims, 47, 49; racism in, versus Islamic heterogeneity, 181–82; separation of church and state, 147–48; spread of Islam into, 64
Amīn, al-, 35
angels, 12, 13
apostasy (*irtidād*), 49–51
Aquinas, Saint Thomas and Thomism, 115–16
Arabia, 49–50; *ḥarīm,* 51–42; Wahhābism in, 69
Arabic Islam, 87–90, *98–99* (map): language, 90; western, Arabic al-Maghrib, 90, 104
arkān al-dīn (pillars of religion), 62, 129–42. *See also 'ibādāt* (acts of worship)
art of Islam, 226–35; aniconic, 229; Arabic words *fann* and *ṣinā'ah,* 229; derived from the *ḥaqīqah* (inner truth), 228; hierarchy of, 229–30; illustration avoided, 230–31; masterpieces of architecture, 228; music, 231–34; opposition to naturalistic, 230–31; Persian miniatures, 230; revelation and, 227; unity of Islamic community and, 59; Word of God (Quran) and, 229

asceticism, 225
Ash'arism, 81, 82, 241
asmā' al-ḥusnā, 4
Averroës (Ibn Rushd), 82, 83, 118
Avicenna (Ibn Sīnā), 82, 118
Axial Age, 19–20, 21
āyāt (signs), 15
Azerbaijan: Shī'ism in, 65, 72

Bābism, 79, 102
Bahā' al-Dīn Naqshband, 139
Bahā' Allāh, 79
Bahā'ism, 79, 80
Bahrain: Shī'ism in, 65, 72
balance. *See mīzān, al-;* justice
Balkans, 47
Bangladesh, 46, 95
barakah (grace), 24–25; *ḥajj* and, 138; Muḥammadan *barakah,* 38; *Sharī'ah* and, 119–20; of Sufism, 177
bashar, 28
basmalah, 22
Battle of Badr, 260
Battle of Manzikert, 93–94
Bāyazīd Basṭāmī, 212
bazaar, 179–80
"beautiful Names." *See* Divine Names
beauty, 201, 222–27; danger in, 224–25; Divine Name, *al-Jamīl,* 222; goodness and, 223–24; *iḥsān* (spiritual beauty), 60, 61, 62, 235–36, 314; Islamic art and, 226–35; Islam as religion of, 223–25; *Jamāl* (Beauty), 4; as ladder to Divine Beauty, 225–26; Truth and, 222–23
Benares, India, 180–81, 215
Bhagavad Gita, 40
Bible: 1 Cor. *15:55,* 269; Duet. *4:13,* 117; Duet. *11:13,* 116; Exod. *21:1,* 117; Gen., 10; Gen. *2:11–17,* 117; Gen. 9:1–7, 117; Gen. *29:6,* 117; Gen. *26:5,* 116; John *8:32,* 291; Lev. *19–20, 22,* 117; Matt. *5:44,* 253; Matt. *8:34,* 291; Num. *18–21,* 135
bid'ah (innovation), 85–86
Bilāl ibn Rabah al-Ḥabashī, 92
Bīrūnī, al-, 40
Black African Islam, 92, *98–99* (map), 165; Bilāl ibn Rabah al-Ḥabashī and, 92; languages of, 92–93; Mahdīism, 107; Mali Empire and, 92; music, spiritual, in, 234; slavery and, 182; Sudan, 93
Bosnia, 96–97
Brelvi movement, 102, 265
Buddha, 19, 33–34, 39
Buddhism, 8, 18, 21, 40, 52, 208, 221; beauty and, 224; freedom and, 291; Mahayana, 65
Burckhardt, Titus, 108, 185–86, 228
Burma, 46

Cairo, Egypt, 71, 73; holy sites in, 140; Ibn Ṭūlūn Mosque, 228; Khān-Khalīlī bazaar, 180; Mosque of the "Head of Ḥusayn," 139, 140, 180
caliphs and caliphate, 65–66, 149; 'Abbāsid, 73, 89, 178; Fāṭimid, 73; Sokoto, 102; Umayyad, 161
Canada: Ismā'īlīs in, 75
Catholicism (Roman Catholicism), 65; apophatic theology of, 5l *Credo in unum Deum* (I believe in one God), 3–4; Latin Mass and, 25; magisterium, 6
Central Asia: Ḥanafism in, 68; Ismā'īlī in, 75; Māturidism in, 82
charity or almsgiving, 134–36; *fiṭriyyah,* 135; *khums,* 135; *ṣadaqah,* 135; *waāf,* 136; *zakāh,* 134–35. *See also zakāh*
Chinese Islam, 46, 96, 165; Sinkiang or Eastern Turkistan, 96
Chishtiyyah, 64
Christianity, 18, 21, 39; acceptance of ideas in, 6; attacks on the Prophet of Islam, 26–27; Crusades, 257–58; European, 19, 89; evil, concept of, 10; *extra ecclesiam nulla salus* (no salvation outside the church), 21; God is Love, 210–11; hierarchy of believers within, 60; Islam, connection to, 40–41, 42, 60; Islam versus, 12, 21–22; Latin as liturgical language of, 89; marriage and monogamy, 185–86; martyrdom and, 269; as minorities in Islamic countries, 46, 49; missionary activity of, and tensions with Muslims, 47–49, 79; monks, 176; mysticism, 64; Pauline, 89; pilgrimage and, 138–39; prophets, 4; religious dialogue and, 52; rise of, 20; sects, 76; sin of disobedience (original sin), 7, 12; suffering in, 211; tithing compared to *zakāh,* 134–35; Triune God of, 21
cleanliness, 130
community. *See ummah* (community)
Compassion and Mercy (*raḥmah*), 201, 203–9; Divine Names, *al-Raḥmān* (Infinitely Good) and *al-Raḥīm* (All-Merciful) and, 204; function in Islamic life, 205–9; goal of Quranic revelation and, 209; relationship of God to

human and, 205–6; relationship of human to human and, 206–8; relationship of human to nonhuman and, 208; Rūmī poem and, 205; suffering not identified with, 211; Sufism on, 204
Confucius and Confucianism, 19, 21, 40, 52
Coomaraswamy, A. K., 229
Copts, 168
creation, 9–15; anthropogenesis (creation of human beings), 12–15; good and evil, 9–10; humanity, 16; purpose of, 11; world (cosmos), 10–12, 204
The Crisis of the Modern World (R. Guénon), 311

Dādājī Ganjbakhsh, 139
dār al-ḥarb (Abode of War), 163–65
dār al-islām (Abode of Islam), 58, 88, 100, 163–65, 312–13; minorities living in, 166–68. *See also* Islamic culture
dār-al-ṣulḥ (Abode of Peace), 163–64, 217, 221
Darqāwī, Shaykh al-, 105
David, 34
death, 33, 65; shroud, 136
dietary regulations, 126–28
dīn, 16, 62. *See also* religion (dīn)
Divine Comedy (Dante), 11, 31, 245, 247
Divine Names and Qualities, 81, 203; "beautiful Names," 3–5; beauty, *al-Jamīl,* 222; compassion and mercy, *al-Raḥmān* (Infinitely Good) and *al-Raḥīm* (All-Merciful) and, 204–9; human existence as manifestation of, 11, 13–14; justice, *al-ʿĀdil, al-Muqsit, al-Ḥakam,* 241; love, *al-Wadūd,* 209–15; peace, *al-Salām,* 218, 220; truth, *al-Ḥaqq,* 222, 264; world as manifestation of, 11
Divine Nature, 4, 16; femininity and masculinity, 4, 188
Divine Order: masculine and feminine dimensions, 5
Divine Unity. *See tawḥīd* (Divine Unity)
Divine Will, 18
Druze, 77, 78
Duns Scotus, John, 116

East Africa: Ismāʿīlī in, 75; Shīʿism in, 65; Sufism in, 104. *See also* Black African Islam
economics (*al-iqtiṣād*): economic teachings, 144–47; employer-employee relations, 145–46; forbidden practices, 146; mercantile activity, 146–47, 179–80; property, 145; rights and, 283; work ethic, 145
Egypt: Al-Azhar Unversity, 73; Cairo, 71, 73; as center of Arab culture, 88–89; Christians in, 167; *fillāḥīn* in, 181; head covering for women, 196; holy sites in, 139, 140; Islamization of, 106; Mosque of the "Head of Ḥusayn," Cairo, 139, 140; Muḥammad Shāfiʿī and, 69, 73; music, spiritual, in, 234; Muslim Brotherhood in, 106; Napoleonic invasion of, 101, 102; nomads in, 175; reactions to Westernization in, 105; religious pluralism and, 46, 52; Sunnism in, 67; Ṭaḥāwism in, 82
Elijah, 72
Eliot, T. S., 311
Ellul, Jacques, 108
eschatology. *See maʿād* (eschatology)
ethics: *Sharīʿah* and, 155–56; world civilizations and adherence to, 312–14
Europe: Christianity in, 89; church and state, 148; crime and punishment in, 153–54; development of, versus Islamic world, 310–11; Ḥanafism in, 68; imperialism of, and Muslim lands, 100–104; Muslims of, 96–97, 165; spread of Islam in, 64
Eve. *See* Ḥawwāʾ
evil, 9–10, 129
Ezra, Abraham ibn, 210

Fakhr al-Dīn al-Rāzī, 81
family, 183–88; bonds over tribal, but truth over family, 169–70, 183; divorce, 184–85; lack of illegitimate children, 187; male and female, Islamic perspective, 188–89; marriage, 183–84, 185–88; Quran on, 169–70; responsibility to, 279; women and women's rights in, 185, 189–97
Fārābī, al-, 82
farḍ (obligatory actions), 126
Fāṭimah, 30, 140
Fāṭimid, caliphate 73
fillāḥīn, 181
fiqh (rules and regulations), 122–24, 142. *See also muʿāmalāt* (transactions)
firdaws (paradise), 247
fiṭrah, al- (primordial nature), 6–7
freedom, 290–96; contemporary Muslim responses to the issue of, and human rights, 296–99; God as absolute, 291–92; attachments, freedom from, 291; obedience to God and, 292–93; political and social, 293–94; as release

from limitations, 291; religion and freedom from the self, 291, 292, 294; West and, 290–91, 294–95. *See also* human rights
Furqān, al-, 25
Foucault, Père de, 48
free will, 81
Freemasonry, 180
fundamentalism, 9, 40, 46, 106–7, 108–12; Ikhwān al-Muslimīn (Muslim Brotherhood), 106; Jamāʻat-i islāmī, 106; reaction to Westernization and, 105–6; violent extremists and, 106–7, 109, 262–63

Gabriel (Jibra'īl), archangel, 22, 30, 31; *ḥadīth* of, 60–61, 236
Ghadīr Khumm, 66
Ghazzālī, al-, 81, 144, 212–13, 233
Ghulām Aḥmad, 79, 80, 102
Ginān, 74
God. *See* Allah (God)
Goethe, Johann Wolfgang, 28
goodness: beauty and, 223–25; and evil, 9–10, 129
grace. *See barakah*
Grand Mosque of Cordova, 52
Greece (ancient), 19; Platonism, 19; Pythagoras and Phythagoreanism, 19, 21
Guénon, René, 108, 311
Guide for the Perplexed, The (Maimonides), 83
guilds (*aṣnāf*), 180–81
Gulshan-i rāz (The Secret Garden of Divine Mysteries [Shabistarī]), 36

Ḥadīth or ḥadīth qudsī, 10–11, 14, 15, 37–8, 55; on acting justly, 253, 254–55; on animals and vegetal world, 208; on attainment of virtue, 199; on beauty, 201, 227; on consensus and the law, 121; on divorce, 184; economic teachings and, 145; on education, 193; environmental teachings, 143; eschatological, and Mahdīism, 102–3; ethical teachings of, 155–56; *ḥadīth* of Gabriel, 60–61, 236; political teachings, 147; on possession of truth, 76; Prophetic, 237; society, ideal, in, 169; as source for *Sharīʻah,* 120–22; unity in the community of Islam and, 58
Ḥadrat-i Maʻsūmah, 140
Ḥāfiẓ, 44, 316
Hagia Sophia, 51
ḥajj, 32, 71, 136–39; abstention from sexual activity and, 136; becoming *muḥrim,* 136; black stone as sign of the covenant, 137; cloth worn by pilgrims (*iḥrām*), 136; problems of accommodating pilgrims, 138; qualifying for, 138; rites for, 137; season for (*ʻumrah*), 141; unity in the community of Islam and, 59, 137–38
ḥājjī, 171–72
Ḥākim bi'Llāh, al-, 77
ḥalāl (permissible acts), 126, 127–28
Ḥanbalī School, 68, 69, 81
Ḥanafī, 68, 81
ḥaqīqah (truth) and *ḥaqq* (truth and reality) , 281; balance and, 244; beauty and, 222–23; Divine Law and, 156; Divine Truth, *al-Ḥaqq,* 222, 241, 264, 316; hierarchy within, 60; rights and responsibilities and, 281–82
ḥarām (forbidden acts), 126–27; economic, 146
Ḥasan al-Bannā', 106
Hasidic, 64, 210
Ḥawwā' (Eve), 15
Hick, John, 53
Hinduism, 18, 19, 21, 34, 40, 95; Benares, 51; *bhakti* movement, 210; Sat Panth and, 74
hijrah, 31
history: Battle of Badr, 260; Battle of Manzikert, 93–94; European domination of Muslin lands, crisis and eschatological overtones, 100–105; Iranian Revolution, 1979, 107; Islamic, infidels in, 44; Mongol invasion, 174; movements in Islamic, 27, 78–79; of religions, 18–21; revelation's function in, 18–19; spread of Islam, 63–64, 106, 216–17; World War II and Islam, 103, 104–5, 107, 154. *See also* Islamic culture; Ottoman Empire
Hudā, al-, 25
ḥudūd (punishments and restrictive ordinances), 151–54; Jewish law compared to, 151–52; Quran and, 152
human beings and humanity: as *ʻabd Allāh* (God's servant), 13; as central agent of God on earth, 11; creation of, 16; defined in relationship to God, 276–77; diversity of races, 16; dominance on earth, 13; ethical and spiritual nature of, 309–16; freedom to rebel, 15; God as Lord of both East and West, 309; imperfection of, 208–9; intelligence, 7, 13 ; mortal man (*bashar*), 28; primordial nature (*al-fiṭrah*), 6–7; responsibilities of,

277–81; rights of, 281–90; sin (*shirk*), 7; as theophany, 13–14; unity within the diversity, 16; Universal Man (*al-insān al-kāmil*), 28; as vicegerent (*khalīfah*), 12, 13, 15, 76; what does it mean to be human, 275–77; what God wants of humans, 277. *See also* human responsibilities; human rights
human responsibilities, 277–81; to environment, 299; to family, 279; to God, 277–78, 304–5; to oneself, 278–279; to society, 279; universal declaration of, 299; what happens to those who do not fulfill duty, 279–81
human rights, 281–90; choice of spouse, 282–84; contemporary Muslim responses to the issue of, and freedom, 296–99; cultural values and, 287, 303–4; enumeration of, 296–97; God's rights versus, 287–88, 303; *ḥaqq* and *al-Ḥaqq,* 281; immortal souls and, 282–83; Islamic deliberations on, 296, 300; Islamic ideals and understanding of, 297, 301; legal, 284–85; on nonbelievers, 301–2; personal, 282–84; political, 285–87; Quranic and *Ḥadīth* references for, 296–97; secular versus Islamic understanding of, 287–90, 302–3; society's rights versus, 303; West and, 297–98; women and, 288–90
Ḥusayn, Imām (*Sayyid al-shuhadā'*), 139, 140, 269

'Ibādīs, 77, 87, 123
'ibādāt (acts of worship), 129–42; almsgiving (*zakāh*), 134–36; daily prayers (*ṣalāh*), 130–32; fasting (*ṣawm*), 132–34; *jihād* in, 259; others based on *Sunnah,* 141–42; pilgrimage (*ḥajj*), 136–41; sacredness of actions in daily life, 141; as service, 277, 278. *See also* charity or almsgiving; *ḥajj*; Ramaḍān; *ṣalāh*
Iblīs (Devil or Satan), 12–13, 14; misuse of analogy by, 14; nature of fire, 14; power over human beings, 15
Ibn 'Arabī, Muḥyī al-Dīn, 83, 118, 213
Ibn Khaldūn, 173
Ibrāhīm (son of the Prophet), 34
iḥqāq, 281
iḥsān (spiritual beauty), 60, 61, 62, 235–36, 314
ijmā' (consensus in law), 121
ijtihād, 123
Ikhwān al-Muslimīn (Muslim Brotherhood), 106
Illich, Ivan, 108
Imām: first, 66; mausoleums of, 139; martyrdom of, 269; role of magisterium played by, 85–86. *See also* Twelve-Imām Shī'ites; *specific persons*
īmān, al- (faith), 38, 43, 44, 60, 61, 62; leader of daily prayers and honorific title, 67; Sunnism and Shī'ism, difference in meaning, 67]
individuals, divine judging of, 159–60, 245, 248
India, Indian subcontinent, and Indo-Pakistani-Bangladeshi Islam, 94–95, *98–99* (map), 46; Benares silk and Muslim guilds, 180–81; British missionaries and Aḥmadiyyah movement, 79; conquest of Muḥammad ibn Qāsim and, 94; Ḥanafism in, 68; holy sites in, 139; languages of and Urdu, 94–95; music, spiritual, in, 234; Muslim minorities in India, 165; Shī'ism in, 65, 74–75; Sufism in, 94
Indonesia: religious pluralism and, 48, 52; Shāfi'īs in, 69
insān (human being), 7
inshā'a'Llāh, 22–23
inspiration (*ilhām*), 17
Iran: 'Alīallāhī in, 77; bazaar, Tehran, 179–80; holy sites in, 139, 140; Islamization of, 105; *jihād-i sāzandigī,* 257; Mahdīism and Ayatollah Khomeini, 107; Pashtus, 175; reactions to Westernization in, 105; religious pluralism and, 46, 52; Reza Shah and unveiling of women in, 195; rule of jurisprudent (*wilāyat-i faqīh*), 148, 149; rule of *'ulamā',* 149; Sabaeans in, 78; *Sharī'ah* in, 155; Shī'ism in, 65, 71, 72
Iraq: 'Abbāsid caliphate, 89; 'Alīallāhī in, 77; Baghdad, 73, 81; holy sites in, 139; religious pluralism and, 46, 49; Sabaeans in, 78; as Sassanid capital, 89; Shī'ism in, 65, 67, 71, 72; Yazīdīs in, 78
'irfān, 83
Islam: acceptance of ideas in, 6; afterlife, belief in, 244–48; art, as central manifestation of, 228–35; attitude toward other religions in history, 39–42; believers and infidels (*kāfirs*), 42–46; central doctrines, 58, 61; Christianity, connection to, 40–41, 42, 60; Christianity versus, 21–22; community

(*ummah*) in, 157, 159–63; community system (*millat*) of, 125–26, 167–68; conversion and, 49–51, 216; cosmopolitan and worldwide religious perceptive, 40; creation depicted in, 9–15; credo at the heart of, 32, 314–16; cultural zones, 87–100, *98–99* (map); diversity within, 57, 63; eschatological (*ma'ād*) beliefs of, 244–45; evil, concept of, 10; fundamentalism and modernistic currents, 9, 40, 46, 100–112, *111*, 183; God is One, 3–9, 315–16; hierarchy within, 59–65; historic contact with other religions, 39–40; intellectual and theological diversity, 80–84; Judaism and, 41–42; lack of sacerdotal authority in, 6; Law (*Sharī'ah)*, 25, 49–52, 115–56; love for the Prophet, 35–37, 211; Mahdīism, 72, 78–79, 102–3, 107; Man (*insān*), 6–7; name from *al-islām* (surrender), 8, 17; origins and rise of, 20–21, 65–66; orthodoxy and heterodoxy in, 84–87; pillars of (*arkān al-dīn*), 62, 126, 129; primacy of the Sacred, 305–6; as primordial and final religion, 18, 20–21; racial heterogeneity of, 182; reformists, 102–4; as religion of beauty, 223–25; as "religion of the straight path" (*al-ṣirāṭ al-mustaqīm*), 85 as "religion of the sword," 216–18, *see also* war; religious pluralism today and, 46–54; sects within, 76–80; secularism, globalization, and consumerism as threats to, 199; separation of Sunnism and Shī'ism, 63, 65–67; society, 168–81, 197–99; spectrum of Islam, *11*; striving after unity (*tawḥīd*) as the heart of, 6, 197–98; surrender, 7–9, 34, 220; symbolized as a circle whose center is *Tarīqah*, 60; testifications of, 3, 85; theocracy compared to, 148–49; as third Abrahamic religion, 41; traditionalists, 107–12, *111*; unity within the community (*ummah*) of, 37, 58–59, 63; virtues of, 35; Will of God, emphasis on, 10. *See also Sharī'ah*; Shī'ite and Shī'ism; Sufism; Sunnism; *specific topics*

islām, al- (surrender), 8, 17, 34, 60, 61, 62, 220

Islamic culture, 87–100, *98–99* (map); American, 97; Arabic, 87–90; Black African, 92–93; Chinese, 96; European, 96–97; Indo-Pakistani-Bangladeshi, 94–95; Malay, 95–96; Muslim minorities, 165–66; Persian/Iranian, 90–91; racial heterogeneity of, 182; Turkish/Turkic, 93–94

Ismā'īlīs, 44, 64, 73–75, 76, 82, 86, 123; Aga Khānid and the Bohras, 75; assassins, origins of, 74; *fadā'iyān,* 74; Fāṭimid, 77; forts, 74; *kalām,* 82; Ṭayyibiyyah, 74–75

Israel: Arab-Israeli wars, 105; Druze in, 77, 78

Istanbul, 51

istiḥsān (equity), 121

īthār (giving, in the path of God), 135–36

jafr, 26

Ja'far al-Ṣādiq, 26, 68, 72, 73, 123

Jalāl (Majesty), 4–5

Jalālī calendar, 133

Jamā'at-i islāmī, 106

Jamāl (Beauty), 4

Jamāl al-Dīn al-Afghānī. *See* Afghānī, al-, Jamāl al-Dīn

Japan, 19

Jerusalem: celestial, 246; direction faced during prayer and, 32; mosque of the Dome of the Rock, 31; as site of eschatological events, 32

Jesus Christ, 3, 17, 169; God's Will and, 305–6; Europe and, 19; as founder of a religion, 33, 34; Islamic eschatology and, 246; miracles of, 24; Quram compared to, 23; as prophet, 3, 18; *ummah* of, 160; virgin birth, 40–41

jihād, 256–66; as armed struggle, 262–63; as defense (*difā'ī*), 262, 266; greater, 260–61; legitimate and absence of hate and anger, 264–65; lesser, 261; lesser and greater, famous saying of the Prophet, 260; life cycle and daily life of a Muslim and, 259; *mujāhid* (holy warrior), 257, 265; popular meaning versus theological and juridical sense, 257–57; term in Arabic, 256, 258; in transactions, 259–60; who can declare, 263–64

jizyah (religious tax), 166

John of the Cross, 214

Jordan, 52; Islamization of, 106

Joshua, 41

Judaism, 19, 21, 39; apophatic theology of, 5; *barak,* 24; dialogue with Muslims, 52–53; dietary laws, compared to Islamic, 128; Hasidim, 64, 210; Islam and, 40–41; law, *Halakhah,* 41, 116–17, 151–52; original sin, 12; prophets, 3, 4, 41; revelation of God to, 3; sacred language, Hebrew, 41;

sexuality and marriage in, 184; suffering in, 211; tithing compared to *zakāh,* 134–35
justice, 81, 237, 240–43; 'Alī, views on, 248–52; on acting justly, 252–55; the balance and, 243–44; centrality of to moral and spiritual life, 239; combating oppression and injustice, 255–271; Day of Judgment, 159, 243; Divine Names, *al-'Ādil, al-Musqsit, al-Ḥakam,* 241; God is just, and justice is related to him, 240; human, and its modes, 252–56; innate human sense of justice and the search for justice, 239–40; peace and, 272; *Sharī'ah* and, 253–56; sources for guidance, 253, 255

Ka'bah (House of God), 30, 32, 136–37, 141
Kabbala, 26; Kabbalistic tradition, 64
Kafirestan, 78
kāfirs (nonbelievers), 42–46
kalām (theology), 81–84. *See also* theology
Kamāl (Perfection), 4
Karbalā', tragedy of, 71
Khadījah, 29–30, 34, 140, 146, 179, 193
khalīfah or *khalīfat Allāh* (vicegerent), 12, 13, 15, 152
khalīfah rasūl Allāh, 65
Khalwatiyyah, 64
Khawārij, 44, 66, 86
Khayyām, 'Umar, 133
Khomeini, Ayatollah, 107, 149, 288
Khurasn, 82, 212
Khwājah 'Abd Allāh Anṣārī, 139
Kindaī, al-, 82
kitāb (book), 17
Krishna, 34, 40
kufr (infidelity), 44, 45
kuffār (infidels), 44
Küng, Hans, 53
Kurds, 168

Lā ilāha illa'Llāh, 3, 39
Ladakh, 46
Lahore, Punjab, Pakistan, 214–15
Lao-Tze, 19, 40
law: Christianity and, 118; Divine Islamic Law (*Sharī'ah),* 16, 25, 41, 49–52, 59, 69, 80, 108, 115–56; Divine Will versus reason, 115–16; Ja 'farī School, 68, 69; Jewish, 41, 116–17; minorities living within *dār al-islām,* 166–68; Muslim minorities living outside of *dār al-islām* and, 165–66; natural, 115–16; nonreligious Islamic law (*qānūn*), 122; philosophy of, in Islam, 115–20; Quran and, 27; schools of (*madhhab*), 67, 68–69, 120, 123–24; secularization of, 116; Thomism, 115–16. *See also Sharī'ah*
Lebanon, 52; Christians in, 167; Druze in, 77, 78; Shī'ism in, 65, 71, 72
Lings, Martin, 108
Lote Tree of the Uttermost End, 32
love, 201, 209–16; Divine, 209–11; Divine Name, *al-Wadūd,* 209; creation and, 11; in and for God, 211–12, 214; Islamic literature of, 213–15; poems of Rābi'ah al-'Adawiyyah and, 212; poems of Rūmī, 213; for the Prophet, 35–37, 211; Quranic references, 209–10; suffering and, 211; Sufism and, 212–15
Lover and the Beloved, The (Lull), 213
Lull, Raymond, 213
lunar calendar, 133–34
Luther, Martin, 135

ma'ād (eschatology), 81, 244–48; Christ's role in, 246; Day of Judgment, 159, 243, 244; individual and, 245–46; heaven, hell, and purgatory, 246–47; human history and, 245–46; Jesusalem as site of eschatological events, 32; Mahdīism, 72–73, 78–79, 102–3, 107; unity in the community of Islam and, 58
ma'ṣūm (inerrant), 67
madhhab (schools of Law), 67
madrasahs, 181
maghāzī (early wars in defense of the faith), 32
Mahdīism, 72–73, 78–79, 102–3, 107; Brelvi movement, 102, 265; Ghulām Aḥmad and Bābism, 79, 102
Maimonides, 82
makrūh (abominable acts), 126, 127
maktūb ("it is written"), 9
Malay Islam, 95–96, *98–99* (map); Islamization of, 106; languages, 95; religious pluralism and, 46, 52, 53; Shāfi'īs in, 69; Sufism in, 95, 96
Malcolm X (El-Hajj Malik El-Shabazz), 97
Mālik al-Ashtar, 250–52
Mālik ibn Anas, 68
Mālikism, 68, 81
Maḥmūd Shaltūt, 262
man (human, *insān*). *See* human beings and humanity

mandūb (recommended actions), 126, 127
Manichaeism, 39
Mansa Mūsā, 92
maqām (mausoleum), 140
Maraboutism, 181
marriage, 183–84, 185–88; choice of spouse, 283; polygamy, 185–86
martyrdom, 268–71; in Christianity, 268–69; *shahīd,* 270; suicide bombers, 268, 270–71; who are martyrs, 269
Mashhad, Iran, 139, 140
maṣlaḥah mursalāh (law and the public interest), 121
Māturīdism, 82
Mawdūdī, Mawlānā Abu'l-'Alā', 106
Mawlawiyyah, 64
Mecca: direction faced during prayer and, 32; Grand Mosque takeover, 1980, 107; *ḥajj* and, 136–39, 141; Ka'bah (House of God), 30, 32, 136–37, 141; migration by the Prophet (*al-hijrah*), 31; non-Christians and, 51; the Prophet and, 29, 30, 31; Wahhābism and, 69
Medina, 31, 32–33, 66; Mālikism in, 68; Mosque of the Prophet, 33; pilgrimage sites in, 139; Wahhābism and, 69
men: choice of spouse and, 283; marriage and polygamy, 185–88; rights and role of, 188–89, 192
Menuhin, Yehudi, 232–34
mercy. *See* compassion and mercy
merchant class and mercantilism, 146–47, 179–80
mi'rāj, 31–32
Mian Mir, 214
millat or community system of, 125–26, 167–68
mīzān, al-, 243–44
modernists, 9, 40, 46, 103–5, 140, 183; Jamāl al-Dīn al-Afghānī, 103; independence movements and, 103–4; Marxism and, 105, 295; Muḥammad 'Abduh, 103; Muḥammad Iqbāl, 103; Sir Sayyid Aḥmad Khān, 103; Young Turk movement, 103
Morocco, 52, 68, 234
Moses, 18, 24, 34; Mr. Nebo as resting place, 41; *ummah* of, 160
mosques: conversion of, 52; Dome of the Rock, 31; Grand Mosque of Cordova, 52; Ibn Ṭūlūn Mosque, Cairo, 228; masterpieces of architecture, 228; Mosque of the "Head of Ḥusayn," Cairo, 139; Mosque of the Prophet, 33
mu'āmalāt (transactions), 152–51; economic teachings, 144–47; environmental teachings, 142–44; *jihād* in, 259–60; political teachings, 147–51
Mu'īn al-Dīn Chishtī, 139
mu'min (possessor of faith), 43, 60, 62
Mu'tazilite school, 81, 82, 241
mubāḥ (permissible acts), 126, 127
Muḥammad, 35. *See also* Prophet of Islam, the
Muḥammad 'Abduh, 82, 103
Muḥammad al-Bāqir, Imām, 72, 123
Muḥammad al-Mahdī, 72; in occultation (*ghaybah*), 72
Muḥammad, Elijah, 97
Muḥammad ibn 'Abd al-Wahhāb, 102
Muḥammad ibn Qāsim, 94
Muḥammad Iqbāl, 103
Muḥammadan *barakah,* 38
Muḥammadun rasūl Allāh, 3, 39
muḥsin (possessor of virtue), 60, 62
mujāhid (holy warrior), 257, 265
mujāhidah (state of combating distractions of the soul), 257
mujtahid, 123
Mūsā al-Kāẓim, Imām, 73
music, 231–34; allowed, 232–33; connecting with God and, 233; Taliban's banning of, 233–34; types of in, Islamic world, 234; West influenced by, 233
muslim (possessor of surrender), 60, 62
Muslims: acceptance of the messengership and prophethood of Muḥammad, 39; acceptance of *Sharī'ah* and, 118, 119; anger over Westernization and globalization, 48; dynasties, 66; equality before the law and, 124–26, 253–54, 284; exclusivism and, 53; *jihād* and daily life, 258–59; as minorities (outside *dār al-islām*), 165–66; *mu'min,* 43; persecution, oppression, and bias against, 47, 49; rationalism or skepticism of the West and, 13; religious life of, 5; religious pluralism and, 46–54; respect for and faith in prophets, 36–37, 38–39; *shahādahs* (testifications) of, 3, 39, 85, 272; *Sunnah* as model for living, 37, 38; as *ummah wasaṭah* (middle community), 161–62; unity of, 37, 58–59, 100. *See also* Islamic culture
Musta'lis, 73–74
Mustanṣir bi'Llāh, 73
mysticism, 82, 213

Nādir Shāh, 91
nafas al-Raḥmān, 11, 204

Naqshbandiyyah, 64
Naṣīr al-Dīn Ṭūsī, 82
nature: compassion and mercy and, 208; environmental teachings, 142–44; Islamic rites harmonized with, 12; Western destruction of, 310–11
Niʿmatullāhiyyah, 64
Niẓām al-Dīn Awliyā', 139
Nizārīs, 73, 74
Nocturnal Journey (*al-miʿrāj*), 31–32
nomads, 173–75
North Africa: al-Maghrib, 68; Mālikism in, 68; Maraboutism, 181
Nuṣayrīs, 78
Nuṣrat Fātiḥ ʿAlī Khān, 234
Nutrition, 9

Oman, ʿIbādīs in, 77
Orthodox Christian Church, 87; apophatic theology of, 5; in Ottoman Empire, 167
orthodoxy and orthopraxy, 84–87; extremists, 86, 262–63; formal and exoteric level, 87; levels of practice and, 85; middle of the spectrum, Sunnism and Shīʿism of the Twelve-Imām School, 86; role of magisterium played by *ummah* and the Imām, 85–86; "straight path" (*al-ṣirāt al-mustaqīm*), 85
Ottoman Empire, 77, 94; Battle of Lepanto, 101; caliphs, 66; Europeans as *kuffār*, 44; fall of, 150; Ḥanafī scholars, 45; *millat* or community system of, 125–26, 168; minorities living in, 167; Twelve-Imām Shīʿism and, 76

Pakistan: Aḥmadiyyah movement, 79–80; Islamization of, 105; link to Afghānīstan, 68; music, spiritual, in, 234; reactions to Westernization in, 105; religious pluralism and, 48, 53; Shīʿism in, 65; Ḥanafism in, 68; Urdu language, 95
Palestine, 46
paradise, 14, 26, 31, 245–48
Path of Eloquence (*Nahj al-balāghah* [ʿAlī]), 248
peace, 201, 215–22; difficulty in attaining, 219; Divine Name, *al-Salām,* 218, 220; justice and, 272; Quran on seeking of, 218–19; refutation of Islam as "religion of the sword," 216–18; surrender to God (*taslīm*) and, 220. *See also* justice; war
Peripatetic (*mashshā'ī*) school, 82
Persian Empire, 19, 89, 178
Persian Islam, 89, 90–91, *98–99* (map); Iranian languages (Kurdish, Baluchi, Pashtu), 91; Iranian race, 90; Ismāʿīlīs in, 75; language (Farsi, Dari, and Tajik), 90–91; music, spiritual, in, 234; Persian Gulf War, 49; Salmān-i Fārsī, 91; Shīʿism in, 65, 67, 71, 91; Sunnism in, 91. *See also* Iran
Philippines, religious pluralism and, 46
philosophy: great Islamic philosophers, 82; Greek and Syriac texts, translations, and incorporation of Greek philosophies into the Quranic worldview, 82; influence of Islamic on the West, 82–83; Ismāʿīlī school, 82; of law, in Islam, 115–20; Peripatetic (*mashshā'ī*) school, 82; Quran and, 27, 82; School of Illumination (*ishrāq*), 83; Sufism (gnosis), 83; "the transcendent theosophy," 83
pilgrimages: Christian, 138–39; *ḥajj,* 136–39; Jerusalem, 139; loci of grace, various, 139–40; tomb of the Prophet, Medina, 139; Wahhābī opposition, 140–41. *See also ḥajj*
Plato, 241
political teachings, theory, structure, 147–51; ʿAlī on, 249–50; human rights and governmental power, 285–87; Islam as nomocracy, 148–50; oppression (*ẓu*lm), 249; Quran, basic principles in, 147, 149; role of government, 149–50; secularist governments, 151; theocracy compared to Islamic ideal, 148–49*; ʿulma* ¯', 148, 149
prayer. *See ṣalāh* (daily prayers)
predestination, 81
Prophet of Islam, 27–39; animals, kindness to, 208; battle of Badr, 260; benediction invoked upon mention of, 35–36; character and stature of, 28; Christian attacks on, 26–27; death, 33, 65; descendents of (*sayyids* or *sharīfs*), 30, 91; fasting and, 133; grace of (Muḥammadan *barakah*), 38; *ḥadīth* of Gabriel, 60–61; *ḥadīth qudsī* of, 10–11, 14, 37–38; *ḥajj* and, 32, 136; importance of, traditional, 28, 33; "initiatic" chain, or *silsilah,* 64, 67; on *jihād,* 260; life of, 29–33, 146, 179; love for, 35–37, 38; as Logos and manifestation of Logos, 36; Mecca and, 29, 30, 31, 32; Mecca migration (*al-hijrah*), 31; names of, 35; Nocturnal Journey (*al-miʿrāj*), 31–32; polygamy of, 187; purification

of the Ka'bah, 32; Quran revealed to, 8, 22, 24, 30, 32; rules of war, 267; sayings of (*aḥādīth*), 37; as the "Seal of Prophets," 18, 28; slavery and, 181; succession to, 66; Sufi poem on, 28; *Sunnah* (doings) as model for living, 37, 38; testification, 3, 39; *ummah*, bonds of, and, 173; unification of Arabia and, 33; virtues of emulated, 35; wives of, 29–30

prophets and prophecy (*nubuwwah*), 15–22; Adam, 13, 17; belief in, 38–39; false, 17; Hebrew, 3, 19, 34, 41; Jesus Christ, 3, 17, 24; as living realities in the Islamic universe, 4; miracles given to corresponding to the era, 24; Moses, 18, 24; multiplicity of, 15–16, 21, 36, 53; Muslim respect for, 36–37; number of, 17; unity in the community of Islam and, 58, 100. *See also* Prophet of Islam, The

punishments and restrictive ordinances. *See ḥudūd*

purgatorial states, 246

Qādiriyyah, 64

qiblah, 32

qiyās (analogy, case law), 121

Qom, Iran, 139, 140

Qualities of God, 4

Quran (*al-Qur'ān*, the Recitation), 2, 22–27; on acting justly, 253, 254–55; the balance, 243–44; as central theophany of Islam, 22; chapters (*sūrahs*) and verses (*āyahs*), 26; Christ compared to, 23; commentaries (*tafsīr* and *ta'wīl*), 26, 37; on compassion and mercy, 204; cosmos and world of nature in, 11–12; on dress, covering, veil, 195; effect of, 24–25; eloquence of, 24; economic teachigns, 144–45; environmental teachings, 143; ethical teachings of, 155–56; family bonds in, 169–70; interpreting, 85; on justice of God, 242–43; as *kitāb* (book), 17; on love, 209–10; language of, 26; levels of meaning, 26; on martyrdom, 269; names of, 25; numerical symbolism of, 26; origins and preservation of, 24; paradise described in, 246–47; on peace, 218–19, 221; phrases from, repeated throughout life, 22–23; political teachings, 147, 149; psalmody and chanting, 230, 232; punishments and restrictive ordinances (*ḥudūd*), 152; recitation of, and beauty, 224, 229–30; rites and rituals ordained by, 37; sacredness of inner meaning and outer form, 23; single form of, 23; size of, 24; society, ideal, in, 169; as source of Islamic Law (*Sharī'ah)*, 25, 120–22; Surah 96 ("The Clot,"), 30; *Sūrat al-Fātiḥah* (Opening Chapter), 131; themes of, 25–26; *Umm al-kitāb* ("the Mother Book") and, 17, 25; unity in the community of Islam and, 58, 59, 100; universalist in understanding of religion, 21, 40, 43, 53–54; as verbatim Word of God (revelation), 4, 17, 22; Virgin May in, 40–41. *See also* Index of Quranic Sources

Rābi'ah al-'Adawiyyah, 212

Rama, 34, 40

Ramaḍān: fasting and, 132–33; lunar calendar and, 133–34; unity in the community of Islam and, 59

raḥmah, 201, 203–9

Raḥmān, al-, 11, 204

Raḥīm, al-, 204

reason, 81–82

Reformists, 102–4; Salafiyyah, 102. *See also* modernists

religion (*dīn*): authentic, 3, 8; founders of, two types, 33–34; history of, 18–21; Islam's attitude toward other religions in history, 39–42; multiplicity of, necessity for, 16, 53–54; oneness of God and, 3; virtues of the adherents and founders of the religion, 35

religious pluralism, 46–54

Republic (Plato), 241

revelation (*waḥy*), 16–20, 81; creation as first, 12, 15; diversity of, 16; human state, 15; *kitāb* and, 17; multiplicity of, 21, 54; Quran as, 17; religions, 15; three grand "books," 15; *Umm al-kitāb* ("the Mother Book") and, 17, 25

Revelation of St. John, 246

Riḍā, Imām, 140

Rifā'iyyah, 64

rites and rituals: harmonized with natural phenomena, 12; ordained by the Quran, 37; tragedy of Karbalā' commemoration, 71; unity in the community of Islam and, 59. *See also ḥajj*; Ramaḍān; *other specific rites*

Roszak, Theodore, 108, 311

Rūmī (Jalāl al-Dīn Rūmī), 44, 139, 205, 213, 221, 264–65, 273

Rushdie, Salman, 288

Russia: Caucasus, 46–47; Ḥanafism in, 68; Muslim minorities in, 165

Sabaeans, 78
Ṣadr al-Dīn Shīrāzī, 83
Safavids, 77, 91
St. Augustine, 9
Saladin, 265
Salafiyyah, 102
ṣalāh (daily prayers), 130–32; content, 131; direction faced during (*qiblah*), 32, 130–31; as gate to universal, 132; *imām* leading, 131; individual prayer (*du'ā*), 132; prayer of the heart, 132; as rejuvenation, 132; ritual ablution, 130; *Sūrat al-Fātiḥah* (Opening Chapter) of the Quran, 131
Salāmah al-Raḍī, Shaykh, 105
Salmān-i Fārsī, 91, 92, 181
salvation, 81
Sanūsiyyah Order, 104–5
Sat Panth (True Path,) 74
Satan. *See* Iblīs
Saudi Arabia: punishment in, 153; *Sharī'ah* in, 154; Shī'ism in, 65; teaching of theology (*kalām*) forbidden in, 81; Wahhābism in, 69–70
ṣawm (fasting), 132–34; Ramaḍān and, 132–33
Sayyid Aḥmad Khān, 103
Sayyid Muḥammad Bāb, 79
Sayyidah Nafīsah, 140, 194
sayyids, 30
School of Illumination (*ishrāq*), 83
Schuon, Frithjof, 53, 108, 273
sects (*firaq*), 76–80, 87; Aḥmadiyyah, 79, 87; 'Alawīs of Syria (Nuṣayrīs), 78; 'Alawīs of Turkey, 77; 'Alīallāhī, 77; Bābism, 79, 102; Druze, 77, 78; Kāfirestānīs, 78; Khawārij, 77; Sabaeans, 78; Taliban, 78, 233–34; Yazīdīs, 78
secularism, 45–46, 53–54, 195, 196; criticism of, 108; family and, 198; feminism and, 196–97; human rights, versus Islamic culture, 287–90; peace and, 220
Senegal, 64
sexuality, 26; abstention during *ḥajj*, 136; charges of sexual licentiousness, 187; extramarital, Islamic versus the West, 187; human rights and, 284; laws pertaining to, 126–27; marriage and, 184–87; promiscuity, 187; as sacred and a blessing, 184; Western mores and, 183
Shabistarī, Maḥmūd, 36, 44
Shādhiliyyah, 64
Shāfi'ī, Imām Muḥammad, 68–69, 123; *Risālah* (Treatise), 123
Shāfi'ī School, 68–69, 81
shahādahs (testifications), 3, 39, 85, 270, 272
shāhid (witness), 270
shahīd (martyr), 270
Shāmil, Imām, 104, 110, 265
Sharī'ah (Islamic Law, Divine Law), 16, 25, 41, 115–56; acting justly and, 253–56; acts of worship, 129–42; application of, 154–55; *barakah* and, 120; building churches and synagogues outside the *ḥarīm*, 51–52; categories of actions and values (obligatory, recommended, forbidden, abominable, and permissable), 126–29; court, 153, 254; environmental crisis and, 144; ethical and spiritual teachings of, 155–56; God as *al-Shāri'*, 119; hierarchy of, 60; human custom (*'urf* or *'ādah*) and law as distinct from Divine law, 121–22, 243; human law, confrontation with, 154–55; human rights and, 284; *ijtihād*, 123; methodology, (principles of jurisprudence, *uṣūl al-fiqh*), 122–24; *mujtahids*, 123; new challenges to, 123–24; philosophy of, 115–20; punishment for apostasy, 49–51; punishments and restrictive ordinances (*ḥudūd*), 151–54; sacred sites and non-Muslims, 51–52; sources of, 120–22; sources, hierarchy of, 122–23; suicide forbidden by, 270–71, 278; Sunni Law, major schools, 123–24; transactions, 142–51; tree symbol and, 124; unity in the community of Islam and, 59, 100; whom it applies to, 124–26. *See also* *'ibādāt* (acts of worship); *mu'āmalāt* (transactions)
sharīfs, 30
Shi'ite Muslims and Shī'ism, 24, 37, 44, 70–76; branches of, 71–76; caliphate and, 66, 149; countries where notable, 65; *dār al-ḥarb* and principle of dissimulation (*taqiyyah*), 164–66; extremists (*ghulāt*), 86; 'Ibādī, 77, 87, 123; Imāms in, 67, 70–72; Ismā'īlī branch, 64, 73–75, 76, 82, 86, 123; *jihād* and, 262; *kalām*, 82; Mahdīism, 72–73; martyrdom and, 269; as minority, 65; Musta'līs, 73–74; name, origins of, 65; Nizārīs, 73, 74; religious tax (*khums*), 135; Sat Panth (True Path), 74; split

with Sunnism, 63, 65–66; Sufism and, 63; sultanate and, 140; tragedy of Karbalā', 71; Twelve-Imām, 44–45, 68, 71–72, 75–76, 79, 82, 86–87, 123, 140, 262; Zaydī, 75, 76, 82, 86, 123
Shintoism, 19
shirk, 7
silsilah ("initiatic" chain), 64, 67
sin, 7; differences with Christianity, 12; *shirk*, 7. *See also ḥarām* (forbidden acts); *makrūh* (abominable acts)
Singapore, Shāfi'īs in, 69
slavery, 181–83; absence of racism and, 182
society: absence of monasticism in Islam, 176; administrators, 178–79; bazaar, 179–80; caliphs and caliphate, 65–66, 149, 179; cities and, 174; classes, 175–81; compassion and mercy in, 207–8; family bonds, 169–70; goal of, 170; global orders (Seljuqs and Ottomans), 174; guilds (*aṣnāf*), 180–81; hierarchy based on *taqwā* and knowledge, 170; ideal and historic Islamic, 168–72; Islam and integration of, 197–99; Islamic conception of, 167; *khawāṣṣ* (spiritual elite) and '*āwāmm* (commoners) in, 177; merchant class, 179–80; military class, 179; nomadic element, 173–75; peasantry, 181; responsibility toward, 279–80; social mobility in, 172–73; structure of Islamic, 172–81; Sufism and spiritual elite, 177–78; sultanate, 149, 179; support and help of the poor, 170–71; tribalism, 173–74; *'ulamā'*, 175–76, 178. *See also ummah* (community)
Sokoto Caliphate, 103
Solomon, 34
Sri Lanka, 46, 95
Suarez, Francisco, 116
sub-Saharan Africa, 48
Sudan, 64, 93; Islamization of, 106; Mahdīs of, 78, 103
suffering, Islam versus Judaism and Christianity, 211
Sufism, 11, 27, 28, 43–44, 59, 62–63; "Breath of the Compassionate" as substance of cosmic existence, 11, 204; countries in which present, 64; freedom from self and, 292; function of, 64–65; as group within Islamic society, 177–78; on hierarchy of the *Sharī'ah*, 60, 62; *iḥsān* and, 62; independence movements and, 104; Indian subcontinent and, 94; "initiatic" chain, or *silsilah*, 64; *khawāṣṣ* and *'āwāmm* in, 177; love and knowledge in, 212–13; love poetry and literature, 213–15; Malay world and, 95; Maraboutism, 181; Muḥyī al-Dīn ibn 'Arabī, 83; orders of, 64; orthodoxy and, 87; saints of, commemorations at holy sites, 139–40; *Sharī'ah* and, 62–63; spread of Islam and, 63–64; *'ulamā'* among, 176
Suhrawardī Shaykh Shihāb al-Dīn, 83
suicide and suicide bombers, 270–71, 278
sultanate, 149
Sunnah of the Prophet, 28, 37; *Ḥadīth*, 37–38; interpreting, 85; rites based on, 141; source for *Sharī'ah*, 120–22; Sunnism and, 65; unity in the community of Islam and, 58, 59
Sunnism, 24, 37, 44–45, 65–70; Ash'arism, 81, 82, 241; caliphate and, 66, 149; division of followers according to schools of Law (*madhhab*), 67–70; gate of *ijtihād*, 123, 155; Ḥanbalī, 68, 69, 123; Ḥanafī, 68, 123; imām in, 67; *jihād* and, 262; Mālikī, 68, 123; martyrdom and, 269; Mu'tazilite school, 81, 82, 241; name, origins of, 65; orthodoxy of, 86–87; Shāfi'ī, 68–69, 123; split from Shī'ism, 63, 65–66; sultanate and, 149; Wahhābism, 45, 69–70
Sūrat al-Fātiḥah (Opening Chapter) of the Quran, 131
surrender (*islām, al-*) , 7–9, 17, 34, 60, 61, 62, 220; fallacious sense of, and acts with calamitous consequences, 9; peace and, 220; *taslīm*, 220
Syria, 46, 52; 'Alawīs (Nuṣayrīs) in, 78; Druze in, 77; Ḥanbalīsm in, 69; holy sites in, 139; Ismā'īlī in, 75; Shī'ism in, 65

ta'wīl (spiritual hermeneutics), 26
tasfīr (commentary), 26
Ṭaḥāwism, 82
taḥqīq, 281
Tajikistan, 90
Taliban, 78; banning of music, 233–34
Taoism, 19
Ṭarīqah (spiritual path), 63, 107; Divine Law and, 156; hierarchy within, 60, Islam as a circle and, 60; prayer of the heart, 132; Sufis and, 64
taslīm (surrender to God), 220
tawḥīd (Divine Unity), 3, 6, 7, 16, 20, 44, 81, 85, 197–98; unity in the community of Islam and, 58, 100

Ṭayyibiyyah, 74
Teresa of Avila, 214
terrorism: September 11, acts on, 263; suicide bombers, 270–71
testifications of faith. *See shahādahs*
Thailand, 46; Shāfiʿīs in, 69
thawāb (reward from God), 126
theology (*ʿilm al-kalām*), 81–84; Ashʿarism, 81, 82; Ḥanbalī school, 68, 69, 81; Ismāʿīlī, 82; Māturīdism, 82; Muʿtazilite school, 81, 82; mysticism, 82, 213; Ṭaḥāwism, 82; Twelve-Imām Shīʿite, 82; Wahhābism, 45, 69–70; Zaydīs, 82
Tibetan *Book of the Dead,* 246
Tijāniyyah Order, 104
tobacco use, 121
transcendence, 5; *Sharīʿah* and, 119
Transcendent Dimension in human life, 159–60
"transcendent theosophy, the" (*al-ḥikmat al-mutaʿāliyah*), 83
"transcendent unity of religions," 53
truth. *See ḥaqīqah*
Tunisia, 109
Turkey; ʿAlawīs in, 77; Ataturk's secularism in, 105, 109, 195; Ḥanafism in, 68; holy sites in, 139; music, spiritual, in, 234; reactions to Westernization in, 105; religious pluralism and, 46, 53; women in, 195, 196; Young Turks, 103
Turkish, Turkic Islam, 93–94, *98–99* (map); Altaic languages, 93; Battle of Manzikert and, 93–94; Ottoman Empire, 94
Twelve-Imām Shīʿism, 44–45, 71–72, 75–76, 86–87; *jihād* and, 262; *kalām,* 82; Law (Jaʿfarī Law), 68, 123; Qom, Iran, and, 140; Shaykhī, 79

ʿulamāʾ, 148, 149, 175–76; *bāzārī* and, 179; declaration of *jihād* and, 263–64
ʿUmar al-Mukhtār, 265
ʿUmar O ibn al-Khaṭṭāb, 30, 61, 66
Umm al-kitāb ("the Mother Book"), 17, 25
ummah (community), 58, 60, 157, 198; concept of, 159–63; in *dār al-ḥarb,* 163–65; in *dār al-islām,* 163–65; multiplicity of nations and, 161; Muslim minorities, 165–66; Quran on, 157, 159, 160, 161; recognized according to religious affiliation, 160; role of magisterium played by, 85–86; secularism and, 198; unity of Islamic, 161; *wasaṭah* (middle community), 162
Universal Man (*al-insān al-kāmil*), 28
universe, as combination of Divine Names, 5
Upanishads, 40
ʿurf (human customs), 121–22, 243
ʿUthmān Dan Fadio, 78, 103
ʿUthman ibn ʿAffān, 30, 66
Uzbekistan, 90

vertical triumphalism, 21
Virgin Mary, 40–41

Wadūd, al-, *209–15*
Wahhābism, 45, 69–70; opposition to visits to saints' tombs, 140
wājib (obligatory actions), 126
walāyah/wilāyah (spiritual and initiatic guidance), 63, 67, 225–26
war: combating oppression and injustice, 255–56; conditions under which war can be fought, 266–68; inner or spiritual, 260–61; *jihād,* 256–66; martyrdom and, 268–71; no peace without justice, 272; the Prophet on, 267; Quran on, 266–67; weapons of mass destruction, 267–68
Wasteland, The (T. S. Eliot), 311
Weil, Simone, 129
West Africa, 78, 104; Maraboutism, 181; tomb of Aḥmad Bamba, Touba, 139. *See also* Black African Islam
Where the Wasteland Ends (Theodore Roszak), 311
Women: choice of spouse and, 283; creation of, 14; economics and economic rights of, 147; education of, 193–94; employment of, 192–93; equality before the law, 124–26, 190, 284; in family and society, 189–97; feminism, 196–97; Islamic understanding of womanhood and woman's roles, 14, 188–89, 191; marriage and, 185–88; rights of, 185, 191; veil and covering, 194–97
world (cosmos): creation of, 10–12, 204; signs of God (*vestigia Dei*) seen in, 12

Yathrib, 31. *See also* Medina
Yazīdīs, 78
Yemen: *Sharīʿah* in, 154; Ṭayyibiyyah in, 74; Zaydī in, 75, 82

zakāh (almsgiving), 134–35
Zaydī, 75, 76, 82, 86, 123
Zayn al-ʿĀbidīn al-Sajjād, Imām, 71–72

Index of Quranic Sources

Al-Fātiḥah
1:2–7, 131

Al-Baqarah
2:30–32, 12
2:62, 43
2:115, 5
2:124, 254
2:143, 162
2:187, 152, 189
2:190, 263, 266
2:192, 266
2:213, 157
2:229, 152, 254
2:230, 152
2:256, 49, 262
2:285, 32

Al-ʿImrān
3:18, 242
3:31, 210
3:57, 254
3:108, 254
3:110, 170
3:159, 101
3:169, 269
3:171, 269

Al-Nisāʾ
4:13–14, 152
4:19, 192
4:58, 253
4:90, 266
4:136, 38
4:163–65, 54

Al-Māʾidah
5:1, 145
5:8, 237, 253, 264
5:16, 219
5:32, 266
5:42, 237
5:45, 266
5:54, 210, 214
5:69, 43
5:108, 242

Al-Anʿām
6:62, 152
6:57, 149, 242
6:114, 242
6:115, 242
6:141, 273
6:152, 244, 253

Al-Aʿrāf
7:6, 242
7:29, 253
7:34, 160
7:46, 219
7:156, 201
7:172, 7, 278
7:180, 4, 235

Al-Anfāl
8:190, 10

Al-Tawbah
9:29, 166

Yūnus
10:19, 160
10:48, 16

Hūd
11:18, 255
11:90, 210

Yūsuf
12:80, 242
12:40, 149

Al-Raʿd
13:41, 242

Ibrāhīm
14:24, 124

Al-Ḥijr
15:19
15:29, 12

Al-Nahl
16:120, 160

Banī Isrāʾīl
17:44, 11
17:81, 84

Maryam
19:62, 219
19:96, 201

Ṭa Ha
20:14, 277

Al-Anbiyāʾ
21:25, 4
21:47, 244
21:92, 157

Al-Ḥajj
22:34, 160

Al-Muʾminūn
23:14, 235

Al-Qaṣaṣ
28:88, 242

Al-ʿAnkabūt
29:8, 170
29:69, 227

Al-Sajdah
32:21, 28

Al-Aḥzāb
33:35, 125
33:56, 36

Ya Sīn
36:36, 188
36:58, 219

Al-Zumar
39:6, 16
39:9, 60
39:46, 242

Hā Mīm Al-Sajdah or *Fuṣilat*
41:34, 264
41:53, 15

Al-Shūrā
42:8, 161

Al-Jāthiyah
45:16, 242
45:18, 113

Al-Fatḥ
48:23, 113
48:4, 221

Al-Ḥujurāt
49:9, 161
49:13, 55

Al-Dhāriyāt
51:56, 277

Al-Raḥmān
55:9, 244
55:26–27, 8
55:60, 235

Al-Wāqiʿah
56:26, 219

Al-Ḥadīd
57:25, 244
57:27, 175

Al-Mujādilah
58:7, 159

Al-Ḥashr
59:13, 60
59:23, 201

Al-Ṣaff
60:8, 253

Al-Nabāʾ
78:8, 188

Al-Buruj
85:14, 210

Al-Ṭīn
95:4, 7
95:8, 242

Al-Zilzāl
99:7–8, 248

Al-Ikhlāṣ
112:1–4, 1